A Tale of Two Parties

Since 1952, the social bases of the Democratic and Republican parties have undergone radical reshuffling. At the start of this period southern Blacks favored Lincoln's Republican Party over suspect Democrats, and women favored Democrats more than Republicans. In 2020 these facts have been completely reversed. *A Tale of Two Parties: Living Amongst Democrats and Republicans Since 1952* traces through this transformation by showing:

- How the United States society has changed over the last seven decades in terms of regional growth, income, urbanization, education, religion, ethnicity, and ideology;
- How differently the two parties have appealed to groups in these social cleavages;
- How groups in these social cleavages have become concentrated within the bases of the Democratic and Republican parties;
- How party identification becomes intertwined with social identity to generate polarization akin to that of rapid sports fans or primitive tribes.

A Tale of Two Parties: Living Amongst Democrats and Republicans Since 1952 will have a wide and enthusiastic readership among political scientists and researchers of American politics, campaigns and elections, and voting and elections.

Kenneth Janda is Payson S. Wild Professor Emeritus of Political Science at Northwestern University. He is co-founder of the international journal *Party Politics*; co-author of *The Challenge of Democracy: American Government in Global Politics*, 15th ed. (2021); author of *Party Systems and Country Governance* (2011) and *The Emperor and the Peasant* (2018). He received the Samuel J. Eldersveld Lifetime Achievement Award from the American Political Science Association's Political Parties and Organizations Section in 2000, and the APSA's Frank J. Goodnow Award for service to the discipline and profession in 2009.

Routledge Research in American Politics and Governance

20. Congressional Communication in the Digital Age
Jocelyn Evans and Jessica Hayden

21. Reforming the Presidential Nominating Process
Front-Loading's Consequences and the National Primary Solution
Lisa K. Parshall

22. Public Debt and the Common Good
Philosophical and Institutional Implications of Fiscal Imbalance
James Odom

23. Removal of the Property Qualification for Voting in the United States
Strategy and Suffrage
Justin Moeller and Ronald F. King

24. The Rise of the Republican Right
From Goldwater to Reagan
Brian M. Conley

25. Interest Group Design
The Foundation and Evolution of Common Cause
Marcie L. Reynolds

26. Pop-Up Civics in 21st Century America
Understanding the Political Potential of Placemaking
Ryan Salzman

27. A Tale of Two Parties
Living Amongst Democrats and Republicans Since 1952
Kenneth Janda

28. Homeland *In*Security
Terrorism, Mass Shootings, and the Public
Ann Gordon and Kai Hamilton Gentry

"A pioneer of the modern social sciences offers a remarkable tale of how American political parties have developed over the past 17 presidential elections. He draws on his own experiences as a citizen, political scientist, student, and mentor, as well as analyses of nearly 70 years of data. Charting the evolving composition of the parties, Professor Janda shows how the social bases of the parties have changed and how social features, rather than ideology, have come to define the Democrats and Republicans. While this raises questions about how well responsible party government works, Professor Janda ends with an optimistic view of the future. This book is a social science masterpiece from which we will all learn."

James Druckman, *Professor, Northwestern University*

"Kenneth Janda inventively examines survey data to uncover the extent to which Republicans and Democrats today are different from those in the 1950s. He documents changes as to how different groups identify with the parties as well as in which groups constitute the base of each party. Janda presents the numbers, but then he delightfully adds his own perspectives on these seven decades of politics. As to be expected, the answer is that there has been change in some of the sociological differences between the parties, but the surprise is how many have stayed the same."

Herbert Weisberg, *Professor Emeritus, Ohio State University*

"Drawing upon social identity theory, Janda helps us understand why—at a time when the policy differences between the two parties have never been more stark—their support bases are driven more by social identity than by policy. With analysis covering the period from 1952 to 2020, the already-interesting story is made even more interesting with touches of autobiography and analogies from—believe it or not—the world of sports. In an era marked by hyperpartisanship, extreme polarization, and political tribalism, this is an entertaining and highly informative book that should be read by all serious students of American party politics."

Robert Harmel, *Professor, Texas A&M*

"I loved this book. Full of engaging writing and personal insights, Janda takes us on a highly informative and highly readable tour of the evolving two-party system of the past seven decades. This book will be valuable to scholars and students of American political parties and political parties' history, but its straightforward and accessible presentation should recommend it to an even wider audience."

Steven Greene, *Professor, North Carolina State University*

"This is an excellent study of partisan identity, with important new insights into the nature of identity, the ways demographic bases of partisans' identities have evolved over time, and especially, into how partisan identity relates to ideology. Janda draws on identity theory to develop the close affinity of partisan identity to team identification in sports, with fruitful results. Among other things, this helps him to develop the idea that parties largely cause ideology rather than the other way around. All that, and it is also a good read!"

W. Phillips Shively, *Professor Emeritus, University of Minnesota*

A Tale of Two Parties
Living Amongst Democrats and
Republicans Since 1952

Kenneth Janda

NEW YORK AND LONDON

First published 2021
by Routledge
52 Vanderbilt Avenue, New York, NY 10017

and by Routledge
2 Park Square, Milton Park, Abingdon, Oxon OX14 4RN

Routledge is an imprint of the Taylor & Francis Group, an informa business

© 2021 Taylor & Francis

The right of Kenneth Janda to be identified as author of this work has been asserted by him in accordance with sections 77 and 78 of the Copyright, Designs and Patents Act 1988.

All rights reserved. No part of this book may be reprinted or reproduced or utilised in any form or by any electronic, mechanical, or other means, now known or hereafter invented, including photocopying and recording, or in any information storage or retrieval system, without permission in writing from the publishers.

Trademark notice: Product or corporate names may be trademarks or registered trademarks, and are used only for identification and explanation without intent to infringe.

Library of Congress Cataloging-in-Publication Data
A catalog record for this title has been requested

ISBN: 978-0-367-32222-9 (hbk)
ISBN: 978-0-367-69876-8 (pbk)
ISBN: 978-0-429-31736-1 (ebk)

Typeset in Times New Roman
by Newgen Publishing UK

To Ann Janda, my wife, resident copy editor, and former head of Northwestern University's Social Science Data Services. She also served as Northwestern's Official Representative to the Inter-University Consortium for Political and Social Research. For decades, Ann disseminated data from the ICPSR and the American National Election Studies to students and faculty until retiring in 2006.

Contents

List of Figures xi
List of Tables xiv
List of Boxes xv
Preface xvii
Acknowledgments xx

1 Stability and Change in the American Polity 1

2 Partisan Identities 15

3 Party Organization and Social Groupings 34

4 Region: Once Primary, Now Secondary 52

5 Income: Slight, Steady, and Increasing Difference 59

6 Urbanization: Shifting Effects 67

7 Education: Incremental Reversal 76

8 Religion: Important and in Flux 82

9 Ethnicity: Dwindling Whites 93

10 Ideology: Partisan Cause or Partisan Effect? 104

11 Reviewing the Survey Data 121

12 Baneful Effects 133

13 Donald Trump's Last Hurrah 147

Appendix A: Equal Group Appeal Formula	154
Appendix B: Party Base Concentration Formula	156
Appendix C: Poll Questions Asking Respondents' Ideology, 1935–1969	158
References: Books, Articles, and Papers	160
References: Popular Periodicals and Websites	167
Index	172

Figures

1.1	U.S. Population Counts and Projections: 1950–2020	3
1.2	U.S. Population Growth Rates, 1950–2020	4
1.3	Winning President's Percentage of Popular Vote, 1952–2016	9
1.4	Winning President's Percentage of Electoral Vote, 1952–2016	10
1.5	Map of 2016 Electoral Votes in Contiguous States	11
1.6	Population Changes in State Electoral Votes by Region, 1950–2020	12
2.1	Distribution of Political Party Identifiers on Seven-Point Scale, 1952–2020	21
2.2	Distribution of Political Party Identifiers on Three-Point Scale, 1952–2020	24
2.3	Percentage of Party Identifiers Voting for Their Party's Presidential Candidates	25
2.4	Percent of Voters Who See Differences Between the Two Major Parties	26
2.5	Percent of Voters Saying Which Party Is More Conservative	27
3.1	Party Appeal to Gender Groups, 1952 and 2016	41
3.2	Party Composition by Gender Groups, 1952 and 2016	41
4.1	Regional Distribution of Respondents, 1952–2020	53
4.2	Percentages of Party Identification by Regions, with Equal Group Appeal Scores	55
4.3	Regional Groups as Proportion of Party Identifiers, with Party Base Concentration Scores	56
4.4	Parties' Equal Group Appeal and Base Concentration Scores, Regions 1952–2020	57
5.1	ANES Respondents' Distribution of Occupations in the U.S., 1952–2004	59
5.2	ANES Respondents' Distribution of Income in the U.S. by Centiles, 1952–2004	60
5.3	Percentages of Party Identification by Income, with Equal Group Appeal Scores	61
5.4	Proportions of Party Identifiers by Income Centiles, with Party Base Concentration Scores	62

5.5	Parties' Equal Group Appeal and Party Base Concentration Scores, Income 1952–2020	63
6.1	U.S. Census Estimate of Percent Urban-Rural Population, 1950–2010	68
6.2	Population in Rural, Suburban, and Urban Areas, 1952–2018	69
6.3	Percentages of Party Identification by Urbanization, with Equal Group Appeal Scores	71
6.4	Proportions of Party Identifiers by Urbanization, with Base Concentration Scores	72
6.5	Parties' Equal Group Appeal and Base Concentration Scores, Urbanization 1952–2018	73
7.1	Distribution of Educational Levels, 1952–2020	77
7.2	Percentages of Party Identification by Education, with Equal Group Appeal Scores	78
7.3	Education Groups as Proportion of Party Identifiers, with Party Base Concentration Scores	79
7.4	Parties' Equal Group Appeal and Party Base Concentration Scores, Education 1952–2020	80
8.1	Distribution of Religious Affiliations, 1952–2020	84
8.2	Attendance at Religious Services, 1952–2016	85
8.3	Percentages of Party Identifiers by Religion, with Equal Group Appeal Scores	87
8.4	Religious Groups as Proportions of Party Identifiers, with Party Base Concentration Scores	88
8.5	Parties' Equal Group Appeal Scores, Religion 1952–2020	88
8.6	Parties' Base Concentration Scores, Religion 1952–2020	89
8.7	Parties' Equal Group Appeal and Party Base Concentration Scores, Religiosity 1952–2016	90
9.1	Distribution of Ethnic Responses, 1952–2020	95
9.2	Percentages of Party Identification by Ethnicity, with Equal Group Appeal Scores	96
9.3	Ethnic Groups as Proportion of Party Identifiers, with Party Base Concentration Scores	97
9.4	Parties' Equal Group Appeal Scores, Ethnicity 1952–2020	97
9.5	Parties' Base Concentration Scores, Ethnicity 1952–2020	98
10.1	Number of Mentions of "Liberal" and Its Forms in Party Platforms Since 1840	105
10.2	Ideological Distribution, 1952–2020	108
10.3	Percentages of Party Identification by Ideology, with Equal Group Appeal Scores	111
10.4	Ideology Groups as Proportion of Party Identifiers, with Party Base Concentration Scores	112
10.5	Parties' Equal Group Appeal Scores, Ideology 1952–2020	112
10.6	Parties' Base Concentration Scores, Ideology 1952–2020	113
10.7	1972–2008: "Are you Liberal, Conservative, or Haven't Thought Much About It?"	117

11.1	A Box Plot	122
11.2	Democrats' Group Appeal Box Plots Since 1952, with Median Values	123
11.3	Republicans' Group Appeal Box Plots Since 1952, with Median Values	124
11.4	Democrats' Base Concentration Box Plots Since 1952, with Median Values	126
11.5	Republicans' Base Concentration Box Plots Since 1952, with Median Values	127
11.6	Percentages of 2019 Electorate and Proportions of Party Bases by Ethnicity, Religion, Urban, and Education	129
13.1	Changes in the American Electorate, 1952–2019	148

Tables

3.1	1952 and 2016 Party Identification by Gender,* Percentages by Columns	40
3.2	1952 and 2016 Party Identification by Gender, Proportions by Rows	40
10.1	1970 Gallup Poll on Meaning of "Liberal" and "Conservative"	109
11.1	Partisan Assignments of Four Social Cleavages	128

Boxes

3.1 Explaining the Equal Group Appeal Score 44
3.2 Explaining the Party Base Concentration Score 46

Preface

I write as a political scientist and as a citizen who since 1952 has witnessed major changes in party politics. At age 16 in 1952 and a junior in high school, I listened to the radio's comprehensive coverage of the Democratic and Republican nominating conventions. That does not single me out. Some 6.5 million Americans living in my age group (85 or older) heard the conventions too. However, they are too smart to put their recollections and reminisces in a book about contemporary politics.

My personal experience figures into this story another way. As a 24-year-old predoctoral student at Indiana University, I spent the 1959–1960 academic year at the University of Michigan's Survey Research Center, where I was privileged to observe Angus Campbell, Warren Miller, Phillip Converse, and Donald Stokes analyze national 1952 and 1956 election surveys. Although my doctoral research dealt with roll-call voting in the Kentucky state legislature, not electoral behavior, my influential mentor at Indiana, Professor Charles S. Hyneman, arranged for my appointment anyway. Professor Campbell, head of Michigan's SRC, was suitably accommodating, while Warren, Phil, and Don treated me like a member of their research family. I learned a lot that year as the four published what became arguably the most influential book in the study of American politics, *The American Voter* (1960).

I never did write my thesis on roll-call voting in Kentucky, nor did I switch to study electoral behavior. My Michigan experience led elsewhere. I persuaded Henry Teune, my fellow IU PhD candidate, to join me in designing and conducting a survey of all candidates for the Indiana General Assembly in 1960.[1] That summer before the November election, Henry and I traveled across the state interviewing House and Senate candidates. We collected data on 238 out of 277 candidates, which we used in our 1961 dissertations: Henry's on legislative interest groups and mine on representational behavior. So I did survey research, but on legislative candidates, not voters.

For decades after, I maintained contact with Miller, Converse, and Stokes through the Inter-University Consortium for Political Research, which was created in 1962 to share data from the SRC's national election surveys with researchers across the nation.[2] The SRC had already conducted national voter surveys in the presidential elections of 1948, 1952, and 1956. Treating the 1948 survey as a pilot study, *The American Voter* relied mainly on the 1952 and 1956 data. Those surveys formed the basis of what became known as the American National Election Studies (ANES), a collection of all election surveys since 1952 now available online.[3]

Using ANES data for 1952–2016, the National Opinion Research Center General Social Survey data for 2004–2018, a 2019 Voter Study Group survey, and a Nationscape survey for 2020,[4] this book examines the social traits of political party identifiers—i.e., citizens who, when asked, say they consider themselves as Democrats or Republicans. It analyzes their party identifications according to region of the country, economic status, urbanization of residence, level of education, religious affiliation, and ethnicity. It also examines citizens' ideological self-placement. This book is about people's political identity, not their voting behavior.

It began as an update to my 2013 Apple iBook, *The Social Bases of Political Parties: Democrats and Republicans 1952–2012 and 2032*. My iBook was fully interactive, allowing readers to navigate within the text by clicking on underlined phrases, but it was only available in electronic form for Mac users.[5] In printed form, this book lacks that capability, but it extends the analysis to include the 2020 presidential election years.

A Tale of Two Parties also offers a different perspective on the social traits of those who identify with the Democratic and Republican parties. Whereas my iBook treated parties as reflecting their social bases, this book evaluates the social bases of parties in terms of social identity theory. People from different social groups often identify as Democrats or Republicans so they can belong to what they perceive as a desirable social crowd.

Sports researchers also use social identity theory to explain partisanship in sports. Fans don't deliberate on their choices of teams; they identify with local teams already favored by their friends and neighbors. Sports fans form a supportive crowd. They love their players (who can do no wrong) and hate their opponents (who do no right). Green Bay Packers fans in Wisconsin wear cheesehead hats to solidify their identity with their professional football team, not because they like cheese. This book develops at some length the similarity between the considerable research on sports fans and the study of political partisanship.

Democrats readily tell interviewers that they are politically liberal and Republicans say they are politically conservative. People tend to think that liberal voters identify as Democrats and conservatives as Republicans. In contrast, this book argues that many voters become Democrats and then say they are liberal, and even more become Republicans and then say they are conservative. Because many voters don't clearly understand the liberal and conservative positions on an ideological continuum, partisanship influences their ideological claims as much as ideology influences their partisanship.

Finally, I speculate on why partisanship in 2020 differs so much from partisanship in 1952. Technological changes in communication over the past seven decades account for much of today's political polarization.

Notes

1 Kenneth Janda, Henry Teune, Melvin Kahn, and Wayne Francis, *Legislative Politics in Indiana: A Preliminary Report to the 1961 General Assembly* (Bloomington, IN: Bureau of Government Research, Indiana University, 1961).
2 See "About ICPSR" at www.icpsr.umich.edu/web/pages/about/. I served as an ICPSR Council Member from 1965 to 1967.
3 See "About Us" at https://electionstudies.org/about-us/.
4 See Nationscape at www.voterstudygroup.org/nationscape.
5 *The Social Bases of Political Parties* is available as an iBook at https://books.apple.com/us/book/social-bases-political-parties/id602462683?mt=13. It also can be downloaded as a PDF at www.janda.org/bio/parties.htm. That book assessed the relationship between the parties' social bases and their aggregation and articulation of issues in congressional voting. This book does not pursue that connection.

Acknowledgments

As stated in the Preface, I am indebted to Angus Campbell, Warren E. Miller, Philip E. Converse, and Donald E. Stokes at the University of Michigan's Survey Research Center who allowed me to observe them completing work on *The American Voter* (1960). They would be surprised, and I hope pleased, to know that I finally did some serious analysis of survey data on presidential elections.

Their work at Michigan's Survey Research Center led to the creation of the National Election Studies, now the American National Election Studies (ANES). The 1952–2016 Cumulative File of ANES surveys provided most of the data analyzed herein. Jamie Ventura at the University of Michigan office of ANES in Michigan and Matthew DeBell at Stanford University's ANES office patiently answered my several questions about sampling and coding.

Unfortunately, ANES stopped including a variable on the urban-rural nature of the respondents' residence in 2004. I used urbanization and party identification data from the General Social Survey for presidential election years since then and for 2018, to stand for 2020. "The GSS Team" anonymously provided help with their new cumulative file. Before his retirement in 2019 as head of the General Social Survey, Tom W. Smith answered many of my questions. He was also helpful to Ann when she headed Northwestern's Social Science Data Services.

Writing before the 2020 presidential election, I relied on survey data for the first quarter of 2020 collected by the Nationscape project at UCLA, with Lynn Vavreck and Chris Tausanovitch, principal investigators.[1] Professor Vavreck kindly arranged for Tyler Reny, Project Coordinator, to produce cross tabulations needed to include that year. He also patiently answered queries about the data. I also used data from the 2019 Voter Study group to examine effects on the parties' bases of combining social groups.

Several political scientists filled in gaps and helped bring me up to speed on electoral behavior research—often sending me electronic copies of publications. I thank my Northwestern colleagues Jamie Druckman and Daniel Galvin; my old friend, Herbert Weisberg; and others who provided useful information, specifically Bryce Dietrich, Patrick Egan, John Flynn, Donald Green, Steven Greene, Michael Hogg, Verlan Lewis, Christopher

Ojeda, Lilla Orr, and W. Phillips Shively. Scholars in several disciplines guided me through the social identity literature. Political scientist Lilliana Mason was especially helpful in directing me to readings on social identify theory, along with social psychologists Michael Hogg and Kay Deaux. Biological researchers John Bryden and Dar Meshi enlightened me on the relationship of social media to social identity. Social psychologist Beth Diets-Uhler introduced me to research on sports fans. Dan Wann, a pioneer in creating scales to measure sports fans' identification, shared various studies on the topic.

Longtime friends Robert Feldman and Jerry Goldman helped me continue writing more than they realize. Finally, Natalja Mortensen, Senior Editor in Political Science at Routledge, and Charlie Baker, Editorial Assistant, were unfailingly supportive and helpful in realizing this publication.

Note

1 "Nationscape is designed and conducted by UCLA researchers led by political scientists Lynn Vavreck and Chris Tausanovitch. The Nationscape survey is fielded by Lucid. Analysis is conducted by UCLA researchers and Democracy Fund Voter Study Group." See "Netscape Research Collaboration" at www.voterstudygroup.org/nationscape/researchers.

1 Stability and Change in the American Polity

Charles Dickens began his classic novel, *A Tale of Two Cities*, with the famous sentence, "It was the best of times; it was the worst of times." Dickens wrote in 1859 about London and Paris during the 1789 French revolution. His opening influenced my thinking about American party politics. I'm no Dickens, but here is my take: "Since its beginning, the American polity has been very stable, but it has greatly changed." Certainly, American party politics have changed greatly in my lifetime.

The contradictory themes of stability and change run through this chapter. I begin by making a case for the United States' governmental stability over more than two centuries. As I write at age 85, I describe how our party politics have changed during my life span. When I was in high school in 1952, Dwight Eisenhower was elected president by a landslide. He won while most southern states in the old confederacy remained solidly Democratic and voted for his opponent, Adlai Stevenson. In the 1950s, Republican voters were more likely than Democratic voters to hold college degrees. Republicans were also more likely to be women than men, and voters in small towns and rural areas were almost twice as likely to be Democrats than Republicans. In 2016, all states in the old confederacy voted for Republican Donald Trump. Today, voters with college degrees are apt to be Democrats, women favor Democrats over Republicans, and Republicans are more common than Democrats in small towns and rural areas.

I marvel at how much has changed in politics during my lifetime. All my grandparents were European immigrants. I lived in a metropolitan area (Chicago) and attended its public schools before moving to a rural area and graduating from a small town high school in Wilmington, Illinois. I feel close to various social groups that identify with Democrats and Republicans and as qualified as anyone to account for their party identifications. My tale of two parties begins by documenting the party system's stability during the nation's lifetime.

The Case for Stability

The American polity has been remarkably stable for over 230 years, despite enormous geographical and demographic changes. The United States grew from 13 colonies clustered along the northeastern coast in the eighteenth century to 50 states extending from the Atlantic to the Pacific oceans. The new nation expanded commensurately in population. It evolved from an agricultural economy at the end of the eighteenth century, to an industrial economy at the start of the twentieth century, to a twenty-first-century economy based on electronics and information technology. It won a civil war to end slavery in the 1860s, a legislative war in the 1960s to grant civil rights to descendants of former slaves, and political battles later that insured civil rights for women, the disabled, and homosexuals. It welcomed millions of immigrants from Europe in the nineteenth and early twentieth centuries and millions from Latin America and Asia afterward. Since 1788—without interruption by wars or national calamities—our country has held national elections for president every four years and national elections for Congress every two years. By persevering during social change and political conflict, the United States has demonstrated its stability as a nation.

Although its 1787 Constitution established an untried form of national government, the United States has also been remarkably stable in its politics. While unelected monarchs governed other nations, elected officials governed the United States. Unlike the direct democracy of ancient Athens, where citizens participated directly in government, the new government was designed as a representative democracy, in which elected officials would act on voters' behalf. Citizens in each state, according to population, were empowered to directly elect delegates to a House of Representatives. Citizens would also indirectly elect the new President of the United States by choosing a number of "electors" equal to their state's representation in the House and the Senate.[1]

Those who wrote the Constitution lacked clear visions of how their unprecedented electoral system would operate. The Constitution does not mention political parties. Although parties or political factions existed then in Europe, they had a bad reputation.[2] George Washington was elected and re-elected president without party affiliation or organized political opposition. Indeed, he warned about parties' "baneful effects" in his 1796 Farewell Address. Nevertheless, political parties soon formed, and a party system became integral to American government and—perhaps like a necessary evil—proved crucial to its functioning as a democracy. From a centuries-long viewpoint, political parties contributed to the nation's stability.

The Case for Change Within My Lifetime

Media moguls classify me as belonging to the "Silent Generation," people born between 1928 and 1945. Born during the Great Depression in 1935, I don't remember living during that time of deprivation, but I vividly recall the later years of World War II, which ended when I was ten years old. My political memory starts with the decade of the 1950s. The war had destroyed or crippled former powers in Europe and Asia, and the United

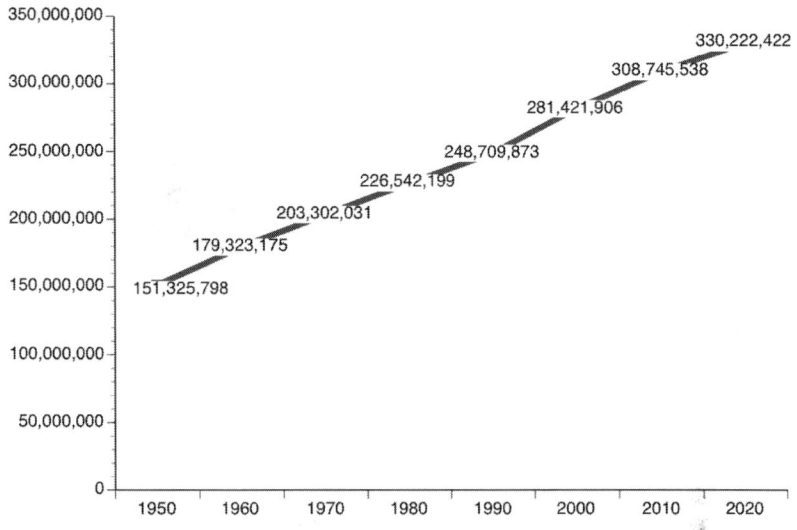

Figure 1.1 U.S. Population Counts and Projections: 1950–2020*

States was the world's preeminent military power. Only China and India, both underdeveloped countries, had populations demonstrably larger than the United States' 150+ million. The Soviet Union may have been larger, but its data were suspect.[3] Everyone expected America's population to grow, and Figure 1.1 shows that—70 years later—the U.S. population had doubled in almost a straight line from 1950 to 2020.

Despite World War II's costs, the nation was the wealthiest on earth. In 1950, the United States' Gross Domestic Product was $1.5 trillion, three times that of the Soviet Union, five times the United Kingdom's and Germany's, and six times China's.[4] Americans were vigorous and optimistic. Moreover, 73 percent of the respondents said they could "trust the government in Washington to do what is right" when asked in the American National Election survey.[5]

By 2020, the United States population growth rate had slowed, as shown in Figure 1.2. Its 0.5 percent growth rate in 2019 was the lowest in history. In part, this is due to people in the Millennial Generation (born 1981–1996) having fewer children. Also, the nation added only 600,000 immigrants, versus more than a million three years earlier, before President Trump's administration.[6] Today, the United States remains the world's wealthiest nation but may not remain so for long. Its GDP in 2019 was $21 trillion, but China at $15.5 trillion was second and closing fast.[7] Despite its wealth, U.S. citizens have lost trust in their government. Only 17 percent in a 2019 national survey said they could "trust the government in Washington to do what is right," versus the 73 percent in 1958.[8]

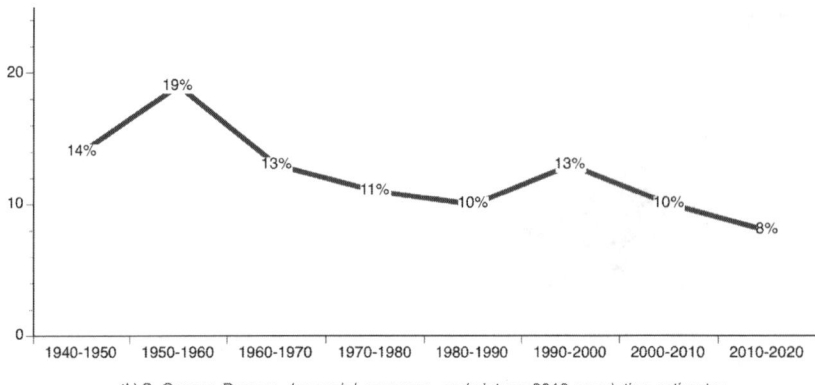

Figure 1.2 U.S. Population Growth Rates, 1950–2020*

By the summer of 2020, the 2020 COVID-19 pandemic had caused over 200,000 deaths in the United States, left over 20 million unemployed during the year, and cost over $3 trillion in government expenditures (and debt). Americans who identified with the Democratic and Republican parties differed substantially in how they viewed the health crisis and subsequent economic calamity and how government should respond to both. In mid-May, Gallup poll's senior scientist, Frank Newport, reported on "The Partisan Gap in Views of the Coronavirus."[9] He found that Democrats and Republicans turned to different sources for cues on virus-related issues and that they differed on government's role in dealing with the pandemic. While recognizing that "partisan differences in view of issues and policies are built into the American system, and can be a plus," Newport warned that Democrat and Republican differences "in their acceptance of and adherence to government mandates" hampered dealing with both the health crisis and the economic calamity.

For decades, the media had described American party politics in terms of "political polarization." Political scientists now said that partisan groups were demonstrating a special type of polarization, a general animosity toward each other called "affective polarization."[10] Democrats and Republicans did not just differ on policy, they increasingly disliked and distrusted those from the other party. "Democrats and Republicans both say that the other party's members are hypocritical, selfish, and closed-minded, and they are unwilling to socialize across party lines."[11]

That was not true of Democrats and Republicans after World War II nor for decades afterward. In 1948, both parties courted General Dwight D. Eisenhower as a possible presidential candidate. Democrat Sam Rayburn, Speaker of the House 1949–1953 and 1955–1961, enjoyed good working relationships with Republicans. In 1946, after Republicans won the election and Rayburn temporarily lost his Speaker's private automobile, 50 Republican congressmen contributed to the Democrats' fund to purchase a car for him as Minority Leader.[12] In 1972, Republican Senator Bob Dole headed the Republican National Committee when his good friend, George McGovern, lost to Richard Nixon, but Dole and McGovern remained friends until McGovern's death in 2012.[13] In the 1980s, Republican President Ronald Reagan enjoyed a close "after six" drinking relationship with Democrat Tip O'Neill, Speaker of the House. In the 1990s, Democratic Senator Ted Kennedy and Republican Senator Orin Hatch shouted at each other on the Senate floor but worked together in Senate Committees.[14]

If members of Congress in opposite parties form close friendships today, they are not publicized. One study of C-SPAN videos of the House floor from 1997 to 2016 showed members of one party increasingly unlikely to "cross-the-floor" to speak to members of the other across the aisle.[15] Before trying to understand how such partisan enmity developed, we should briefly review the history of party politics in the United States.

The Origin of American Political Parties

After George Washington declined to run for a third term, ambitious politicians organized with other elites to seek the presidency and fill Congress. Equally ambitious political aspirants organized in opposition. Even if avoiding the term, these nascent groups met the formal definition of a political party: a political organization that seeks to place its avowed representatives in government positions.[16] That Americans would form political parties was a foregone conclusion.

Democratic government inevitably produces political parties. Why inevitably? As John Aldrich explained in his classic book, *Why Parties?*:

> Election requires persuading members of the public to support that candidacy and mobilizing as many of those supporters as possible. This is a problem of collective action. How do candidates get supporters to vote for them—at least in greater numbers than vote for the opposition—as well as get them to provide the cadre of workers and contribute the resources needed to win election? The political party has long been the solution.[17]

Winning a majority of votes from a large number of voters requires organized collective action from a set of individuals, hence the need for political parties. In democratic governments, contests for political office typically engender multiple parties, hence the creation of a party system. Every nation classified as a democracy has a system of at least two parties that seek to place its members in government by competing in elections. As E.E. Schattschneider wrote nearly 80 years ago, "Political parties created democracy, and modern democracy is unthinkable save in terms of the parties."[18]

Since George Washington left the presidency and despite his warning about parties, the United States has had at least three distinct party systems. I trace their history to show continuity, and thus stability, in our national politics.

The First Party System, 1796–1816: Those who backed John Adams in the 1796 election became known as "Federalists," but they avoided referring to themselves as a political party. They were opposed by "Democratic Republicans" (no relation to either the Democrats or Republicans of today) who backed Thomas Jefferson. Federalist and Democratic-Republican candidates contested presidential elections until the election of 1820, when the Federalists faded away.

A Brief Non-party Era, 1820–1824: Lacking a Federalist challenger, Democratic-Republican President James Monroe was re-elected in 1820 without opposition. That election and the election of 1824 encompassed a brief "Era of Good Feeling," during which presidential competition occurred within the Democratic-Republican Party. Today we might liken their intra-party jockeying to primary contests. The "Good Feeling" ended after the 1824 election. Although Andrew Jackson won pluralities of the popular and electoral vote, he lacked an electoral vote majority, throwing the decision into the House of Representatives. There, he lost the presidency to John Quincy Adams, who had come in second in both popular and electoral votes.

The Second Party System, 1828–1856: In 1828 Andrew Jackson formed the Democratic Party to support his successful presidential campaign against incumbent John Quincy Adams. Jackson was supported by farmers and newly enfranchised voters in western states, Adams by manufacturing interests in the northeast ones. Jackson carried every state west of New Jersey and Delaware, winning the electoral vote 178 to 83. The new Whig Party furnished the Democrats' principal opposition during this period. Meanwhile, the slavery issue grew more contentious. Today's Republican Party was formed in 1854 in opposition to the Kansas-Nebraska Act, which allowed slavery to expand into new states.[19] The Republicans and Whigs unsuccessfully ran candidates against the winning Democrat in the 1856 presidential election.

The Third Party System, 1860-present: The slavery issue split the Democratic Party in 1860. A united Republican Party ran Abraham Lincoln, seen as opposing slavery in new states but accepting it in the South. Lincoln carried virtually every northern and western state. Former Democrats representing three parties won electoral votes, mostly from southern states. Since 1860, every U.S. president has been either Democratic or Republican. Other parties have backed presidential candidates in every election and occasionally have influenced the outcome, but no one from another party has ever been elected president.

Social and Party Changes During the Current Party System

There were only 28 states in 1828, and just 33 in 1860. In 2020, citizens in 50 states plus the District of Columbia could vote in federal elections. Enormous social changes have occurred since the Civil War. Many millions of immigrants swelled the nation's population, and fundamental technological changes altered the way people live and work. Although the same two parties have dominated the electoral scene for more than 150 years, both have experienced changes in the social bases of their support. Over the last 50 years, the parties' social bases have flipped in critical respects.

For decades after the Civil War, the Republican Party drew its support from business and manufacturing interests in northeastern and midwestern states. The Democratic Party dominated the southern states, which became known as the "Solid South" for steadfastly supporting Democrats. Although Blacks remained loyal to Abraham Lincoln and the Republican Party that freed them from slavery, they were disenfranchised in the South, where most lived, and northern Blacks were not mobilized to vote by either party. Republicans did not need their votes, northern Democrats did not seek their votes, and southern Democrats did not want them to vote.

From 1860 through 1928, Republican presidential candidates won 14 of the 18 presidential elections. They carried the northern urban and industrial states (with the most electoral votes) while Democrats won in the rural, more agricultural, and less populous Solid South. After the 1929 stock market crash punctured capitalist prosperity, voting patterns changed dramatically. Beginning in 1932, voters in all parts of the country turned to the Democratic Party during the Great Depression and elected Franklin D. Roosevelt to four consecutive terms.

From 1932 through 1948, the Democratic Party won all five presidential elections, backed by the fabled "Roosevelt coalition" of blue collar workers, urban voters, white southerners, intellectuals, and social minorities—racial, ethnic, and religious. Republicans, in contrast, fared better with higher income, well-educated, and suburban voters. While these groups were fewer in numbers, they were part of the white majority.

In 1952, I began to pay attention to politics, but not too seriously, being a teenager in a small-town high school with only 200 students. However, I do clearly remember the string of Democratic presidents ending with the election of Republican candidate Dwight Eisenhower. Notably, the Republican Eisenhower won 4 of the 11 states in the formerly "Solid South." By an even larger margin, he was re-elected in 1956. That was my last year at Illinois State Normal University and I was headed toward graduate school at Indiana University to study political science. By then, I was paying close attention to elections.

The 1960s civil rights movement upset the established patterns of party support. In 1963, President John F. Kennedy, a Democrat, proposed legislation to end segregation in public places and to ban employment discrimination on the basis of race, color, religion, sex, or national origin—in keeping with the winning Roosevelt coalition. After Kennedy's assassination late that year, his successor, Lyndon Johnson (a southerner himself) steered those proposals into law as the 1964 Civil Rights Act. Johnson handily won election himself later that year, but he lost five southern states to Republican Barry Goldwater, who vigorously opposed the 1964 legislation.

Democratic losses continued in 1968, when George Wallace won eight southern states as a third-party candidate. Texas was the only southern state captured by Democrat Hubert Humphrey while Republican Richard Nixon won most of the other states and the presidency. Running for re-election in 1972, Nixon won every state but Massachusetts. The Democrats' winning "Roosevelt coalition" had evaporated. Nevertheless, Democrats won 5 of the 11 subsequent presidential elections, while the Republicans won 6. Since 1860, the same two parties—at least two with the same names—have dominated American party politics.

Stability and Changes in Political Parties and Presidential Voting

The persistence of a two-party system in the United States is unique among the world's democracies. Scholars generally attribute the U.S. two-party system to its prevailing electoral system, specifically to two factors: (a) single-member districts and (b) use of plurality rule to determine winners.[20] Their net effect is to increase representation of the larger party and to discourage the formation of minor parties. Most other nations employ multimember districts and electoral rules that insure proportional representation, which encourages multiple parties. While presidential elections are ultimately decided by majority rule in the Electoral College, nearly all states award their electoral votes by plurality rule. As the nation has grown and changed, both major parties have adjusted to working within this electoral system. They have alternated in power in controlling both houses of Congress and in winning the presidency.

Since 1952, both parties have enjoyed a rough balance over 17 presidential elections to 2016. Republican candidates won ten elections (1952, 1956, 1968, 1972, 1980, 1984, 1988, 2000, 2004, 2016) and Democrats seven (1960, 1964, 1976, 1992, 1996, 2008, 2012). Moreover, the winner often did not win by much over this period. Republican presidential candidates averaged winning 52 percent of the vote, and Democratic winners averaged 51 percent. Figure 1.3 plots the percentage of the popular vote won by successful Republican and Democratic presidential candidates from 1952 to 2016.

Figure 1.3 portrays both a picture of stability and one of increasing division. Two features document the stability of American electoral politics. First, the parties alternated in winning. Second, most elections were relatively close; the winner getting more than 55 percent of the votes only

Stability and Change in the U.S. Polity 9

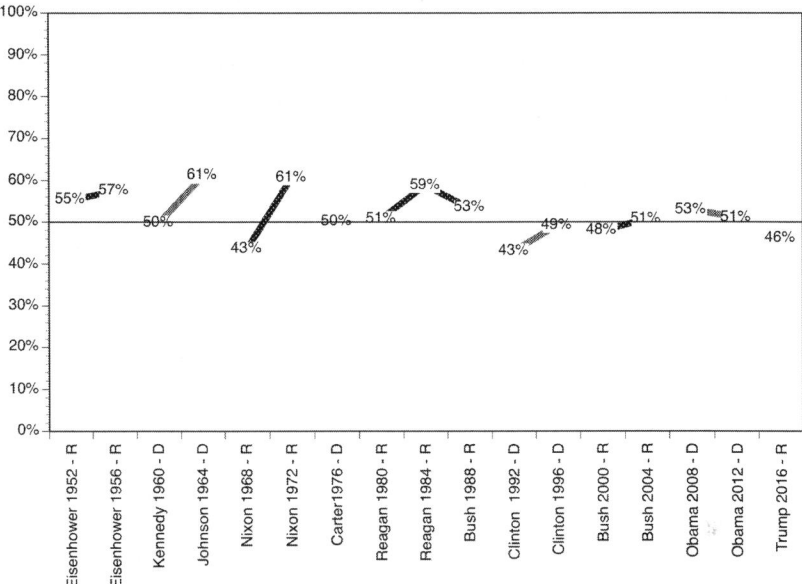

Figure 1.3 Winning President's Percentage of Popular Vote, 1952–2016

4 of 17 times. Scholars contend that a two-party system is supposed to work that way. Candidates should propose policies that appeal to most of the voters—those in the political center, not at the extremes. Consequently, elections should be relatively close because voters do not view choices between presidential candidates as critical. If, however, nearly equal groups of voters are deeply divided over policies and candidates, then close elections have a different meaning.

Figure 1.3 also shows how divided the American electorate has become in the last quarter century. In the seven presidential elections from 1992 to 2016, no candidate won more than 53 percent of the popular vote; four candidates won the presidency with less than a majority of the popular vote; and two won office while losing the popular vote. Republican George W. Bush won in 2000 with 547,000 fewer votes (0.5 percent) than Democrat Al Gore. Republican Donald Trump won in 2016 with 2,869,000 fewer votes (2.1 percent) than Democrat Hillary Clinton.

Presidents are not elected to office by winning the popular vote cast by citizens but by the electoral votes cast by states. The U.S. Constitution specifies that the successful candidate must win a majority—not a plurality—of the total state electoral vote. Since the electoral vote was fixed at 538 for the 1964 election,[21] 270 votes have been needed to win the presidency. Throughout most of our history, most presidential candidates have won a larger percentage of the electoral vote than the popular vote, which

10 Stability and Change in the U.S. Polity

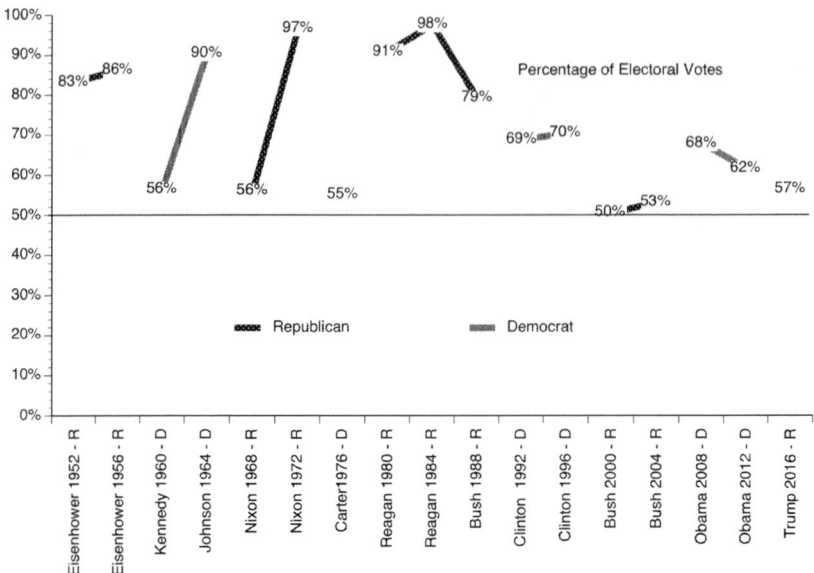

Figure 1.4 Winning President's Percentage of Electoral Vote, 1952–2016

magnified the appearance of a candidate's victory. Figure 1.4 illustrates that effect.

For example, after the 2000 election, Republican George W. Bush and Democrat Al Gore were nearly tied in the popular vote nationwide and virtually tied in Florida's popular vote. After a protracted recount of Florida's popular votes was held in selected counties—and then stopped by the Supreme Court—Bush was declared the winner by only 537 votes (0.01 percent of the total). By winning the contested Florida recount, George W. Bush won all of Florida's electoral votes, pushing him one vote above the 270 required for a majority. That made Bush president although Gore won a slight majority of the popular vote.

Donald Trump's victory was decidedly different. Although getting nearly 3 million fewer popular votes than Hillary Clinton, he won 30 states to her 20 (plus the District of Columbia). As shown in Figure 1.5, Trump won nearly all the states in the South, Midwest, and plains, while Clinton carried most of the more heavily populated states on both coasts.

One cannot compare presidential elections by states from 1952 to 2016 without allowing for changes over time in the allocation of electoral votes. Each state's electoral vote is equal to its representation in Congress. States get two electoral votes for their two U.S. senators and additional electoral votes equal to their seats in the House of Representatives. Every state has one seat in the House, but some get additional seats based on their population as determined in each decennial census. States that gain or lose

Stability and Change in the U.S. Polity 11

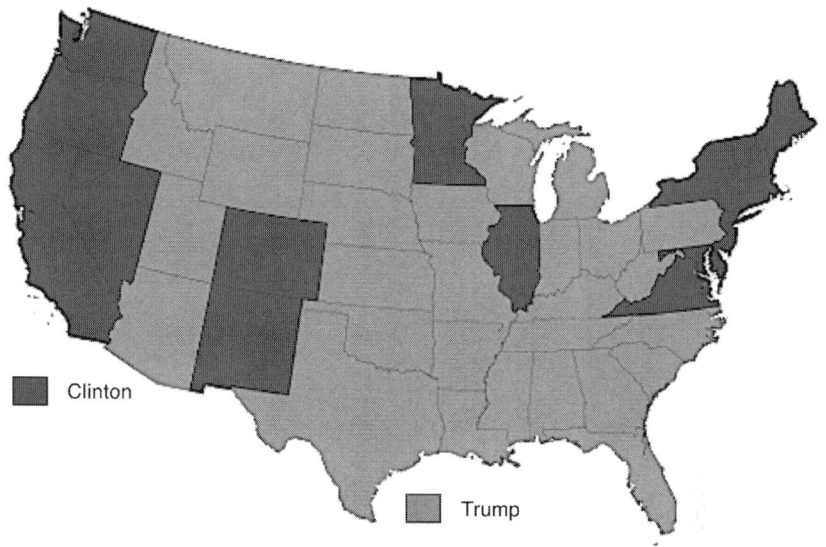

Figure 1.5 Map of 2016 Electoral Votes in Contiguous States

population relative to other states can gain or lose one or more seats in the House of Representatives, resulting in a gain or loss of electoral votes for president. Over the years, northern states have systematically lost population to states in the south and west, resulting in corresponding losses and gains of electoral votes. Figure 1.6 plots the losses and gains by regions according to the seven decennial censuses from 1950 to 2010 and U.S. Census Bureau estimates for the 2020 census, which will determine the 2024 electoral vote distribution.

In stark terms, Figure 1.6 illustrates how population movement from the north to the south and west has produced a commensurate shift in presidential election politics. Trends at work for the 2012 and 2016 elections will also influence the 2020 presidential election, and the 2020 census will magnify their effects on subsequent presidential elections.

The unusual distribution of the states' electoral votes in 2016 between the Democratic and Republican candidates suggests that the country was divided in unprecedented fashion. In 1952, Democrats counted on solid support from blue collar workers in North Central manufacturing states and on some support from agricultural workers in rural states. In 2016, these former Democratic voters appeared to vote for Donald Trump and for Republican congressional candidates who grasped his coattails. Elected president with a minority of the popular vote, Donald Trump cultivated fierce loyalty among his supporters (many former Democrats) and equally fierce disapproval among his opponents (some former Republicans). Support for, and opposition to, President Trump pervaded Congress.

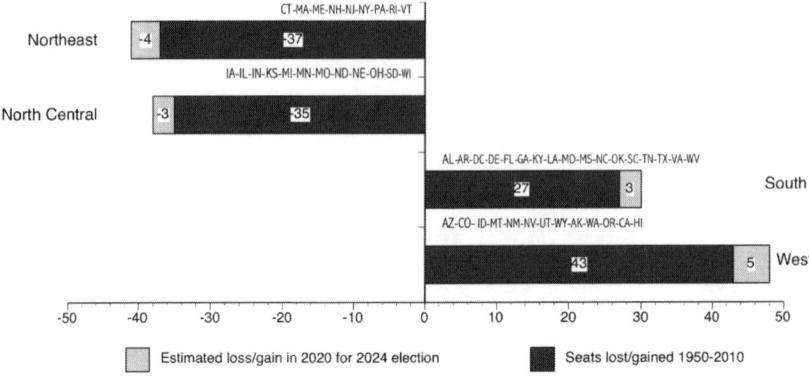

Figure 1.6 Population Changes in State Electoral Votes by Region, 1950–2020

Under control of Democrats, the House of Representatives voted, almost perfectly along party lines, to impeach the president. The Senate voted, almost perfectly along party lines, not to convict him. At the end of 2019, the Pew Research Center's 130+ page report on politics at the end of the decade said: "Partisanship continues to be *the* dividing line in the American public's political attitudes, far surpassing differences by age, race and ethnicity, gender, educational attainment, religious affiliation or other factors."[22]

These social differences are linked to partisanship to varying degrees. When political analysts speak of the "base" of the Republican Party, they identify groups of people such as farmers, coal miners, Evangelicals, rural whites. Pundits may talk less about the base of the Democratic Party, but they describe its strongholds as women, city-dwellers, the college-educated, minorities. Some analysts describe these social categories as potential social cleavages. The rest of this book investigates the extent to which such potential social cleavages underlie the basis of partisanship that might last beyond the Trump presidency. Is there such a thing as the "Trump coalition" that could affect future American electoral politics as long as the Roosevelt coalition lasted from 1932 to 1952?

Conclusion: A Tale Informed by Personal Experience

Charles Dickens did not live during "the best of times" and "the worst of times" described in his *A Tale of Two Cities*. Born in 1812, Dickens lived in London while writing about the 1789 French Revolution in Paris. He was only 47 years of age in 1859 when his book was published. Of course, people a half century later knew about the revolutionary period in France from print media. One widely read pamphlet, *Reflections on the Revolution in France* by the British statesman Edmund Burke, appeared in November 1790, early in the rebellion. Burke opposed the violence and disorder in France and praised English traditions, including social rank and accumulated wealth. Burke's pamphlet was a well-crafted statement of political theory that was very influential in its time and is still important today.

Although Dickens did not live during the revolution, he drew on his friendship with Thomas Carlyle, the 65-year-old author of *The French Revolution: A History* (1837). Carlyle, whose book remains a standard source, even provided Dickens with a cartload of books on the topic.[23] Without question, Dickens was informed about the revolution, but he did not experience it. I have the advantage of having lived throughout my tale about the Democratic and Republican parties. I hope my reminiscences serve the reader.

Notes

1 Senators were not universally elected until 1914, after the passage of the 17th Amendment to the Constitution in 1913.
2 Piero Ignazi's book, *Party and Democracy: The Uneven Road to Party Legitimacy* (Oxford: Oxford University Press, 2017), traces the popular acceptance of the role of political parties in democratic government from their origin in early Greece.
3 1939 Soviet census reported a population of 170.6 million, but its accuracy was disputed. Moreover, millions died during World War II. The next census, in 1959, reported 208 million. See https://en.wikipedia.org/wiki/Soviet_Census_(1959).
4 Angus Maddison statistics of the ten largest economies by GDP (PPP) at https://en.wikipedia.org/wiki/Angus_Maddison_statistics_of_the_ten_largest_economies_by_GDP_(PPP).
5 Pew Research Center, "Trust in Government, 1958–2019," (April 11, 2019).
6 U.S. Census Bureau, "2019 U.S. Population Estimates Continue to Show the Nation's Growth Is Slowing" (December 30, 2019).
7 List of countries by GDP (nominal), at https://en.wikipedia.org/wiki/List_of_countries_by_GDP_(nominal).
8 Pew Research Center, "Trust in Government, 1958–2019," (April 11, 2019).
9 Frank Newport, "The Partisan Gap in Views of the Coronavirus," *Polling Matters* (May 15, 2020).
10 Shanto Iyengar, Yphtach Lelkes, Matthew Levendusky, Neil Malhotra, and Sean J. Westwood, "The Origins and Consequences of Affective Polarization in the United States," *Annual Review of Political Science*, 22 (2019), 129–146. See also Lilliana Mason, *Uncivil Agreement: How Politics Became Our Identity* (Chicago: University of Chicago Press, 2018).
11 Iyengar et al., p. 129.
12 "Sam Rayburn," *Wikipedia*, at https://en.wikipedia.org/wiki/Sam_Rayburn.
13 Bob Dole, "My Friend, George McGovern: He Was a Man Who Never Gave Up," *Minneapolis StarTribune* (October 22, 2012) at www.startribune.com/bob-dole-my-friend-george-mcgovern/175246371/.
14 Newsweek Staff, "Sen. Orrin Hatch Remembers Ted Kennedy," *Newsweek* (August 26, 2009), at www.newsweek.com/sen-orrin-hatch-remembers-ted-kennedy-78653.

15 Bryce J. Dietrich, "Using Motion Detection to Measure Social Polarization in the U.S. House of Representatives," *Political Analysis* (2020) at www.brycejdietrich.com/files/papers/Dietrich_cspan.pdf.
16 Kenneth Janda, *Political Parties: A Cross-National Survey* (New York: The Free Press, 1980), p. 5.
17 John Aldrich, *Why Parties?* (Chicago: University of Chicago Press, 1995), p. 23. See also *Why Parties? A Second Look* (Chicago: University of Chicago Press, 2011), p. 21.
18 E.E. Schattschneider, *Party Government* (New York: Rinehart, 1942), p. 1.
19 Earlier parties also used "Republican" in their names—"Democratic" too. In fact, Thomas Jefferson and James Madison founded the "Democratic-Republican" Party in the 1790s in opposition to the dominant Federalist Party. The Democratic-Republicans split into factions in the early 1820s. One group morphed into the Democratic Party, and another into the National Republicans. After Andrew Jackson's re-election in 1832, National Republicans, Anti-masons, and others formed the Whig Party, united in their opposition to Jackson. There is no lineage from the National Republicans to today's Republican Party.
20 Article I, Section 2 of the U.S. Constitution says merely, "The House of Representatives shall be composed of Members chosen every second year by the People of the several States." Similarly, the Twelfth Amendment for the popular election of Senators says: "The Senate of the United States shall be composed of two Senators from each State, elected by the people thereof." It does not prescribe voting procedures.
21 The Constitution specified that the electoral college should be based on the states' representation in Congress: one vote for each Representative and Senator. After World War II and before Alaska and Hawaii were admitted into the Union, the electoral vote totaled 531. For the 1960 election, it rose to 537. The 23rd Amendment to the Constitution gave Washington, DC three electoral votes, equal to the smallest state.
22 Pew Research Center, "In a Politically Polarized Era, Sharp Divides in Both Partisan Coalitions," (December 17, 2019) at www.pewresearch.org/politics/2019/12/17/in-a-politically-polarized-era-sharp-divides-in-both-partisan-coalitions/.
23 A.N. Wilson, "Afterword" in Charles Dickens, *A Tale of Two Cities* (New York: Signet Classics, 2007), pp. 387–388.

2 Partisan Identities

The United States has the world's oldest party system. It also has the world's only true two-party system. The United Kingdom also has two major parties, but several other parties have won seats in the British parliament over the last seven decades, during which fewer than ten persons ever sat in the House of Representatives as other than a Democrat or Republican.[1] The United States also differs from most other countries by having a decentralized and thus weak national party organization. The "American mold" has been described as "decentralized, undisciplined, and, by comparison with the European mass parties, ideologically incoherent."[2] European mass parties and most others have formal members who pay dues, which entitles them to participate in selecting party officials and candidates. In contrast, American parties have no formal members, only voters who self-identify as Democrats and Republicans. That simple act allows party identifiers to help choose their parties' candidates.[3] Sports fans also self-identify with athletic teams, but they do not get to choose their teams' players. Otherwise, political partisans and sports partisans have much in common.

Politics and Sports

Political scientists have often likened political partisans to sports fans. In their book on political parties and voters' social identities, Green, Palmquist, and Schickler say, "*partisanship* is something of a double *entendre*, calling to mind both partisan cheering at sports events and affiliation with political parties."[4] Later, they elaborate:

> Whether we examine survey responses or rates of political participation, it is clear that partisans feel engaged by electoral competition. Like long-standing fans of a local sports team, they have a clear sense of which team to root for. Their team is embedded in how they think of themselves. They take an interest in political news in much the same way that sports fans follow the fortunes of various teams and players. The sports analogy aptly captures the manner in which partisan spectators get caught up in team competition ...[5]

Political scholars Bartle and Bellucci draw an analogy between identifying with a political party "and supporting a football team. Both identifier and fan like to see 'their side' win."[6] Mason, author of a later study on party identity, notes that a political partisan, being emotionally involved with the party's welfare, "behaves more like a sports fan than like a banker choosing an investment."[7]

In contrast, sociologists, psychologists, and others who study sports fans rarely connect them to political partisans. The scholarly analysis of sports fan identities by Dietz-Uhler and Lanter does not mention the words "party" or "parties."[8] The index to the 275+ page edited volume on sports fandom (2008) that includes their study contains no reference to "political." That term is also absent in the index to a more recent (2013) 300-page collection of studies, *Sports Fans, Identity, and Socialization*.[9]

Although political scientists often relate party identifiers to sports fans, they fail to study that relationship. The index to the recent (2017) and massive (550-page) *Routledge Handbook of Elections, Voting Behavior and Public Opinion* has no entry for "sports fans."[10] However, one of its 40 chapters grudgingly recognizes a connection between the studies of political and sports partisans. Writing on "Party Identification," Bowler admits: "At the risk of some over-simplifying, there are at least some analogies between party identification and sport fandom, although it is possible to over-state the correspondence."[11] He then quoted from the Dietz-Uhler and Lanter study referenced above:

> When sports fans identify strongly with a team, they tend to experience more extreme feelings than those who identify weakly with a team. Among the affective consequences of sports fan identification ... are level of arousal, sympathy, post-game affect and enjoyment.[12]

Although Bowler says, "it is possible to over-state the correspondence" between party identification and sports fandom, no one on either side has overstated the relationship. Both political scientists and sports researchers are impressively oblivious of the correspondence between these two forms of partisan identities. The two areas of research exist in virtually parallel, unconnected universes.

By my count, *Sports Fans, Identity, and Socialization* lists 524 references. There are 368 entries (combined) in two recent books on party identification, *Partisan Hearts and Minds: Political Parties and the Social Identities of Voters* (2002), and *Uncivil Agreement: How Politics Became Our Identity* (2018). Among the 524 and 368 references in these sports and political books, there are only four citations in common and only two sources appear in all three books. One is *Bowling Alone*, Putnam's classic study of social disengagement in America.[13] The other common source is work by the social psychologist Henri Tajfel, a pioneer in social identity theory during the 1970s, and his student John Turner.[14] That reference by both groups of scholars marks the fork in the road that separated each group's travel.

Today, leading researchers in political and sports partisanship employ social identity theory—as reflected in the titles of the books cited above. Back in 1979, Tajfel and Turner applied "social identity" to "those *aspects of an individual's self-image* that derive from the social categories to which he perceives himself as belonging."[15] As applied to politics and to sports, social identity theory suggests that people identify with political parties (and with sports teams) less for the policies that they advocate (or for their athletic prowess) than for inclusion in their desirable social crowds.[16]

Social Identity Theory and Sports Partisans

Political science emerged as a discipline separate from history at universities in the nineteenth century. When the American Political Science Association was founded in 1903, political scientists were already studying elections and electoral behavior. Sociology was also a recognized discipline in the nineteenth century. Although the American Sociological Association was founded in 1905, sports sociology was not recognized as an organized, legitimate field of study until the 1970s. The North American Society for the Sociology of Sport was not formed until 1978. So it is not surprising that political scientists studied partisan identification long before sociologists, social psychologists, and other scholars began studying the identities of sports fans. Nevertheless, sports researchers more quickly structured their studies around social identity theory.

Political scientists may discount studies of sports partisans, regarding the research as less significant than studies of political partisans. As academics, political scientists should realize that far more countries have sports teams than political parties, and that live sporting events regularly outdraw live political events even in countries with parties. Moreover, "mediated" sport events—those covered by electronic media—regularly draw even larger audiences and greater interest from a variety of academic fields outside of the liberal arts. Scholars in journalism, communications, and business study various aspects of sports fandom. A recent compendium lists

> research pertaining to factors associated with fans' identification with teams, athletes, and fellow fans; the social and psychological effect of fan identification; coverage of sports and gender and racial differences in coverage; sports marketing; portrayals of sports, teams, and to fans; audience motives for viewing sports; and an array of cognitive, emotional and behavioral effects.[17]

Sports partisanship quickly captured the attention of academic researchers, and social identity theory provided "the basis for the study of sports fan identification."[18] One group writing in the *International Journal of Sport Management and Marketing* said that "the fundamental human need to feel a sense of belongingness with others may be related to sport team identification."[19] Others wrote, "[T]he extent to which a fan feels a psychological connection to a team and/or player is a central component of one's overall social identity."[20] Social scientists' interest in studying fans' identifications with sports team increased in the late 1980s.[21]

In 1993, working within the framework of social identity theory, Wann and Branscombe created a Sport Spectator Identification Scale (SSIS) consisting of seven questions, each scored from 1 to 8 using a Likert-type format. Applied to a sample of 358 introductory psychology students, the seven items were sufficiently intercorrelated to generate a scale with high *alpha* value of 0.93.[22] Psychologists Dietz-Uhler and Lanter say that the SSIS scale, rooted in social identity theory, is "the most widely and extensively used tool for measuring sports fan identification."[23] By 2012, the SSIS scale was translated into German, Dutch, Japanese, and French.[24]

As alternative approaches to measuring other aspects of "allegiance between a sports fan and a team" emerged, the SSIS underwent closer psychometric scrutiny.[25] Subjecting SSIS to Item Response Theory (IRT) as well as Classical Test Theory (CRT), scholars found limits to the scale's ability to capture very high levels of fan identification but that it provided "adequate information for spectators with low to moderate levels of identification with their teams."[26]

Research on sports fans tends to focus on how they deal with the success or failure of their teams: "For those with a deep psychological attachment to a team, emotions such as enjoyment, happiness, satisfaction, and anxiety can fluctuate dramatically depending on the success or failure of the highly-valued team."[27] Researchers recognize that "Fans identify with each other through their shared passion forming bond stemming from shared experiences of team success and failure."[28]

One argument against those who liken sports fans to political partisans considers the stakes of the contest: "Football fans win nothing of material significance when their team wins the world championship, whereas partisans may win desired policy outcomes."[29] The counter argument is that both sets of partisans desperately want their sides to win "even if they do not produce benefits in office or play attractive football," which recognizes the "'primitive' or 'tribal' element" to partisanship.[30] As a political scientist notes, "When partisans lose an election, they take a hit to their self-esteem, which is wrapped up in their partisan identity."[31]

Of course, sports partisans do differ from political partisans in several ways. Three differences are especially important:

1. While both identifiers are rooted in parental socialization, partisan identity of sports fans is strongly influenced by other factors. Dietz and Uhler write that one major study

    showed a variety of reasons for original interest in a team, including (in order of importance) parental interest in a team, talent of the team players, geography and the influence of friends, and the success of the team. Other investigations ... find similar reasons for identifying with a particular team, although not necessarily in the same order ...[Others found] that geographical location was the predominant reason given for being a fan of a team ...[and] that the success of a team was the primary reason for team identification.[32]

Concerning geography, team proximity was one element but sense of "place" was another.[33] In contrast to sports teams, political parties have no home towns.

2. True sports fans typically follow both their sports and their teams more closely than strong political partisans follow politics and their parties. Gill contends:

> An individual's knowledge of a sports organization is a defining aspect of being a fan. ... Acceptance of an individual as a "real" or "authentic" fan partially relies on one's ability to articulate the critical historical moments that have developed and shaped the experiences, memories, and identification of the fan community.[34]

Daily newspapers in metropolitan areas often devote more pages to sporting events than political news. True sports fans usually talk more knowledgeably about the composition and record of their favorite teams than strong political partisans can discuss the composition and performance of their favorite parties. Political partisans seldom need to demonstrate political knowledge to prove their status.

3. Sports fans in the United States can identify with many different teams playing many different games, while political partisans are limited to choosing between the Democratic and Republican parties. As a result, European scholars in multiparty countries find the American measure of party identification of little use, whereas sports researchers across the world measure fan identification with multiple favorite teams.[35] One study of 986 students from several U.S. universities found that the average student followed "approximately three teams closely, two teams moderately, and one and a half teams casually."[36]

Social Identity Theory and Political Partisans

Beginning with our first general election in the eighteenth century, political observers scrutinized election records to divine voters' partisanship. By the first decades of the twentieth century, researchers were systematically analyzing votes cast in precincts, towns, and counties to determine where Democrats, Republicans, and other partisans clustered. Not until the advent of sample survey research in the 1930s were researchers able to link votes cast with voters' attitudes and opinions. World War II prevented political scientists and sociologists from developing and applying this new methodology until after 1945. Others have documented the history of electoral behavior research in the late 1940s and early 1950s.[37]

We skip to 1960, with the publication of *The American Voter*, by Angus Campbell, Warren E. Miller, Philip E. Converse, and Donald E. Stokes at the University of Michigan's Survey Research Center. Described in the late 1970s as a "paradigmatic" work that set boundaries and standards for subsequent research in electoral behavior,[38] *The American Voter* remains today the touchstone for voting studies. Mine is based on two of *The American Voter*'s salient contributions: (a) its measurement of citizens' identification with political parties and (b) its legacy of data—seven decades of national election studies.

In every presidential election from 1952 to 2016, the American National Election Studies (ANES) asked a national sample of voters, *"Generally speaking, do you usually think of yourself as a Republican, a Democrat, an independent, or what?"* That question was followed by an additional pair. Those who answered "Republican" or "Democrat" were asked: *"Would you call yourself a strong (REP/DEM) or a not very strong (REP/DEM)?"* Those who answered "independent" were asked: *"Do you think of yourself as closer to the Republican or Democratic party?"* The authors fashioned this set of three questions into a seven-point scale of "party identification":

1	2	3	4	5	6	7
Democrat Strong	Democrat Weak	Independent Democrat	Independent	Independent Republican	Republican Weak	Republican Strong

Figure 2.1 displays how the American electorate distributed along this scale from the 1952 presidential election to early in the 2020 election year, thanks to the Voter Study Group asking a representative sample of the population nearly the identical set of questions from January through April, 2020.[39]

Two generations of political scientists have relied on national survey data collected on voting behavior in national elections by the American National Election Studies.[40] They used these questions as the measure of party identification, sometimes called the "Michigan Model,"[41] to study American voting behavior. The ANES data provided an invaluable collection of comparable data on American politics. The original study was conceived in the early 1950s without much attention to developments in psychometrics. Consequently, its questions were not designed with thoughts about classical test theory or item response theory, under development at the time.[42] Campbell, Converse, Miller, and Stokes simply viewed answers as indicating whether the respondent had a "psychological attachment" to a political party.[43]

Although they wrote more than a decade before the emergence of social identity theory, later researchers found that only the first question had a social identity interpretation. Greene said: "In asking, responses to the

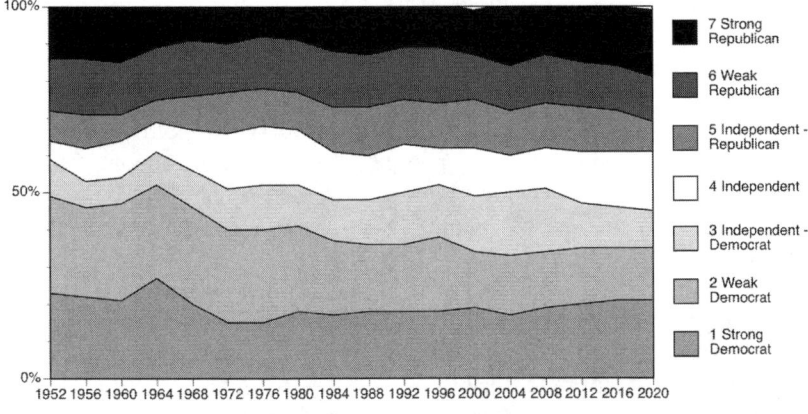

Figure 2.1 Distribution of Political Party Identifiers on Seven-Point Scale, 1952–2020*

first question ('do you think of yourself as') are clearly relying on *self-*categorization as a group member—a central element of social identity theory."[44] The second pair of questions—asking respondents if they were strong/weak DEM/REP partisans, or, if independent, were "closer" to either of the parties—suggested strength of psychological attachment, as the authors claimed. Thus, Greene said, they had conflated "two related, yet conceptually distinct, elements of partisanship into a single measure."[45] In hindsight, Warren Miller, an architect of the ANES questions, agreed that the follow-up questions "blurred the clarity of the basic concept of identification with a political party."[46]

Although *The American Voter* was based on voters' attitudes and not on their social characteristics, Weisberg and Greene contend it also reflected reference group concepts of the 1950s.[47] Indeed, some researchers argue that the Michigan School was "forward-looking" about social identities "before the social identity theory" of Tajfel and Turner."[48] Despite dispute over whether the classic text was rooted in social identity and despite using a measure called "party identification," most researchers treated the Michigan scale of partisanship as assessing a political attitude, not a group identity.[49]

Before proceeding further, we must separate social identity theory as applied to politics from the more popular and emotionally charged term, "identity politics." Bernstein says:

> The term identity politics is widely used throughout the social sciences and the humanities to describe phenomena as diverse as

multiculturalism, the women's movement, civil rights, lesbian and gay movements, separatist movements in Canada and Spain, and violent ethnic and nationalist conflict in postcolonial Africa and Asia, as well as in the formerly communist countries of Eastern Europe.[50]

Whereas "identity politics" is commonly associated with political demands to grant rights to disadvantaged people,[51] "social identity theory" regards party identification as an individual's emotional attachment to a social world, "a sense of shared identity with a particular group."[52] Huddy, Mason, and Aaroe state:

> A social identity involves a subjective sense of belonging to a group that is internalized to varying degrees, resulting in individual differences in identity strength, a desire to positively distinguish the group from others, and the development of ingroup bias. Moreover, once identified with a group or, in this instance, a political party, members are motivated to protect and advance the party's status and electoral dominance as a way to maintain their party's positive distinctiveness.[53]

Prior to this sociological explanation of party identification, scholars explained voters' preferences in terms of politics. In 1957, Anthony Downs' highly influential book, *An Economic Theory of Democracy*, advanced the "axiom" that "each citizen casts his vote for the party he believes will provide him more benefits than any other."[54] The supposed benefits came in the form of economic policies (tax rates, subsidies, regulation, welfare), social policies (education, race relations, immigration) or foreign policies (anticommunism, free trade).[55] To identify with the party that served your politics was the rational course of action.

In historical and cross-national perspective, this rational-choice model of party identification in America clashed with European party models. In their heyday, European "mass" parties had formal members drawn from sectors of society and appealed to their voters' sense of social and political solidarity.[56] In a sense, the electorate was separated into sociopolitical "silos" or "pillars," in a process called "pillarization": "the cultural, political, and cultural organization of society into separate strata" in the party system.[57] In contrast, American parties were characterized in the contemporary, postwar literature as socially rootless. In a series of publications in the 1950s and 1960s, Otto Kirchheimer characterized American parties as "catch-all" parties that sought to bridge the "socioeconomic and cultural cleavages among the electorate in order to attract a broader 'audience.'"[58]

If American parties followed the "catch-all" model in the 1950s and early 1960s, they have not for the last few decades sought to become a "big tent" for all sorts of voters. Analysts today speak instead of political polarization, of Democrats and especially Republicans, being "sorted" into socially distinct groups. Mason writes:

Partisan Identities 23

In particular, the Republican Party is now largely made up of White, Christian, self-identified conservatives, while the Democratic Party is generally characterized by non-White, non-Christian, self-identified liberals. ...

In Democratic congressional districts, citizens were more likely to buy food at stores like Whole Foods, Dunkin Donuts, and Trader Joe's. In Republican congressional districts, hungry shoppers headed to Arby's, Cracker Barrel, and Kroger. Clothing shoppers went to American Apparel and L.L. Bean in Democratic districts and to Dillard's and Old Navy in Republican districts.[59]

This resembles the party pillarization that occurred in Europe. Why have some American voters switched from choosing political parties because of their policies to identifying with them because of their social characteristics? Along with others, I try to explain using social identity theory, which contends that many voters derive social benefits from identifying with a party. They may regard these social benefits as important or more important than the parties' policies.

Party Identity in the United States Since 1952

Political scientists generally agree that voters who claim to be Democrats or Republicans acquire their party identifications through parental influence.[60] However, children do not automatically "acquire" parental party loyalties; partisanship comes from their other "life experiences,"[61] which involves "a process of largely informal learning ... as a consequence of interactions with parents, family, friends, neighbors, peers, colleagues, and so forth."[62] Ojeda and Hatemi contend that the "social milieu" in which children grow into adults substantially reduces parental influence on their party identifications.[63] In later work, Ojeda and Hatemi found "the transmission of party identification from parents to children occurs less than half the time on average."[64] Often, the social milieu leads children to reflect the politics of friends and neighbors as they form their own political and social identity.

Tajfel and Turner say that a person's "social identity" consists of "those aspects of an individual's self-image that derive from the social categories to which he perceives himself as belonging."[65] About party identity, Druckman and Levendusky say, "Identifying with a party divides the world into a liked ingroup (one's own party), and a disliked outgroup (the opposing party)."[66] Researchers agree that the sense of belonging in politics is addressed by the first question in the ANES set, "*Generally speaking, do you usually think of yourself as a Republican, a Democrat, an independent, or what?*"

The two other questions get at strength of partisanship. One asked Democrats and Republicans if they were "strong" or "not so strong" identifiers, but they were still identifiers. The other asked "Independents" whether they were closer to either party. Research shows that those who admit "leaning" more to one party than the other often favor that party in policy opinions and voting choice. Nevertheless, Greene says, they "lack a group identification as a Democrat or Republican."[67] Voters may insist on being classified as "independent" for various reasons—prizing individualism, viewing parties negatively, regarding the two parties as undesirable outgroups, and being politically neutral—but they still reject identifying with a party.[68]

These arguments call for using data only from the first question in our analysis of the parties' social bases. Voters who think of themselves as a Democrat or Republican (whether "strong" or "weak") will be regarded as having adopted such partisanship as their social identity. Figure 2.2 displays the distribution of party identities in the American electorate over 68 years involving 17 presidential elections to the summer of 2020. It shows that the percentage of citizens identifying with the Republican Party has been fairly stable over time, while the percentage identifying as Democrats has dropped somewhat. Increasingly, more respondents claim to be Independent—a term henceforth capitalized to treat it as a third category when we study the parties' appeal to social groups.

Does simply asking respondents whether they "think" of themselves as Democrats, Republicans, and Independents have any construct validity, any meaningful relationship to their voting behavior? Yes, it does. Consider how partisans voted for president in the 17 elections from 1952 to 2016. Except for McGovern's disastrous loss to Nixon in 1972, those who

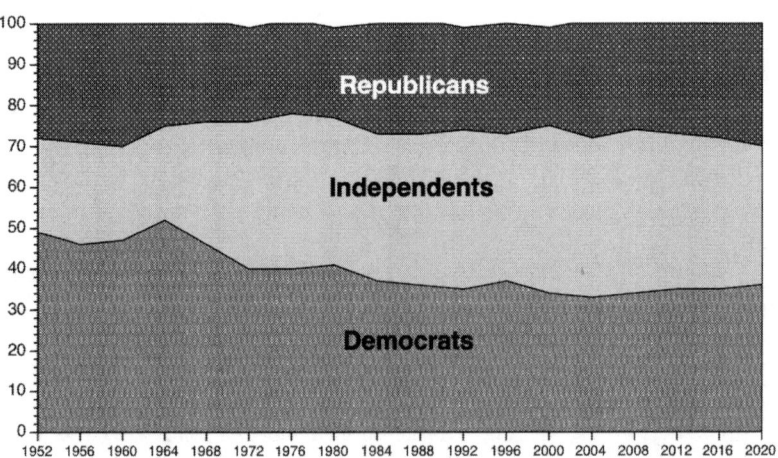

*Data for 1952 to 2016 come from the American National Election Studies (www.electionstudies.org) supported by the National Science Foundation under grant numbers SES 1444721, 2014-2017, the University of Michigan, and Stanford University. Data for 2020 come from January-April Surveys by Democracy Fund and UCLA Nationscape.

Figure 2.2 Distribution of Political Party Identifiers on Three-Point Scale, 1952–2020*

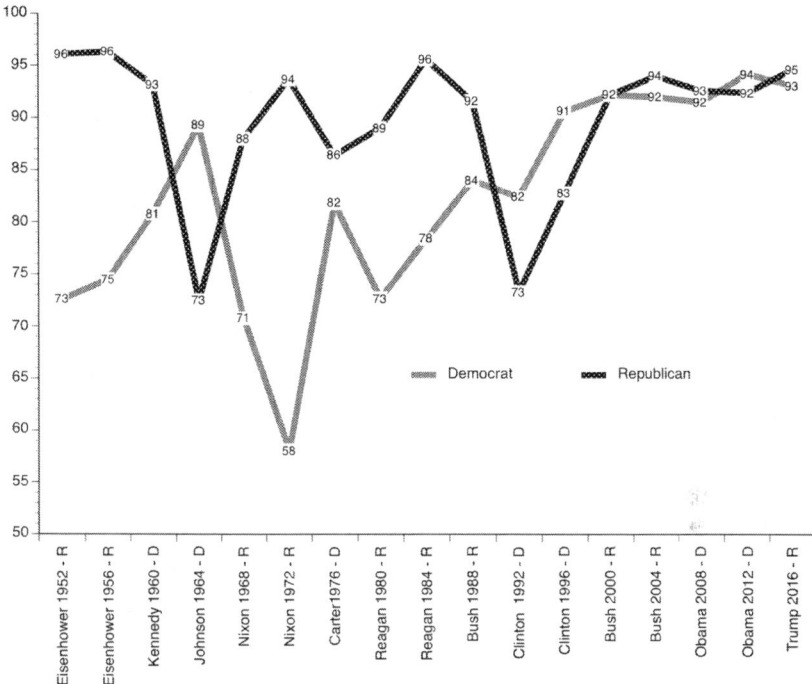

Figure 2.3 Percentage of Party Identifiers Voting for Their Party's Presidential Candidates

thought of themselves as Republicans or Democrats were highly loyal in their party voting. As illustrated in Figure 2.3, 90 percent of self-identified Republicans and 82 percent of self-identified Democrats voted for their own party's candidates. Moreover, in the five presidential elections since 2000, the voting consequences of partisanship intensified, as an average of 93 percent of Democrats and 93 percent of Republicans voted for their party's presidential candidates.[69]

Two hundred and fifty years ago, a British philosopher and member of parliament defined a political party as "a body of men [*sic*] united for promoting by their joint endeavours the national interest upon some particular principles in which they are all agreed."[70] Such "particular principles" may be more salient to small parties in multiparty systems, perhaps like the Green Party's concern with environmental issues in European parliaments. However, major parties in two-party systems tend to take broader and less definitive stances on government policies, often confusing voters about what they "stand for." American voters' perceptions of differences between the Democratic and Republican parties have changed dramatically over the 16 elections during which the ANES asked, "*Do you think there are any important differences in what the Republicans and Democrats stand*

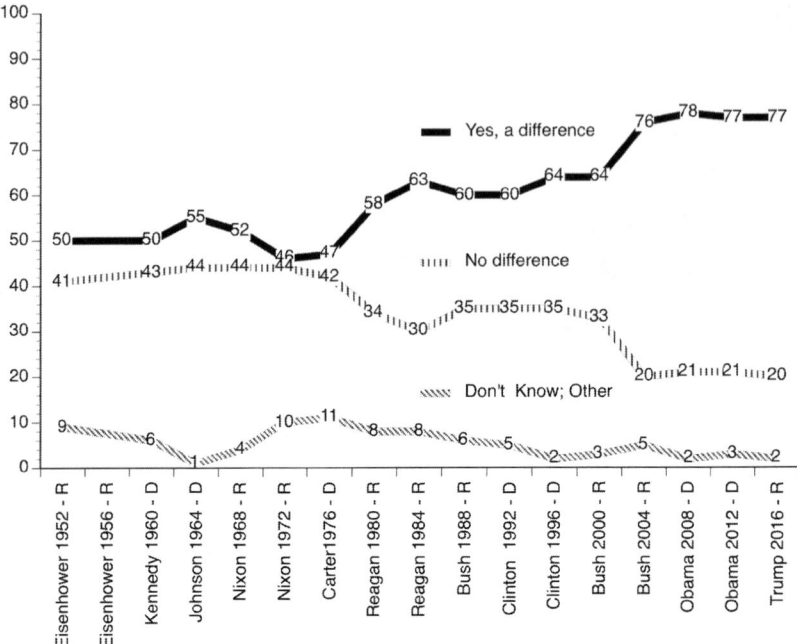

*American National Election Studies, Cumulative Data File, Variable VCF0401, not available for 1956.

Figure 2.4 Percent of Voters Who See Differences Between the Two Major Parties*

for?" Figure 2.4 shows that only half the voters saw any difference in the parties in 1952 but the difference jumped to over 75 percent in 2004 and remained there.

Do not expect the American electorate to explain how the two parties differ, much less to agree on their explanations. Studies show that Americans have widely different understandings of "liberal" and "conservative," two important concepts in American politics.[71] (I discuss ideology at length in Chapter 10.) Nonetheless, when asked which of the two major parties "is more conservative," most voters named the Republican Party, as depicted in Figure 2.5.[72]

Unfortunately, the question (which party is more conservative) was not asked every year. In years it was, from 10 to 20 percent of the voters consistently but strangely saw the Democratic Party as more conservative. While prior to the Clinton presidency almost a third of the electorate said they were both the same or did not know of any differences, that percentage was sliced in half during George W. Bush's presidency and remained low since. Meanwhile, about 70 percent of voters say that the Republican Party is the more conservative, providing more evidence of recent party differences.

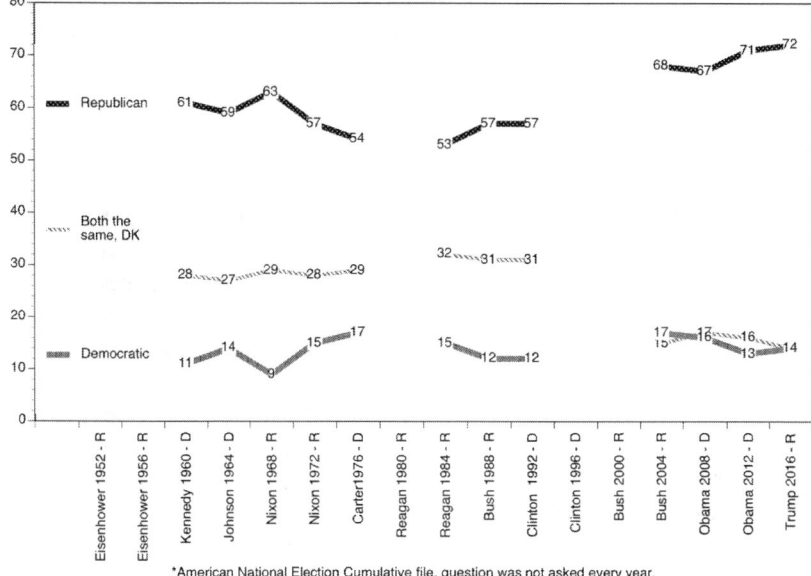

Figure 2.5 Percent of Voters Saying Which Party Is More Conservative*

Emotions in Social Identities

We expect sports fans to identify with athletic teams for social reasons: the teams play nearby, the players are skillful, they win frequently, and the fans' friends are also team fans. In contrast, we expect citizens to identify with the Democratic or Republican parties for political reasons: voters like their governmental policies or philosophy. However, citizens become partisans in politics for social reasons too. According to social identity theory, people identify with both political parties and sports teams out of a desire to be part of their social world. Green, Palmquist, and Schickler contend that "people perceive the parties to have distinct group bases ... and that elections confer status and power on a party and its constituent social groups."[73] They want to belong to those groups.

Recent research by Orr and Huber suggests that "pure partisan animosity in the contemporary public" is "overstated," because much of the animosity is based on "disagreement about contentious issues and not simply teamism."[74] Nevertheless, social identity theory also admits negative motivation. People may align with groups opposed to others they dislike.[75] Consider disliking the New York Yankees, a baseball team that won five World Series from 1949 to 1953. Millions of baseball fans outside New York disliked the Yankees. The 1955 Broadway musical, *Damn Yankees* (later a movie), tells of a man who sold his soul to the devil just to beat the New York Yankees. Consider disliking the Dallas Cowboys, a football team that won the national championship in 1993, 1994, and 1996. Football fans outside Texas found solace in reading the 1997 collection of essays, *I Hate the Dallas Cowboys*.[76] Democrats can feed their group loathing by curling up with *The I Hate Republicans Reader*,[77] and Republicans can bristle at their opponents by reading *Guilty by Reason of Insanity: Why The Democrats Must Not Win*.[78] So political partisans show "teamism" too.

Elites in both parties structure voters' attitudes toward parties, and studies show that both parties' partisans dislike and distrust other party elites more than other party voters.[79] Moreover, all Americans have stereotypic misconceptions of the two parties' composition. Based on a national 2015 survey, Ahler and Sood wrote: "Americans believe that 32% of Democrats are gay, lesbian, or bisexual (only 6.3% are in reality), and that 38% of Republicans earn over $250,000 per year (just 2.2% do in reality)."[80] So voters may become Republicans because they dislike LGBT people or may become Democrats because they abhor rich capitalists.

Today, partisanship is so toxic that candidates no longer disclose party identifications in their advertisements. In 1952, Dwight Eisenhower had bumper stickers exhorting citizens to "Vote Republican," and Adlai Stevenson implored them to "Vote Democratic." In the summer of 2020, the principal candidates did not even mention their parties on their campaign websites.

Reminiscing and Summarizing

If asked to answer the ANES question about party identification, I would say that "generally speaking," I consider myself a Democrat. I do not owe that to my parents, who did not identify with either party and rarely discussed politics. My father did not like the Democratic Party "machine" in Chicago, where he grew up and raised his family, so I presume that he mostly voted Republican. My mother probably voted to support my father, and I have no idea who my parents' friends and relatives favored politically. Nevertheless, survey data (Figure 2.2) show that over 75 percent of the electorate identified as Democrats or Republicans in 1952. Thus, most of our relatives and family friends must have had party identities. As I recall, few people in our circle knew who was a Democrat or a Republican and fewer cared, probably because party differences were no big deal. The "social milieu" of my college experience led me to think of myself as a Democrat.

Readers who did not live during the 1950s may not appreciate how different society was then. Only about 20 percent of homes had television. Most people got national political news from newspapers and radio. While most newspaper owners editorially endorsed Republican candidates,[81] many reporters covered Democrats more favorably to balance the ledger. Three networks (ABC, CBS, and NBC) dominated radio and television broadcasts. Every night, mature, white, pedigreed males read similar news stories selected, edited, and framed by network news gatekeepers. Across the nation, Democrats and Republicans got essentially the same information. Media did not drive partisanship.

Today, there are five major television broadcast networks (adding FOX and PBS) and two major cable news networks (CNN and MSNBC) that offer a greater range of views reported by women, men, and minorities. They reflect a variety of social backgrounds and political persuasions. With fewer gatekeepers, and no one controlling the news gate on the Internet and social media, Democrats and Republicans can feed on alternative sources of information and opinion to selectively reinforce their party identifications.

Because individual citizens have more options to get political information, today's political parties face new challenges in mobilizing and directing their supporters. Alas, neither national party organization is designed to take on that task. Both organizations are empty vehicles awaiting presidential drivers to come every four years.

Notes

1 Wikipedia, "Third Party Members of the House of Representatives," at https://en.wikipedia.org/wiki/Third-party_members_of_the_United_States_House_of_Representatives#1949-present:_Modern_era.
2 Nicol C. Rae and Juan S. Gil, "Party Polarization and Ideology: Diverging Trends in Britain and the US," in Terrence Casey (ed.), *The Legacy of the Crash: How the Financial Crisis Changed America and Britain* (New York: Palgrave Macmillan, 2011), 159–178 at p. 168.
3 Democratic and Republican party members may enjoy the privilege of voting in primary elections to help choose party candidates, but recent research finds that party identifiers in the United States and party affiliates in other countries do not offer a functional equivalence to being party members. See Marc Hooghe and Ann-Kristin Kölln, "Types of Party Affiliation and the Multi-speed Party: What Kind of Party Support Is Functionally Equivalent to Party Membership?" *Party Politics*, 26 (2020), 355–365.
4 Donald Green, Bradley Palmquist, and Eric Schickler, *Partisan Hearts and Minds: Political Parties and the Social Identities of Voters* (New Haven, CT: Yale University Press, 2002), p. 1.
5 *Ibid.*, p. 219.
6 John Bartle and Paolo Bellucci, "Introduction: Partisanship, Social Identity and Individual Attitudes," in Bartle and Bellucci (eds.), *Political Parties and Partisanship: Social Identity and Individual Attitudes* (London: Routledge, 2009), 1–25 at p. 9.
7 Lilliana Mason, "'I Disrespectfully Agree'": The Differential Effects of Partisan Sorting on Social and Issue Polarization," *American Journal of Political Science*, 59 (January, 2015), 128–145 at p. 130.
8 Beth Dietz-Uhler and Jason R. Lanter, "The Consequences of Sports Fan Identification," in Lawrence W. Hugenberg, Paul M. Haridakis, and Adam C. Earnheardt (eds.), *Sports Mania: Essays on Fandom and the Media in the 21st Century* (Jefferson, NC: McFarland, 2008), 103–113.

9 Adam C. Earnheardt, Paul M. Haridakis, and Barbara S. Hugenberg (eds.), *Sports Fans, Identity, and Socialization: Exploring the Fandemonium* (Lanham, MD: Lexington Books, 2013). Citations are to the paperback edition; the hardback came out in 2012.

10 Justin Fisher, Edward Fieldhouse, Mark N. Franklin, Rachel Gibson, Marta Cantijoch, and Christopher Wlezien (eds.), *The Routledge Handbook of Elections, Voting Behavior and Public Opinion* (London: Routledge, 2017).

11 Shaun Bowler, "Party Identification," in Justin Fisher, Edward Fieldhouse, Mark N. Franklin, Rachel Gibson, Marta Cantijoch, and Christopher Wlezien (eds.), *The Routledge Handbook of Elections, Voting Behavior and Public Opinion* (London: Routledge, 2017), 146–157 at p. 154.

12 Quotation from Dietz-Uhler and Lanter, p. 106; cited in Bowler, p. 154.

13 Robert Putnam, *Bowling Alone: The Collapse and Revival of American Community* (New York: Simon & Schuster, 2001).

14 Tajfel and Turner published several influential studies. Green et al. cited Tajfel's edited book, *Differentiation Between Social Groups: Studies in the Social Psychology of Intergroup Relations* (London: Academic Press, 1978). Mason cited Henri Tajfel, M.G. Billig, R.P. Bundy, and Claude Flament, "Social Categorization and Intergroup Behaviour," *European Journal of Social Psychology* 1 (1971), 149–178. In their collection of sports fan studies, Hugenberg et al. cited the 1971 Tajfel paper (reprinted in Tajfel's 1978 volume) and two studies by Tajfel and Turner in 1979 and 1986.

15 Henri Tajfel and John Turner, "An Integrative Theory of Intergroup Conflict," in W.G. Austin and S. Worchel (eds.), *The Social Psychology of Intergroup Relations* (Monterey, CA: Brooks/Cole, 1979), 33–47.

16 Here, "social crowds" means desirable friends and not physical crowds. The relationship between social identity theory and crowd psychology is explored in John Drury and Steve Reicher, "The Intergroup Dynamics of Collective Empowerment: Substantiating the Social Identity Model of Crowd Behaviour," *Group Processes & Intergroup Relations*, 2 (1999), 381–402.

The social identity model argues that, in the mass, personal identity becomes less salient and people act in terms of that social identity that is associated with the relevant social category. Control over behavior is not lost but rather governed by the understandings and values that define social identity.

17 Paul M. Haridakis and Adam C. Earnheardt, "Understanding Fans' Consumption and Dissemination of Sports: An Introduction," in Adam C. Earnheardt, Paul M. Haridakis, and Barbara S. Hugenberg (eds.), *Sports Fans, Identity, and Socialization: Exploring the Fandemonium* (Lanham, MD: Lexington Books, 2013), 1–6 at p. 3.

18 Dietz-Uhler and Lanter, p. 103.

19 Nicholas D. Theodorakis, D.L. Wann, P. Nassis, and T.B. Luellen, "The Relationship Between Sport Team Identification and the Need to Belong," *International Journal of Sport Management and Marketing*, 12 (2012), 25–38 at p. 27.

20 Nicholas D. Theodorakis, Daniel L. Wann, and Stephen Weaverat, "An Antecedent Model of Team Identification in the Context of Professional Soccer," *Sport Marketing Quarterly*, 21 (2012), 80–90 at p. 80.

21 Nicholas D. Theodorakis, Nikolaos Tsigilis, Daniel L. Wann, G. Lianopoulos, and Ahmed Al-Emadi, "Sport Spectator Identification Scale: An Item

Response Analysis Approach," *International Journal of Sport Management*, 17 (2016), 178–196 at p. 179.
22 Daniel L. Wann and Nyla R. Branscombe, "Sports Fans: Measuring Degree of Identification with Their Team," *International Journal of Sport Psychology*, 24 (1993), 1–17.
23 Dietz-Uhler and Lanter, p. 105.
24 Theodorakis, Wann, and Weaverat.
25 Theodorakis et al., "Sport Spectator Identification Scale" at p. 178.
26 *Ibid.*, p. 191. Classical Test Theory and Response Item Theory are discussed in Luis Anunciacao, "An Overview of the History and Methodological Aspects of Psychometrics," *Journal for ReAttach Therapy and Developmental Diversities* (August, 2018), 44–58.
27 Dietz-Uhler and Lanter, p. 107.
28 Matthew Gill, "Communicating Organizational History to Sports Fans," in Adam C. Earnheardt, Paul M. Haridakis, and Barbara S. Hugenberg (eds.), *Sports Fans, Identity, and Socialization: Exploring the Fandemonium* (Lanham, MD: Lexington Books, 2013), 151–164 at p. 151.
29 Green, Palmquist, and Schickler, p. 219.
30 Bartle and Bellucci, p. 9.
31 Lilliana Mason, *Uncivil Agreement: How Politics Became Our Identity* (Chicago: University of Chicago Press, 2018), p. 84.
32 Dietz-Uhler and Lanter, p. 105.
33 Joseph Tyson, "Fan Avidity as it Relates to Proximity of Minor and Major League Affiliates," *Sport Management Undergraduate* (2013), Paper 92; and Roger C. Aden and Scott Titsworth, "Remain Rooted in a Sea of Red: Agrarianism, Place Attachment, and Nebraska Cornhusker Fans," in Adam C. Earnheardt, Paul M. Haridakis, and Barbara S. Hugenberg (eds.), *Sports Fans, Identity, and Socialization: Exploring the Fandemonium* (Lanham, MD: Lexington Books, 2013), 9–23.
34 Gill, p. 152.
35 Nicholas D. Theodorakis, Ahmed Al-Emadi, Daniel Wann, Yannis Lianopoulos, and Alexandra Foudouki, "An Examination of Levels of Fandom, Team Identification, Socialization Processes, and Fan Behaviors in Qatar," *Journal of Sport Behavior*, 40 (January, 2017), 1–21.
36 Frederick G. Grieve et al., "Identification with Multiple Sporting Teams: How Many Teams Do Sport Fans Follow?" *Journal of Contemporary Athletics*, 3 (1999), 283–294 at p. 286.
37 See Herbert F. Weisberg and Steven H. Greene, "The Political Psychology of Party Identification," in Michael MacKuen and George Rabinowitz (eds.), *Electoral Democracy* (Ann Arbor: University of Michigan Press, 2003), 83–124; and Bowler.
38 Gerald M. Pomper, "The Impact of *The American Voter* on Political Science," *Political Science Quarterly*, 93 (Winter, 1978–1979), 617–628.
39 These options were presented online to a demographically representative sample of approximately 110,000 adults from January through March, 2020: "*Generally speaking, do you think of yourself as a Democrat, Republican, [or] Independent?* … [If Democrat or Republican] *Would you call yourself a strong Democrat/ Republican or a not very strong Democrat/Republican?* [If Independent, other, or not sure] *If you had to choose, would you lean more toward the Republican Party*

candidate or the Democratic Party candidate? I thank Professor Lynn Vavreck, Principal Investigator of the Nationscape project at UCLA, for access to these data in advance of general release and to doctoral candidate Tyler Reny for generating the tables and guiding me in using them.

40 Nancy Burns, "The Michigan, then National, then American National Election Studies," (2006) at www.isr.umich.edu/cps/ANES_history.pdf.
41 Weisberg and Greene, p. 2.
42 See Anunciacao.
43 Leonie Huddy, Lilliana Mason, and Lene Aaroe, "Expressive Partisanship: Campaign Involvement, Political Emotion, and Partisan Identity," *American Political Science Review*, 109, No. 1 (February 2015), online doi:10.1017/S0003055414000604 at p. 1.
44 Steven Greene, "The Social-Psychological Measurement of Partisanship," *Political Behavior*, 24, No. 3 (September, 2002), 171–197 at p. 174.
45 *Ibid.*, p. 174.
46 Warren E. Miller, "Party Identification, Realignment, and Party Voting: Back to the Basics," *American Political Science Review*, 85 (June, 1991), 557–568 at p. 558.
47 Weisberg and Greene, p. 2. However, Mason and Wronski argue that group identification receded in importance in following decades. See Lilliana Mason and Julie Wronski, "One Tribe to Bind Them All: How Our Social Group Attachments Strengthen Partisanship," *Advances in Political Psychology*, 39 (Suppl. 1, 2018), 257–277 at p. 258.
48 Warren Miller claimed that *The American Voter* sought "to build on the concept of group (party) identification." See Miller, p. 558.
49 Mason and Wronski write: "In the decades after the publication of *The American Voter*, the central relevance of social group identification in American political behavior receded" (p. 258).
50 Mary Bernstein, "Identity Politics," *Annual Review of Sociology*, 31 (2005), 47–74.
51 Carlos Lozada, "Show Me Your Identification," *Outlook, Washington Post Book Review* (October 18, 2018) at www.washingtonpost.com/news/book-party/wp/2018/10/18/feature/.
52 Mason, "'I Disrespectfully Agree,'" p. 130; and Mason and Wronski, p. 259.
53 Huddy, Mason, and Aaroe.
54 Anthony Downs, *An Economic Theory of Democracy* (New York: HarperCollins, 1957), p. 36.
55 For a short review of political explanations of voter choice, see Georg Wenzelburger and Reimut Zohlhöfer, "Bringing Agency Back into the Study of Partisan Politics: A Note on Recent Developments in the Literature on Party Politics," *Party Politics* (March, 2020) online.
56 Piero Ignazi, *Party and Democracy: The Uneven Road to Party Legitimacy* (Oxford: Oxford University Press, 2017), 224–225.
57 Koen Stapelbroek, "Pillarization," in George Thomas Kurian (ed.), *The Encyclopedia of Political Science, Volume 4* (Washington, DC: CQ Press, 2011), p. 1209.
58 Kirchheimer's work is discussed at length by Andre Krouwel, "Party Models," in Richard S. Katz and William Crotty (eds.), *Handbook of Party Politics* (London: SAGE, 2006), 249–269 at p. 258.
59 Lilliana Mason, "Losing Common Ground: Social Sorting and Polarization," *The Forum*, 16, No. 1 (2018), 47–66 at p. 48.

60 Christopher H. Achen, "Parental Socialization and Rational Party Identification," *Political Behavior*, 24, No. 2, Special Issue: Parties and Partisanship, Part One (June, 2002), 151–170.
61 Bowler, pp. 149–150.
62 Anja Neundorf and Kaat Smets, "Political Socialization and the Making of Citizens," in *Oxford Handbooks Online* (www.oxfordhandbooks.com), (Oxford: Oxford University Press, 2018) at p. 1.
63 Christopher Ojeda and Peter K. Hatemi, "Accounting for the Child in the Transmission of Party Identification," *American Sociological Review*, 80 (2015), 1150–1174.
64 Peter K. Hatemi and Christopher Ojeda, "The Role of Child Perception and Motivation in Political Socialization," *British Journal of Political Science* (February, 2020), published online by Cambridge University Press.
65 Tajfel and Turner, p. 40.
66 James N. Druckman and Matthew S. Levendusky, "What Do We Measure When We Measure Affective Polarization?" *Public Opinion Quarterly*, 83 (Spring, 2019), 114–122 at p. 115.
67 Greene, p. 174.
68 Jack Dennis, "Political Independence in America, Part II: Towards a Theory," *British Journal of Political Science*, 18 (1988), 197–219.
69 Those who said they were Independent were less likely to vote. When they did, they split, voting Republican 52 percent of the time and Democratic 43 percent. Independents were also more likely to vote for third-party presidential candidates on ballots in 1968, 1980, 1992, and 1996.
70 Edmund Burke, *Thoughts on the Cause of the Present Discontents* (1770).
71 Kenneth Janda, *The Social Bases of Political Parties: Democrats and Republicans, 1952–2012 and 2032* (eBook edition 1.0, February, 2013), 72–74.
72 Questions about the parties' ideology were not asked before 1960, and omitted in 1980, 1996, and 2000. Also the wording varied. From 1984 on, it was, "Would you say that either one of the parties is more conservative than the other at the national level? (IF YES:) Which party is more conservative?"
73 Green, Palmquist, and Schickler, pp. 219–220.
74 Lilla V. Orr and Gregory A. Huber, "The Policy Basis of Measured Partisan Animosity in the United States," *American Journal of Political Science*, 64 (July, 2020), 569–586 at p. 584.
75 Shanto Iyengar, Gaurav Sood, and Yphtach Lelkes, "Affect, Not Ideology: A Social Identity Perspective on Polarization," *Public Opinion Quarterly*, 76 (Fall, 2012), 405–431.
76 Bert Sugar (ed.), *I Hate the Dallas Cowboys: And Who Elected Them America's Team Anyway?* (New York: St. Martin's Griffin, 1997).
77 Clint Willis (ed.), *The I Hate Republicans Reader: Why the GOP Is Totally Wrong About Everything* (New York: Thundermount Press, 2003).
78 David Limbaugh, *Guilty by Reason of Insanity: Why the Democrats Must Not Win* (Washington, DC: Regnery, 2019).
79 Druckman and Levendusky.
80 Douglas J. Ahler and Gaurav Sood, "The Parties in Our Heads: Misperceptions About Party Composition and Their Consequences," *The Journal of Politics*, 80 (April 27, 2018) at 965. Published online at http://dx.doi.org/10.1086/697253.
81 Micah Cohen, "Political Newspaper Endorsements: History and Outcome," *FiveThirtyEight* (October 26, 2011) at https://fivethirtyeight.com/features/political-newspaper-endorsements-history-and-outcome/.

3 Party Organization and Social Groupings

Established national political parties are political institutions—like legislatures, courts, and executive agencies. While citizens can visit legislatures, sit in courts, and photograph presidents and cabinet secretaries, they cannot readily experience or "see" a political party. They only see candidates running under party names. Like "leprechauns in the political forest,"[1] political parties are invisible to most voters. Although imposing buildings in Washington house the Democratic National Committee (DNC) and the Republican National Committee (RNC), their national headquarters seldom appear on television. Each committee has a national chair presiding over a hundred committee members. At the start of 2020, the DNC was chaired by Tom Perez, the RNC by Ronna McDaniel. The media rarely covered either person's activities, and—regardless of which party wins the presidency in 2020—one or perhaps both party chairs will be replaced soon after the election.

The Invisible and Ineffective National Party Committees

As DNC chair during Donald Trump's presidency, Tom Perez was more active and influential within the Democratic Party than was the RNC chair, Ronna McDaniel, within the Republican Party. The national chair of the non-presidential party has always been more prominent than the presidential party chair, because the president, as *de facto* party leader, eclipses the sitting party chair. After the 2016 election, President Trump elevated existing RNC chair, Reince Priebus, to White House chief of staff, and replaced him with loyalist Ronna McDaniel. Appointing a national party chair as the president's chief of staff was unusual, and appointing Priebus was especially strange—as we will see. Priebus lasted only six months in the White House before President Trump replaced him.

Despite their designations as "national" party committees, the DNC and the RNC are not hierarchical organizations towering over Democratic and Republican office-holders in the House and Senate. They have virtually no control over their party members in Congress, who govern themselves through separate party conferences in both houses. Each party in the House and Senate forms separate campaign committees to elect

Democrats and Republicans to their respective chambers. Although the national committees often provide funds to help state party organizations, they have no direct authority over state parties. American national parties are not pyramids of power.

However, the national committees are in charge of their national party conventions held every four years to nominate their presidential candidates. They also determine the dates and rules for debates among individuals seeking the conventions' presidential nomination. The committees select the convention sites, invite their state parties to attend, and so on. Confronted by the COVID-19 pandemic in 2020, both national committees acted to change their summer convention plans. The DNC kept the Democratic convention in Milwaukee but changed it from mid-July to mid-August, and then made it accessible to delegates only over the Internet. The RNC scheduled its convention for late August in Charlotte, North Carolina. When that city limited attendance because of COVID-19, President Trump split the convention, holding opening sessions in Charlotte and closing sessions in Jacksonville, Florida. Further outbreaks in Florida led him to switch the convention back to Charlotte, leaving a harried RNC to handle arrangements.

More importantly than arranging the national party conventions, the DNC and RNC serve as repositories of vital information about the electoral behavior of states, congressional districts, counties, cities, and voters. The party's presidential nominee gets access to this information, to statistical analysts who can interpret the data, and to professional consultants who can provide strategic and tactical advice for the campaign. Sometimes, the party's nominee rejects the professional advice and wins anyway. Consider the advice that RNC chair Reince Priebus presented to his party in 2013, and how 2016 Republican nominee Donald Trump responded to it.

RNC Advice, 2013, and Trump Campaign, 2016

In 2013, RNC chair Reince Priebus confronted the facts. Democratic presidential candidate Barack Obama was elected with 53 percent of the vote in 2008 and re-elected in 2012 with another, though smaller, absolute majority of the popular vote and 62 percent of the electoral vote. Responding to these Republican losses, Priebus launched the Growth and Opportunity Project and charged it with

> making recommendations and assisting in putting together a plan to grow the Party and improve Republican campaigns. We were asked to dig deep to provide an honest review of the 2012 election cycle and a path forward for the Republican Party to ensure success in winning more elections.[2]

The project's authors met with thousands of people "both outside Washington and inside the Beltway," spoke with "voters, technical experts, private sector officials, Party members, and elected office holders," conducted polls, and consulted pollsters before issuing its 100-page report.[3]

The report began by noting: "Republicans have lost the popular vote in five of the last six presidential elections."[4] It urged the party to recognize "the nation's demographic changes":

> In 1980, exit polls tell us that the electorate was 88 percent white. In 2012, it was 72 percent white. Hispanics made up 7 percent of the electorate in 2000, 8 percent in 2004, 9 percent in 2008 and 10 percent in 2012. According to the Pew Hispanic Center, in 2050, whites will be 47 percent of the country while Hispanics will grow to 29 percent and Asians to 9 percent.
>
> If we want ethnic minority voters to support Republicans, we have to engage them and show our sincerity.[5]

On June 16, 2015, Donald Trump announced his candidacy for the Republican Party's presidential nomination. During which, he said:

> When Mexico sends its people, they're not sending their best. They're sending people that have lots of problems, and they're bringing those problems with us. They're bringing drugs. They're bringing crime. They're rapists. And some, I assume, are good people.[6]

If candidate Trump knew about the RNC's advice to "show our sincerity" to "ethnic minority voters," he did not take it. Instead, he explicitly flaunted the professional team's studied advice and appealed directly to the dwindling white portion of the American electorate. Nonetheless, RNC chair Reince Priebus, who sponsored the party study, backed Trump's campaign. Trump won the 2016 presidential election, and Priebus became his chief of staff. The long and expensive RNC report was later purged from the national committee's website.[7] Such is the status of the national party committees in contemporary American politics.

Trump Campaign in 2020

Against most political analysts' expectations, Donald Trump's bold decision to play to disgruntled segments of the white working class electorate paid off in 2016. Entering the 2020 election year, political analysts remained unconvinced that it was a winning strategy for re-election. *Wall Street Journal* reporters wrote:

> President Trump's 2020 election strategy relies largely on the white, working-class base that he excited in 2016. But he faces a demographic challenge: The electorate has changed since he was last on the ballot in ways likely to benefit Democrats.[8]

Of course, that was what the RNC's *Growth and Opportunity* report had warned about. Trump won anyway. He successfully gambled against the 2013 advice of the RNC about where American society and politics stood and where they were moving.

Political observers today often refer to a party's "base." The term appeared in the 2013 RNC *Growth and Opportunity* report, which stressed "the Party's modern vision to expand and diversify the base of the Republican Party" and recommended efforts "to increase the Party base by promoting the inclusion in the Party of traditionally under-represented groups and affiliations."[9] After Donald Trump's surprising election in 2016, the makeup of his political "base" drew special attention.

John Dean, White House counsel during the Nixon administration, wrote:

> much has been made of then-candidate and now-President Donald Trump's core supporters—his so-called base. When referring to Trump's base, reference is to more than merely those who voted for Trump, but those who appear to support him through thick and thin, i.e., those who, in his words, would still vote for him even if he shot someone on 5th Avenue.[10]

Dean said that Trump's base "obviously resides within the collection of voters who supported him at the polls in November 2016" and, after reviewing data from exit polls, concluded that "his base is predominately male." Most analysts who try to define Trump's base adopt Dean's sociological perspective, looking at social groups.[11] Others take a psychological approach. An article in *Psychology Today* found five key traits of Trump's supporters:

1. Authoritarian Personality Syndrome
2. Social Dominance Orientation
3. Prejudice
4. Intergroup Contact
5. Relative Deprivation[12]

Pursuing a different psychological track, some authors characterized Trump's supporters by political ideologies. An article in *Forbes* found that they were

> Staunch Conservatives
> Free Marketeers
> American Preservationists
> Anti-Elites
> The Disengaged[13]

Clearly, die-hard Trump voters share political attitudes. A *Wall Street Journal* column stated:

Trump supporters are supporters as much because of the president's anti-elite rhetoric, his fight against undocumented immigrants and what they see as defense of traditional values as any substantive achievement; the reverse is true for Trump haters.[14]

Knowledge of personal attitudes usually explains human behavior better than knowledge of social traits. Because political analysts cannot see into voters' minds, they rely on what they can observe—voters' social characteristics. Accordingly, they frame Trump's supporters in sociological terms. Progressive activist Sean McElwee asked, "So who the hell is Trump's base? And what is a base?" Answering himself, he named six groups: White men, White evangelicals, White non-college, White over 50, White over $50,000, White rural.[15] Given that men are only half the electorate, that only 70 percent of the men are white, that only about one-quarter of Christians are evangelical, and so on, McElwee envisioned a very small base for Trump's re-election.

As shown in these passages, party base is a popular but vague term. Wikipedia defines it as "a group of voters who almost always support a single party's candidates for elected office." Figure 2.3 in the previous chapter showed that self-identified Democrats and Republicans voted for their party's candidates more than 90 percent of the time since 2000. That would make "base" equivalent to "party identifiers," but analysts mean something different. They mistakenly conflate two concepts—party identification and social grouping—when they refer to a party's base.

Social Groupings

Terminological issues also arise when discussing social groups or groupings. Sociologists often require a "social group" to be more than just a collection or aggregate of individuals; they must exhibit some degree of social cohesion to be called a social group. The term "social grouping" relaxes the cohesion element, recognizing a socially defined collection of individuals as a social grouping. Technically, all Roman Catholics could be called a social grouping but not a social group. Hereinafter, I use both terms interchangeably but in the sense of a socially defined collection of individuals.

When social groupings become political, new terms arise. Groupings become cleavages. Sociologists Brooks and Manza define "a social cleavage as the difference in political alignment among groups constituting a particular dimension of social structure."[16] Tóka's cross-national study identified six such cleavages: gender, age, rural vs. urban residence, social class, religion, and ethnicity.[17] Weakliem's study of cleavages in the United States focused on class and religion, including race, age, and region only as controls.[18] Brooks and Manza studied only four social cleavages: race, class, religion, or linguistic divisions. Except for respondents' ages, which inevitably change over time, and their occasional changes of residence, citizens are thought to remain in these social categories throughout life, but that thought is questionable. Analyzing data from the same individuals interviewed three times between 2006 and 2014, Egan found that they gave different responses to questions about their ethnicity, religion, and even gender often enough to raise concern for research.[19]

I will return to Egan's findings later, but for now I will assume the basic validity of classifying voters in social groups, deleting from and adding to Tóka's cleavage list and the overlapping list of Brooks and Manza. I drop age and gender and add region. This chapter prepares for analyzing party identification in America according to six dimensions of social cleavage: region, economic status, education, urban-rural nature of residence, religion, and ethnicity.

Voters' party identifications are political attitudes. They are invisible—unknown except by asking. Pundits instead look for visible social groupings that strongly voted for Democratic or Republican candidates in recent elections. The *Wall Street Journal* attributed Donald Trump's reliable source of votes to his "white working-class base."[20] Readers could "see" Trump voters by visualizing the white working class—just as voters saw elements of Hillary Clinton's base as college-educated women and minorities.

Readers may raise two questions about citing social groups as sources of party votes. The first deals with how the groupings are made. "White working class" combines two groups, as does "college-educated women." Why not "white college-educated" and "working class women"? The second question pertains to the extent of partisanship. To what degrees do the separate social groupings identify with either the Democratic or Republican parties? Differences in partisan preference are often a matter of degree, and political preferences may shift over time. As mentioned in Chapter 1, women in 1952 favored the Republican Party somewhat more than men did, but in 2016 women favored the Democrats far more strongly than men.

Two Methods of Analyzing Party Support

Measuring the degree of fit between partisanship and social groups is important in electoral politics. This chapter presents two different ways to measure it—by groups and by parties. The standard method of measuring correspondence between group members and their partisanship calculates the percentages of a group claiming to be Democrats, Republicans, or Independents. The less common method computes the proportion of party identifiers coming from each group. The first method suggests how well the party appeals to the group's voters. In effect, it treats them as the party's "customers." The second method indicates how much influence the group has among all party identifiers. In effect, party identifiers are the party's "owners." (Of course, this is not literally true, but the analogy has merit.) Both methods rely on national sample surveys of citizens during presidential elections.

Table 3.1 1952 and 2016 Party Identification by Gender,* Percentages by Columns

	1952 Survey				2016 Survey		
	Male	Female			Male	Female	
Republican	26%	30%		**Republican**	29%	27%	
Independent	26%	20%		**Independent**	40%	34%	
Democrat	48%	50%		**Democrat**	31%	39%	
	100%	100%			100%	100%	
Total Cases	**783**	**906**	**1,689**	Total Cases	**2,017**	**2,173**	**4,190**

* The 2016 ANES survey had a third category, "Other," but very few respondents chose it.

Table 3.2 1952 and 2016 Party Identification by Gender, Proportions by Rows

	1952 Survey				2016 Survey			
	Male	Female		Total Cases		Male	Female		Total Cases
Republican	0.43	0.57	1.0	**478**	**Republican**	0.50	0.50	1.0	**1,185**
Independent	0.52	0.48	1.0	**384**	**Independent**	0.52	0.48	1.0	**1,536**
Democrat	0.46	0.54	1.0	**827**	**Democrat**	0.42	0.58	1.0	**1,469**
				1,689					**4,190**

Because two distinct methods of analyzing party support are used throughout the remainder of this book, the reader need understand their differences. I illustrate both methods for analyzing party support using respondents' gender as an example. Gender is a useful choice for several reasons: it is a familiar trait that divides voters into two categories virtually equal in size embracing nearly all respondents.[21] Tables 3.1 and 3.2 employs both methods in cross-tabulating party identification by gender using data from the 1952 and 2016 American National Election Studies.

Table 3.1 computes, by columns, the *percentages* of males and females identifying as Republicans, Independents, or Democrats. Table 3.2 computes, by rows, the *proportions* of Republicans, Independents, or Democrats from men and women. (Proportions are expressed in decimal values of 1.0, whereas more familiar percentages are proportions times 100.)

Relationships in these data are grasped more readily by graphing them as in Figure 3.1, a vertical bar chart, and Figure 3.2, a horizontal bar chart. Figure 3.1 shows that in 1952 more women (30 percent) than men (26 percent) identified with the Republican Party. In 2016, far more women than men (39 to 31 percent) were Democrats. Expressing voter groups' party preferences in percentages is the "standard" method of analyzing survey data. The media commonly use this method, which expresses the parties'

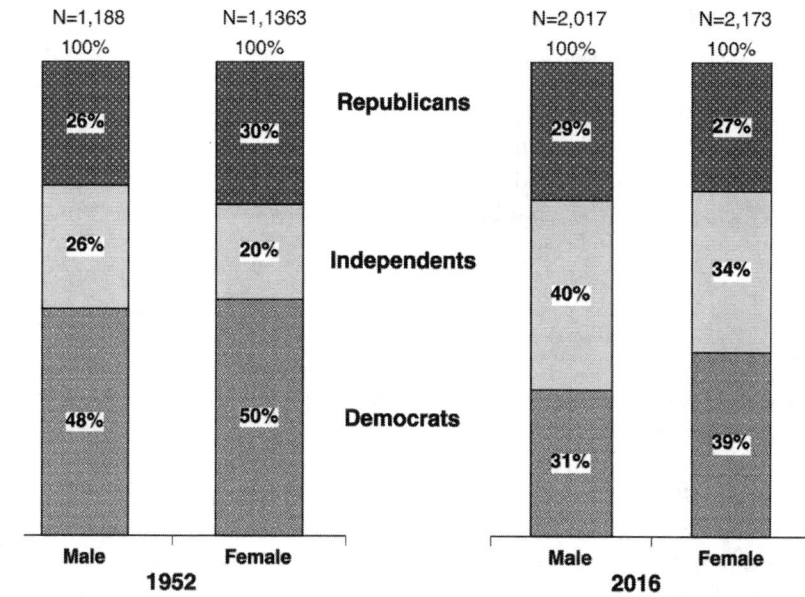

Figure 3.1 Party Appeal to Gender Groups, 1952 and 2016

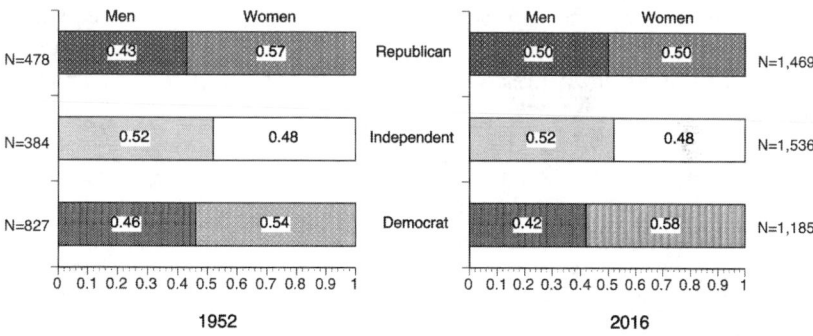

Figure 3.2 Party Composition by Gender Groups, 1952 and 2016

share of each social group's preference. The method treats members of each group as potential voters. It suggests how much the party *appeals* to each group.

Figure 3.2 focuses on the party instead of the group. It displays the proportion of each group in the party base—the set of citizens who self-identify with a political party. This alternative method clearly portrays how the parties' bases have changed over time concerning gender. In 1952, 0.57 of all Republican identifiers were women, but by 2016 the Republican Party consisted equally of women and men: 0.50 to 0.50. In contrast, women in 2016 made up 0.58 of the Democratic base.

I report party composition in *proportions* and group preferences in *percentages* to distinguish between the two different methods for computing group support of political parties. Computing the percentage of a group that identifies with a party suggests the group's voting intentions but not its importance in the party's base. Although I report social groups' percentages of party identifiers, I rely primarily on the proportion of a party's identifiers who come from each group. That is, I concentrate on the party's social group composition—its social base. A social group that dominates the composition of the party "owns" the party concerning issues that affect that social group.

I used gender merely to illustrate both methods for analyzing cross-classifications of social variables with party identification. While the parties' different makeup of men and women is significant, gender is not a critical social cleavage in American politics. Neither men nor women dominate the party base to the extent that one group owns the party's position on gender issues. Also, the United States' gender composition has remained constant over time, so it cannot account for major changes in party politics (although gender differences in candidate preferences can decide elections). Other social variables that do change over time—such as economic status, education, region, urban-rural nature of residence, religion, and ethnicity—lie at the core of party conflict. These social differences often escalate into lasting and intense partisan cleavages. I assess the partisan consequences of these potential social cleavages in Chapters 4–9. First, I must introduce two new summary measures of the relationships between political parties and social groups.

These two measures address two questions an electoral analyst asked about Trump's base:

Which Group Supports Trump the Most?
Which Group Makes Up the Biggest Share of Trump Voters?
If we define the base as a group making up a non-trivial share of the electorate that overwhelmingly prefers one party, it is fair to call white evangelicals Trump's base. If we define the base purely by the size of the coalition, we might prefer instead white non-college voters or whites over 50, both of whom make up more than half of Trump's voters.[22]

To answer "Which Group Supports Trump the Most," I compute Equality of Group Appeal scores. To answer "Which Group Makes Up the Biggest Share of Trump Voters," I compute Party Base Concentration scores. In the chapters to come, I calculate Group Appeal and Base Concentration scores for each party for each year from 1952 to 2020 for each of these social cleavages: economic status, education, region, urban-rural nature of residence, religion, and ethnicity.

Summarizing Group Appeal and Base Concentration

I use the term, "Group Appeal" for the percentage of a social group's party identification, and the term "Base Concentration" for the proportion of the party's base (i.e., all party identifiers) that comes from a social group. All the politically more important social cleavages taken up in the following chapters have multiple categories. The more categories in a social grouping, the more percentages and proportions to study. Because ANES surveys have only two gender categories: male and female,[23] I chose gender to illustrate the alternative methods. Figures 3.1 and 3.2 above calculated the two parties' Group Appeal and their Base Concentration concerning both genders. With only two categories for gender and three for party identification, Figure 3.1 still contained 12 percentages, and Figure 3.2 had six proportions.

Readers would find it tedious to make such comparisons among scores of percentages and proportions generated from seven decades of ANES data. Instead of ferreting out differences in the extent to which parties appeal to voting subgroups—e.g., men and women—and the extent to which subgroups are concentrated in their bases, I employ a more incisive method for analyzing party support. I develop separate measures of "Group Appeal" and "Party Base Concentration" to summarize, in single numbers, the information in all those percentages and proportions seen in Figures 3.1 and 3.2.

A single number for Equal Group Appeal tells how *evenly* the party appeals to all subgroups in the cleavage. Another number for Party Base Concentration tells how *heavily* the group is concentrated among party identifiers.[24]

Equal Group Appeal

Horn, Kevins, Jensen, and van Kersbergen demonstrated that political parties appeal differently to "demographically defined groups."[25] "Equal Group Appeal" is defined as *the extent to which the party appeals equally to each significant voting subgroup within any dimension of social cleavage*. Only the *evenness* of its appeal is considered, not its average strength of appeal. A party's group appeal is perfectly even when it draws equal percentages of support from each category within a social cleavage.

The Equal Group Appeal score has five essential characteristics:

1. It ranges from 0 to 1.0.
2. The higher the score, the more evenly the party appeals to all subgroups.
3. A score of 1.0 occurs only if there is *no* variation in the percentages of support received by the party from the different social groups in the social cleavage. It indicates that the party has broad group appeal concerning that cleavage.

44 *Party Organization and Social Groupings*

4. An Equal Group Appeal score of 0.0 results only if a party receives *all* its support from only one group. That score indicates no appeal to other groups within that social cleavage.
5. This formula has an operational interpretation as evenness in the party's percentage support from social subgroups—the extent of its group appeal within that cleavage.

Box 3.1 Explaining the Equal Group Appeal Score

The percentages in Figure 3.1 are restated in summary form below for easy reference. I drop "Independents" and, from the column percentages, calculate Equal Gender Group Appeal scores for Democrats and Republicans.

Gender Identifications with Parties

	1952		2016	
	Male	*Female*	*Male*	*Female*
Republican	26%	30%	29%	27%
Democrat	48%	50%	31%	39%

A party's Equal Group Appeal score is based on each groups' deviations from their average (mean) level of identification. In 1952, 26 percent of men and 30 percent of women identified themselves as Republicans, for a mean of 28. The average deviation (ignoring signs) of both scores from the mean is 2 points. Those deviations are small, but not as small as produced by the nearly equal 48/50 male/female split for Democrats. Their average absolute deviation is only 1 point from their 49 mean.

We use these average percentage point deviations to measure Equal Group Appeal, but we adjust the raw deviations to take into account the value of the mean. A deviation of 2 points around a mean of 28 counts more than 1 point around a larger mean of 49. Dividing the average deviations by the mean around which they are calculated, 2/28 = 0.07 and 1/49 = 0.02. So in 1952, the Republicans' deviations in male/female appeal were not just twice the Democrats (2 to 1) but almost four times (0.07 to 0.02).

Wanting to measure evenness (not unevenness) in Equal Group Appeal, we subtract 0.07 and 0.02 from 1.0, resulting in 0.93 for Republicans and 0.98 for Democrats. We square these values in creating Equal Group Appeal Scores to normalize their distribution, which otherwise would be negatively skewed—i.e., a few scores tending toward 0.0 with many clustering toward 1.0. Thus, the

Republican Equal Gender Group Appeal score for 1952 was 0.86, and the Democrats' was 0.96.

In 2016, the parties switched in scoring on Equal Gender Group Appeal. The Republicans drew 29 percent of the men and 27 percent of the women for a mean, once again of 28, but with an average deviation of 1. Dividing 1 by 28 = 0.04. Subtracting 0.04 from 1.0 yields 0.96, or 0.92 when squared.

Democrats drew only 31 percent of men and 39 percent of women, averaging 35 percent across genders, with an average deviation of 4. Dividing 4 by 35 = 0.11. Subtracting 0.11 from 1.0 = 0.89, which when squared is 0.79.

Thus, the Republican and Democratic parties scored 0.86 and 0.96, respectively, on appealing to men and women in 1952, but 0.92 and 0.79 in 2016. Both parties appealed differently to gender groups in 2016 than in 1952, but the difference was more pronounced for Democrats.

Appendix A gives the mathematical formula for calculating Equal Group Appeal. That formula also adjusts for different numbers of categories in the social groups.

Box 3.1 explains how the "Equal Group Appeal" measure is calculated. For those who want to know more, see Appendix A for its mathematical formula. Box 3.1 states that the Republicans' gender Equal Group Appeal scores were 0.86 and 0.92, respectively, for 1952 and 2016. The Democrats' gender Equal Group Appeal scores were 0.96 and 0.79 for the two years. The percentages in Figure 3.1 show that women were more likely to identify with the Democratic Party in 2016 than men. That difference in gender appeal is a big change from 1952 and accounts for the Democrats' lower gender Equal Group Appeal score. Republicans' gender Equal Group Appeal hardly changed between those two elections.

Following chapters will occasionally cite percentages of a group that identifies with the parties, but the analysis will rely primarily on the parties' Equal Group Appeal scores as calculated each presidential election year for each of six social cleavages: region, education, income, urban-rural nature of residence, religion, and ethnicity. We will find increasingly greater differences between the parties over time.

Party Base Concentration

"Party Base Concentration" is defined as *the extent to which specific subgroups within any dimension of social cleavage dominate within the party base*. The focus is on the composition of the party's base—on the proportions of party identifiers coming from each group (i.e., proportions calculated by rows in Table 3.2).

Box 3.2 Explaining the Party Base Concentration Score

The proportions reported in Figure 3.2 are restated in summary form below for easy reference. I drop "Independents" and, from the row proportions, calculate the Gender Party Base Concentration score for Democrats and Republicans.

Gender Identifications with Parties, 1952 and 2016 (in proportions)

	1952		*2016*	
	Male	*Female*	*Male*	*Female*
Republican	0.43	0.57	0.50	0.50
Democrat	0.46	0.54	0.42	0.58

The Party Base Concentration score is based on the Herfindahl-Hirschman Index (HHI) of market concentration. HHI squares the market share of each firm competing in a market and then sums the resulting numbers. It usually assumes a fixed number of firms in the market—e.g., 4, 8, 50, and so. We need a measure for comparing Party Base Concentration across social cleavages with varying, but limited, groupings—from two to six. Consequently, I adjust by subtracting from the summed proportions a term that adjusts for the number of subgroups and by dividing the result by another term involving the number of subgroups. The square root of this amount produces the final result. The mathematical formula is in Appendix B.

In 1952, men had a 0.43 "share" (proportion) of Republican identifiers and women had the other 0.57 of identifiers. Thus: $0.43^2 = 0.185$ and $0.57^2 = 0.325$. Summed, $0.185 + 0.325 = 0.51$, from which 0.50 is subtracted given two groups, yielding 0.01. Again given two groups, that value is divided by 0.50, producing 0.02, whose square root is 0.14—for the Republicans' Party Base Concentration score.

Also in 1952, Democratic identifiers divided 0.457 men and 0.543 women. Thus: $0.457^2 = 0.209$ and $0.543^2 = 0.295$. Summed: $0.209 + 0.295 = 0.504$. Subtracting $0.50 = 0.004$ and dividing by 0.5 for two groups results in 0.008, whose square root is 0.09—for the Democrats' Party Base Concentration score.

Applying the Party Base Concentration formula to the 2016 data in Table 3.2, we find the Republicans scoring a perfect 0.00, being equally divided into men and women. The Democrats' score was 0.15, virtually the same as the 1952 Republicans. Given the even proportions of men and women in its base, the Republican Party was not likely to cater to either sex. In contrast, almost three of five Democratic identifiers were women, suggesting that the Democratic Party was more responsive to women's issues in 2016 than the Republican Party.

Appendix B gives the mathematical formula for calculating Party Base Concentration.

The Base Concentration score has five essential characteristics:

1. It ranges from 0 to 1.
2. The higher the score, the greater the Party Base Concentration within the party base.
3. A score of 1.0 is achieved only if all party identifiers come from only one group in the social cleavage.
4. A score of 0.0 results only if all party identifiers are equally distributed across all of the groupings in the social cleavage.
5. This formula has an operational interpretation as the extent of Party Base Concentration within the party's base.

Box 3.2 explains how the "Party Base Concentration" measure is calculated. For those who want to know more, see Appendix B for its mathematical formula. Party Base Concentration scores will also be calculated each presidential election year for each of six social cleavages: economic status, education, region, urban-rural nature of residence, religion, and ethnicity. Occasionally I will refer to the proportion of a given group in the party base, but I will rely on Base Concentration scores, like Group Appeal scores, for most of the analysis—often shortening the terms by eliminating the modifiers, "Party" and "Equal."

Equal Group Appeal and Party Base Concentration scores are negatively related in practice. Parties that score high on Group Appeal tend to score low on Base Concentration, but they are not mathematically related except at the extremes scores of 1.0 for Group Appeal and 0.0 for Base Concentration. Essentially, they differ depending on the distribution of party identification across subgroups of a social group and, more interestingly, on the relative sizes of the subgroups. Think of religion as a social grouping. About 55 percent of Jews in national surveys say they are Democrats, but only about 3 percent of respondents are Jewish. Although the Democratic Party appeals strongly to Jews, they are too few to constitute a large part of the Democratic base—as readers will see later.

Group Appeal, Base Concentration, and Party Politics

Decades ago, Gabriel Almond and James Coleman noted that both political parties and interest groups sought to affect government policy, but they differed in how they aggregated and articulated their members' interests.[26] Parties, seeking to win votes from different groups, largely tend to aggregate interests—that is, they collect and balance conflicting interests within society. Non-party interest groups mainly articulate special interests in the political arena—that is, they express and promote specific interests of businesses, labor, farmers, merchants, and so on.[27]

Almond and Coleman admit, however, "The distinction between interest articulation and aggregation is a fluid one."[28] Some large interest groups—such as the AFL-CIO—represent diverse unions with conflicting interests, requiring the AFL-CIO to aggregate their varying interests before requesting congressional legislation. Conversely, parties whose bases are dominated by specific groups in a political cleavage are apt to articulate in Congress the narrow interests of those groups before the broader interests of the nation. Consequently, parties are expected to respond to groups that dominate its base.

I make two assumptions about the relationship of Equal Group Appeal and Party Base Concentration to interest aggregation and articulation:

> Assumption 1: *Parties that appeal equally to all groups in a social cleavage tend to aggregate the interests of all groups.*
> Assumption 2: *Parties whose base is dominated by any group in a social cleavage tend to articulate the interests of that group.*

According to these assumptions, parties with high scores on Party Base Concentration will articulate (promote) the interests of the dominant groups, while parties with high scores on Equal Group Appeal will aggregate (collect and compromise) the groups' varying interests. After computing and analyzing the parties' summary Group Appeal and Base Concentration scores from 1952 to 2020, I will address how well the Democratic and Republican parties articulate and aggregate the interests of social groups.

The next six chapters will analyze the Equal Group Appeal and Party Base Concentration of six major sociological groupings. They will be taken up in order of their subgroups' importance to the parties, from least important (region) to most important (ethnicity).

Summary and Conclusion

Metaphorically speaking, national political parties are vehicles; presidential candidates are drivers. The candidate who wins the party's nomination sits in the driver's seat and decides where to take the party. Some presidential candidates never get the chance to implement their vision. Take Democrat William Jennings Bryan, the Democrats' presidential candidate in 1896, 1900, and 1908. Bryan had a populist political vision: the federal government should serve the working classes. Bryan did well with farmers and workers in the south and plains states but never could overcome the voting power of the industrial states.

We tend to remember those who win their presidential elections and thus get to steer the nation as well as the party. Historians credit Andrew Jackson, Abraham Lincoln, and Franklin Delano Roosevelt with directing their parties before World War II. Since the war, cases can be made for four presidents having lasting impacts on their parties' fortunes. Lyndon Johnson's successful enactment of civil rights legislation converted many southern Democrats into Republicans. Ronald Reagan's optimism about America's future and his role in dismantling the Soviet Union created thousands of "Reagan Democrats" and refreshed loyalty among long-time

Republicans. Barack Obama, the first Afro-American president, both cemented Democratic ties among minorities and provoked enmity among many whites.

Donald Trump is the fourth president who drove his party in a different direction—one very different from the courses charted by Jackson, Lincoln, and Roosevelt. Ignoring the decline of whites in the American electorate, Trump chose to appeal to ethnocentrism within the dwindling white plurality. He banked on their fears of globalization and their enmity toward Obama. By putting "American First," he could blame coastal financial elites for losing jobs to non-white foreigners and immigrants. Will Donald Trump's presidency have a lasting effect on the Republican Party?

Ironically, some observers have drawn links between Trump and Andrew Jackson, the populist founder of the Democratic Party in 1828, because each saw himself as "a man of the people."[29] Others likened Donald Trump's remake of his own party to William Jennings Bryan's struggle against the opposition Republicans over a century ago. One observer said that Trump offered "the means by which economically distressed, nationalistic voters" could "overthrow the wealthy, cosmopolitan leaders of the Republican Party."[30]

As president, Donald Trump seemed more wedded to cultivating his Republican Party "base" for re-election in 2020 than appealing to the electorate as a whole to insure Republican wins in the future. Daniel Galvin, whose book, *Presidential Party Building*, covered all presidents from Eisenhower to George W. Bush, extended his research in 2020 to include Donald Trump.[31] Galvin said:

> Previous Republican presidents dominated and invested in their party for the explicit purpose of building a new majority in American politics. Reaching out to new demographic groups and trying to persuade them to join the party was integral to this project. Trump, in contrast, has (thus far) predominantly pursued a base-mobilization strategy. Rather than fan out horizontally in search of new groups to join the party coalition, Trump's strategy drills down vertically to penetrate and deepen his base.[32]

What social groups make up the base of the Republican Party, and how do they compare with the social makeup of the Democratic Party? In the next six chapters, we compare the social bases of the Democratic and Republican parties on six dimensions of social cleavage, beginning with the region of the country in which voters live.

Notes

1 Kenneth Janda, "Cross-National Measures of Party Organizations and Organizational Theory," *European Journal of Political Research*, 11 (1983), 319–332, at p. 319.

2 Henry Barbour et al., *Growth and Opportunity Project* (Washington, DC: Republican National Committee, 2013), p. 1.
3 *Ibid.*
4 *Ibid.*, p. 4.
5 *Ibid.*, p. 7.
6 *Washington Post* (June 16, 2013).
7 Google search on January 10, 2020, returned this result: Growth and Opportunity Project – Republican National … https://gop.com › growth-and-opportunity-project. No information is available for this page.
8 Aaron Zitner and Dante Chinni, "Demographic Shift to Test Trump's Strategy," *Wall Street Journal* (January 4–5, 2020), p. A4.
9 Barbour et al., p. 13.
10 John Dean, "Trump's Base: Broadly Speaking, Who Are They?" *Legal Analysis and Commentary from Justia: Politics* (February 15, 2018).
11 For example, see Nicholas Carnes and Noam Lupu, "It's Time to Bust the Myth: Most Trump Voters Were Not Working Class," *Washington Post* (June 5, 2017); and Nicki Lisa Cole, "Meet the People Behind Donald Trump's Popularity," *ThoughtCo.* (June 29, 2019).
12 Bobby Azarian, "An Analysis of Trump Supporters Has Identified 5 Key Traits," *Psychology Today* (December 31, 2017).
13 Karlyn Bowman, "Who Were Trump's Voters? Now We Know," *Forbes* (June 23, 2017).
14 Gerald F. Seib, "For Many Voters, It Isn't About the Economy," *Wall Street Journal* (January 21, 2020), p. A4.
15 Sean McElwee, "Data for Politics #14: Who Is Trump's Base?" *Data for Politics* (August 23, 2018).
16 Clem Brooks and Jeff Manza, "Social Cleavages and Political Alignments: U.S. Presidential Elections, 1960 to 1992," *American Sociological Review*, 62 (December, 1997), 937–946 at pp. 937–938. Also see Jeff Manza and Clem Brooks, *Social Cleavages and Political Change: Voter Alignments and US Party Coalitions* (New York: Oxford University Press, 1999).
17 Gábor Tóka, "The Impact of Cross-Cutting Cleavages on Citizens' Political Involvement," Paper prepared for panel # 11/10, "Cleavages and Party Systems in Post-1978 Democracies" at the 2003 Annual Meeting of the American Political Science Association at Philadelphia, August 27–31, 2003, at p. 19.
18 David L. Weakliem, "The United States: Still the Politics of Diversity," in Geoffrey Evans and Nan Dirk De Graaf (eds.), *Political Choice Matters: Explaining the Strength of Class and Religious Cleavages in Cross-National Perspective* (Oxford: Oxford University Press, 2013), 114–136.
19 Patrick J. Egan, "Identity as Dependent Variable: How Americans Shift Their Identities to Align with Their Politics," *American Journal of Political Science*, 64 (July, 2020), 699–716.
20 Zitner and Chinni.
21 In 2016 (not in 1952) respondents were given "other" as a third category, but very few chose it.
22 McElwee.
23 In the 2016 American National Election Study, 11 respondents refused both options.
24 This approach to measurement and these formulas have a history. See Kenneth Janda and Robin Gillies, "Social Aggregation, Articulation, and Representation

of Political Parties: A Cross National Analysis," paper delivered at the 1975 Annual Meeting of the American Political Science Association, San Francisco; and Kenneth Janda, *Political Parties: A Cross-National Survey* (New York: The Free Press, 1980), chapter 5.

25 Alexander Horn, Anthony Kevins, Carsten Jensen, and Kees van Kersbergen, "Political Parties and Social Groups: New Perspectives and Data on Group and Policy Appeals," *Party Politics* (Paper submitted April 29, 2019; accepted for publication January 15, 2020), at p. 11.

26 Gabriel A. Almond and James S. Coleman, *The Politics of the Developing Areas* (Princeton, NJ: Princeton University Press, 1960).

27 Kenneth Janda, "Interest Aggregation and Articulation," in George T. Kurian (ed.), *The Encyclopedia of Political Science, Volume 3* (Washington, DC: CQ Press, 2011), 798–799.

28 Almond and Coleman, p. 39.

29 Peter Baker, "Jackson and Trump: How Two Populist Presidents Compare," *New York Times* (March 15, 2017).

30 Tim Reuter, "Before Donald Trump, There Was William Jennings Bryan," *Forbes* (June 20, 2016) at www.forbes.com/sites/timreuter/2016/06/20/before-donald-trump-there-was-william-jennings-bryan/#a20c6a527926 forbes.com.

31 Daniel J. Galvin, *Presidential Party Building: Dwight D. Eisenhower to George W. Bush* (Princeton, NJ: Princeton University Press, 2010); and Daniel J. Galvin, "Party Domination and Base Mobilization: Donald Trump and Republican Party Building in a Polarized Era," *Forum* (2020).

32 Galvin, "Party Domination and Base Mobilization," from the abstract.

4 Region
Once Primary, Now Secondary

When regional divisions of a country sharply align with partisanship, politics can get ugly and erupt in violence. Regional conflict was the prime cause of the Civil War in the early 1860s, and North-South political divisions strained America for nearly a century afterward. The defeated South remained solidly Democratic and aligned against the victorious North, led by Republican Abraham Lincoln. For 40 years, from 1880 to 1920, no Republican presidential candidate won even one of the 11 states of the former Confederacy. The moneyed Northeast was thought to control the purse strings of capitalism. The Midwest was long regarded as the stronghold of isolationism in foreign affairs. The South was virtually a one-party region, almost completely Democratic. And the individualistic West pioneered its own mixture of progressive politics.

In the first half of the twentieth century, differences in wealth fed cultural differences between these regions. In their book, *Partisan Hearts and Minds*, Green, Palmquist, and Schickler wrote:

> Southerners associated the Republican Party with the forces of Reconstruction, and non-Southerners associated it with business, farmers, and Protestantism. In the South, the Democratic Party was the party of states' rights and segregation, and in the non-South it was the party of cities, labor, and immigrants.[1]

In recent decades, however, the movement of people and wealth away from the Northeast and Midwest to the Sunbelt states in the South and Southwest has equalized the per capita income of the various regions. One result of this equalization is that the formerly "Solid South" is no longer solidly Democratic. In 1964 Barry Goldwater won five states in the deep South. Since 1968, the South has tended to favor Republican presidential candidates. Regionalism persists in party politics today, but it is of secondary importance and the mirror image of what it had been. Today, the South is mostly Republican, and the northeastern and western states are mostly Democratic.

This switch in party politics has helped Republicans win presidential elections. As southern states grew in population, they also gained electoral votes needed to elect a president. Republican Donald Trump won every southern state in 2016, but he also won all of the Midwest and plains states except Illinois and Minnesota. Indeed, some analysts said the Democrats had to overcome "Donald Trump's base across the Midwest."[2] What is the relationship between the regions in which voters live and their party identifications?

Population Changes Across Regions

Since 1952, the American National Election Studies has coded its interviews by state and then grouped them by regions, using the four broad categories defined by the U.S. Census Bureau:

Northeast: CT, ME, MA, NH, NJ, NY, PA, RI, VT
North Central: IL, IN, IA, KS, MI, MN, MO, NE, ND, OH, SD, WI
South: AL, AR, DE, DC, FL, GA, KY, LA, MD, MS, NC, OK, SC, TN, TX, VA, WV
West: AK, AZ, CA, CO, HI, ID, MT, NV, NM, OR, UT, WA, WY

Figure 4.1 plots the distribution of respondents by regions in presidential election year surveys since 1952.

Over the last half-century, the South and the West gained population relative to the Northeast and North Central regions of the United States. The large population shifts brought distinctive changes in regional patterns of support for the two parties, especially in the South. As the South's population grew relative to the rest of the nation, it became less distinctive

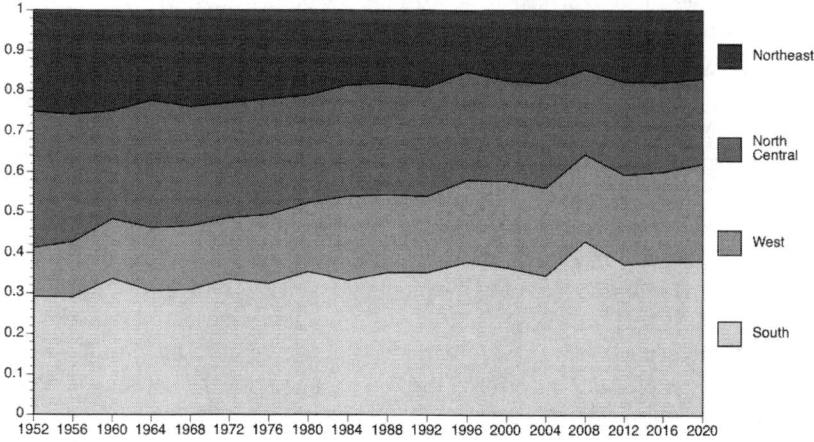

*ANES Presidential Year Surveys 1952-2016; Nationscape Survey January-April, 2020.
These are the data sources for all figures, unless otherwise noted.

Figure 4.1 Regional Distribution of Respondents, 1952–2020*

politically. Near the end of the twentieth century, "region" no longer served as a prime variable for social and political cleavage. In their analysis of social cleavages and political alignments in presidential elections from 1960 to 1992, Brooks and Manza relegated region to a control variable (along with education) as they used gender, social class, religion, and race to explain presidential vote choice.[3] Overall, they found "evidence of a slight increase in social group cleavages in presidential elections from 1960 through 1992," particularly regarding race, and they conclude "Net of change in the race cleavage, the overall social cleavage has been stable during this period." Had Brooks and Manza included region as a social cleavage, extended their analysis to 1952, and studied party identification instead of presidential vote choice, they would have found some significant regional changes.

Equal Group Appeal Across Regions

To help readers follow the analysis, this chapter and following ones employ a common format. Each chapter begins by reporting party support data across regional groupings for 1952 and 2020 in two types of bar charts—one vertical and the other horizontal. Respectively, they correspond to Tables 3.1 and 3.2 and to Figures 3.1 and 3.2 in Chapter 3, which illustrate two ways of computing percentages or proportions in a table—by columns and by rows. Figure 4.2 is a vertical bar chart that computes, by columns, the percentage of each region identifying as Republicans, Independents, or Democrats. The percentage indicates how equally each party appeals to that group of voters and suggests the likelihood of a person in that region voting for its candidates. (Given our focus on parties, no such scores were computed for Independents.)

As shown in the vertical bars, 70 percent of southerners in 1952 identified with the Democrats compared with only 15 percent who thought of themselves as Republicans. Only citizens in the Northeast divided almost equally between the parties. Region definitely served as a social and political cleavage in 1952, but not in 2020. By 2020, southerners split nearly evenly between the Democrats and Republicans, resembling the parties roughly equal within the other regions. Notably, however, significantly fewer voters in the Northeast claimed to be Republicans.

The Equal Group Appeal scores in Figure 4.2 express in single numbers how much the Republican and Democrat percentages of party identification varied by regions in 1952 and 2020. If a party drew equal percentages of party identifiers across all four regions, it would earn an Equal Group Appeal Score of 1.0. Conversely, the lower the score, the greater the variation in percentages of party identifiers across regions. Both parties earned relatively low and almost identical Equal Appeal Scores in 1952: 0.73 for Democrats and 0.72 for Republicans. By 2020, both parties improved substantially in their Equal Group Appeal scores: 0.92 for Democrats and 0.88 for Republicans. Thus, region had lost some effect on partisanship.

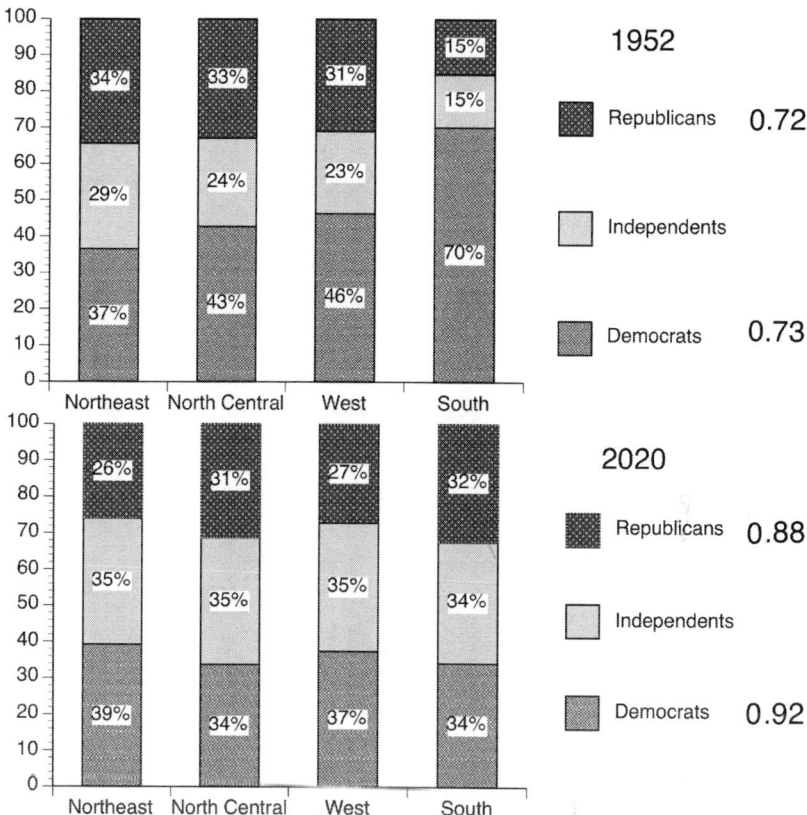

Figure 4.2 Percentages of Party Identification by Regions, with Equal Group Appeal Scores

Party Base Concentration Across Regions

Earlier in this chapter, Figure 4.1 portrayed the population shift from the Northwest to the South from 1952 to 2020. Although Republicans lost identifiers in the declining Northeast, their gains in the South more than compensated for their losses. As a consequence, the party's base switched from being concentrated in the Northeast to being concentrated in the South, as depicted in Figure 4.3.

In 1952, 0.41 of all Republican identifiers came from North Central states, but that proportion dropped to 0.22 in 2020. In contrast, the proportion of Republicans who were southerners rose from 0.14 in 1952 to 0.41 in 2020. After just two generations—from 1952 to 2020—the Republican Party switched from being a northern party, rooted in the North Central states, to one rooted in the South.

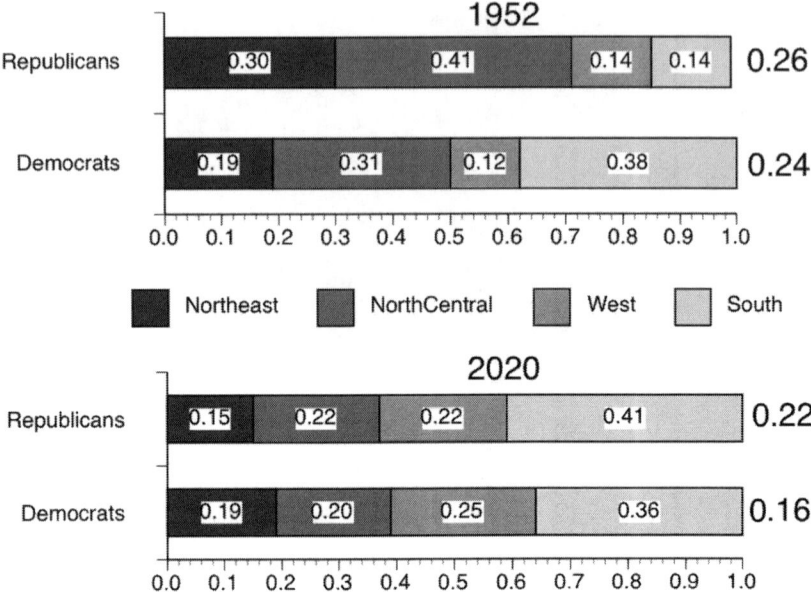

Figure 4.3 Regional Groups as Proportion of Party Identifiers, with Party Base Concentration Scores

The Party Base Concentration scores in Figure 4.3 express in summary numbers the extent to which all party identifiers (i.e., the party's base) come from a single grouping within a social cleavage. The higher the number, the greater the party base is concentrated within a single group. Neither party had distinctly different Base Concentration scores in either period. Republicans scored 0.26 in 1952 and 0.22 in 2020. Democrats scored 0.24 in 1952 and 0.16 in 2020. However, the dominant group in the Republican base switched from the North Central states to the southern states.

Although the Republican Party Base Concentration score changed little between 1952 and 2020, its social composition changed greatly. The Republicans' similar Base Concentration for 1952 and 2020 scores fail to reflect that some (5 percent) of the party's identifiers in 1952 were Black, while nearly all southern Republicans in 2020 were white. Paradoxically, southerners constituted almost the same share of Democrats in 2020 as Republicans. That occurred because Afro-Americans greatly increased their voting registration and switched massively to the Democratic Party between 1952 and 2020.

Equal Appeal and Base Concentration Across Regions Since 1952

Despite the major population shifts during 1952 to 2020 from the Northeast and North Central to the South and West, the parties accommodated

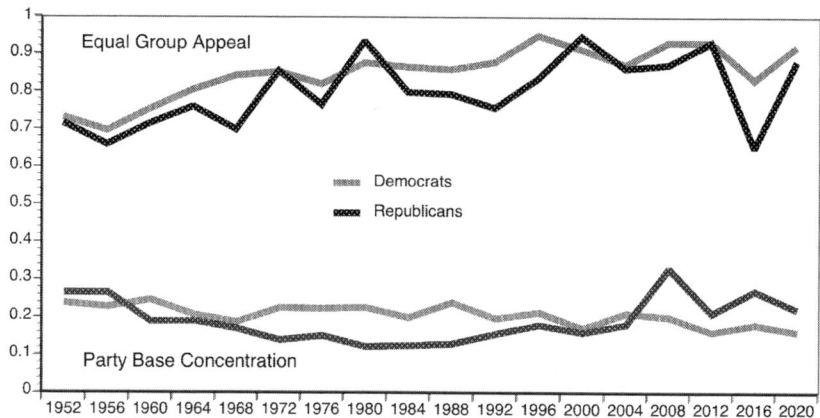

Figure 4.4 Parties' Equal Group Appeal and Base Concentration Scores, Regions 1952–2020

the shifts fairly evenly, as shown in the longitudinal plots of Equal Group Appeal and Party Base Concentration scores in Figure 4.4. The Democratic Party steadily appealed evenly to voters across regions, while the Republicans' appeal experienced more peaks and dips depending on their presidential candidates. Until the election of Barack Obama in 2008, both parties steadily appealed more evenly to voters in the four regions, and regional support failed to become markedly more concentrated in either party. Especially in the Republican Party, however, changes did occur beginning in 2008. By 2020, it shifted from a party whose supporters were centered in the North Central states to one centered in the South.

Some analysts claimed that Donald Trump had a "base across the Midwest," and it is true that in 2016 Trump won elections in the normally Democratic states of Wisconsin, Michigan, and Pennsylvania. Those states' electoral votes gave him the presidency. Moreover, the 2016 ANES survey (not shown here) found more North Central respondents than southerners identifying themselves as Republicans. However, the South's greater population gave the South the larger share of Republican identifiers—40 to 31 percent—in 2016. In 2020, that ratio grew to 41:22. One could argue that the South was Trump's real base in seeking re-election.

Reminiscing, and Summarizing

During my high school years (1949–1953) in Illinois, I came to understand that state governments in the north differed from the south, where public schools were still segregated. During my freshman year at Illinois State Normal University, I learned about the Supreme Court's 1954 decision that segregation of schools violated the Constitution. Not until 1956 did

I witness racial segregation in practice. That summer I took a job as a photographer at Mammoth Cave National Park in Kentucky, which was only a border state, not in the original confederacy. At my first stop for gasoline across the Illinois-Kentucky border, I saw that water fountains were labeled for use as white or colored. Fortunately, the National Park (where I worked for four summers) was desegregated. In 1957, when attending the National Press Photographers Association convention in Washington, DC, I learned that the nation's capital was not. Blacks could not enter a Howard Johnson's restaurant. They could only carry-out at a window for coloreds in the parking lot. Much has changed during my lifetime, and much for the better.

Historically, American party politics divided sharply over regional differences in desirable social and economic policies. Consequences of the Civil War between the North and South remained for nearly a century, as white citizens in southern states voted consistently and overwhelmingly for Democratic presidential candidates, while northerners mostly voted for Republicans. In 1952 and 1956 Republican Dwight Eisenhower was elected and re-elected president despite losing most of the southern states. Still, he won a few, signaling a breakdown of southern political rigidity. As the South "came into play" in national politics, region declined in importance as a factor in party identification. Figures 4.2 to 4.4 demonstrated significant changes in how the Democratic and Republican parties have appealed to different parts of the country and how the parties' bases have changed in their representation of different regions.

Ironically today, southerners are more likely to identify themselves as Democrats than Republicans—although that differs for whites versus nonwhites. Although regional differences in party identification still exist (in reversed form), voters' personal characteristics seem more important than the region in which they live. For example, although southerners contribute about the same proportion (≈ 0.40) of the Republican and Democratic identifiers, the Base Concentration score masks the fact that most the Republicans are white and most of the Democrats are not.

Notes

1 Donald Green, Bradley Palmquist, and Eric Schickler, *Partisan Hearts and Minds: Political Parties and the Social Identities of Voters* (New Haven, CT: Yale University Press, 2002), p. 163.
2 Bradley Beychok, "In 2020, Democracy Will Be Decided at the Margins," *The Hill* (November 18, 2019).
3 Clem Brooks and Jeff Manza, "Social Cleavages and Political Alignments: U.S. Presidential Elections, 1960 to 1992," *American Sociological Review*, 62 (December, 1997), 937–946 at 937.

5 Income
Slight, Steady, and Increasing Difference

Citizens and scholars alike expect political parties to represent their economic and occupational interests. Researchers link these interests to individuals according to their socio-economic status (SES), defined nearly a century ago as a person's "cultural possessions, effective income, material possession, and participation in group activity in the community."[1] Scholars since have used a "wide variety of variables" to measure SES, usually focusing on income, education, and occupation.[2] Often, researchers relied on just one of these indicators. When public opinion polling began in the mid-1930s, pollsters usually asked respondents about their occupations, coding their responses in broad categories such as "professional or managerial," "clerical and sales," "skilled labor," "unskilled labor," "farmers," and so on. Figure 5.1 reports the distribution of such occupational categories in the presidential election surveys from 1952 to 2004—the last year ANES asked the question.

The most striking change over 50-plus years is the decline in the percentage of unemployed homemakers (originally called "housewives"). Also noteworthy are the growth in professional workers and in white collar workers and the decline in the already small categories of unskilled

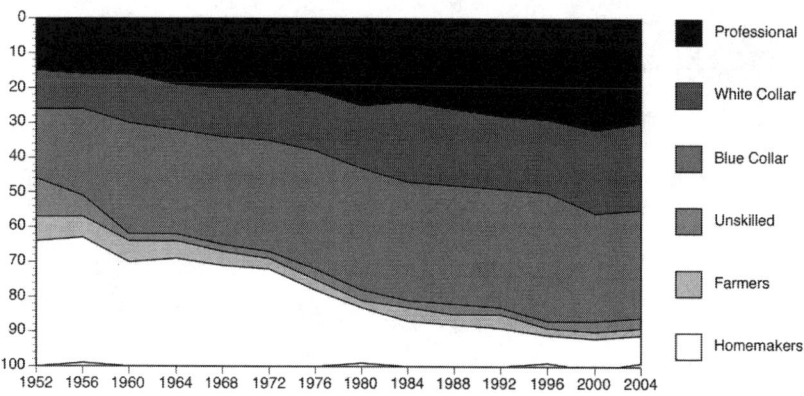

Figure 5.1 ANES Respondents' Distribution of Occupations in the U.S., 1952–2004

workers and farmers—who by 2020 made up less than 2 percent of the U.S. labor force.

As society changed over time so did the nature of employment and the problems of classification. In 2010, the Bureau of Labor Statistics recognized the new and fast-growing occupation, "application software developer," which did not exist prior to the creation of the iPhone in 2007.[3] Due to the changing nature of occupations and the difficulty of classifying responses to questions about occupation, the ANES—like many other polls—replaced occupation with income as a measure of socio-economic status.[4] Consequently, I use income instead of occupation to analyze the relationship between socio-economic status and party identification. One's occupation may be linked more closely to one's politics than income, but income will have to do. Education, another presumed element of SES, will be studied later.

In all ANES surveys since 1952, respondents were not asked about their personal income but about their family's total income. They chose among broad income categories that changed each survey with inflation. To make the income responses comparable from 1952 to 2016, the ANES staff classified responses into five broad percentile categories for each presidential year. The categories were fixed at the 0–16 centiles; 17–33 centiles; 34–67 centiles; 68–95 centiles; and 96–100 centiles. Because the income categories presented to respondents did not correspond exactly to the percentile breakdowns on national income distributions, the graph of income distribution over time by centiles in Figure 5.2 is somewhat jagged.

Figure 5.2 includes data from the 2020 Nationscape survey data recoded into the same set of centiles. In 2020, the 0–16 centiles included those earning less than $30,000, which encompassed the lowest one-sixth of the population. The 17–33 centiles had $30,000–$50,000 income. Those in the 34–67 centiles earned $50,000–$100,000. The last one-third was divided

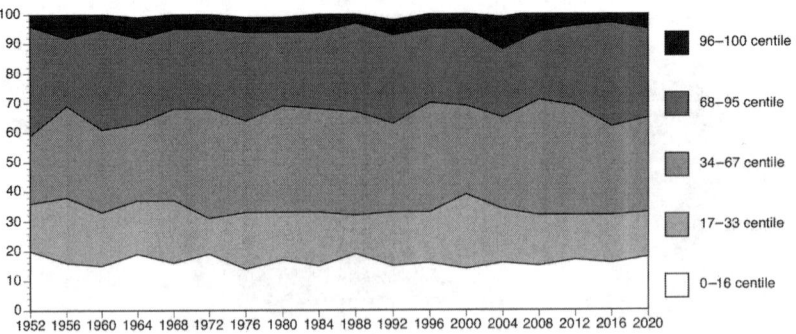

Figure 5.2 ANES Respondents' Distribution of Income in the U.S. by Centiles, 1952–2004

into those making $100,000–$250,000 (68–95 centiles) and the top 96–100 centiles, making over $250,000 in 2020.

In the figures to follow, I reduced the five ANES categories to four percentile groupings—and collapsed the 2020 Nationscape data into the same four categories. I eliminated the top 5 percent as a separate category because the few high income respondents would yield unstable percentages.[5] I show how equally the Democratic and Republican parties appealed to voters in these four income groups from 1952 to 2020 and whether any particular group dominated the base of either party.

Equal Group Appeal by Income

Figure 5.3 is a vertical bar chart that computes, by columns, the percentage of each income group identifying as Republicans, Independents, or Democrats. The percentage indicates how equally each party appeals to that group of voters and suggests the likelihood of a person in that income group voting for its candidates.

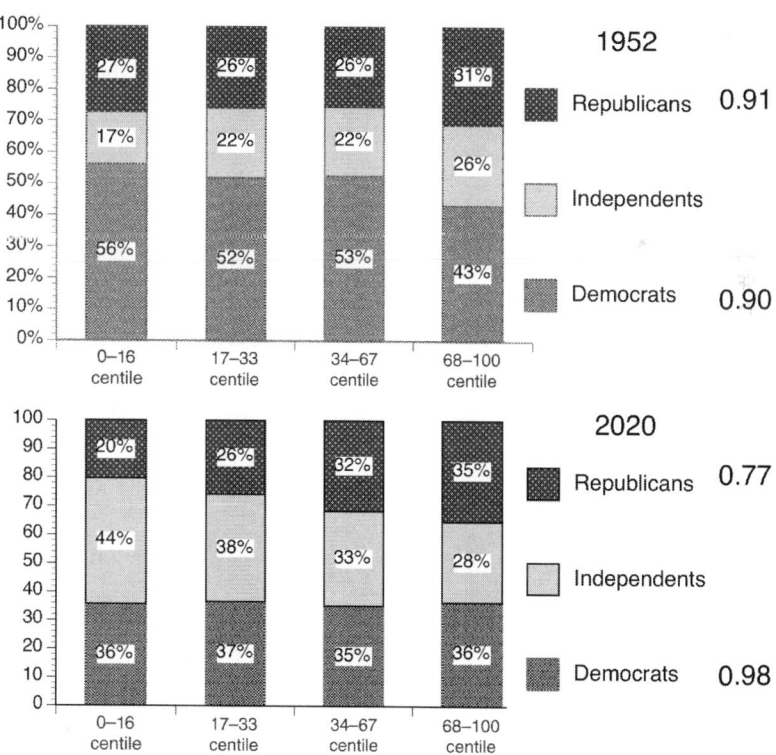

Figure 5.3 Percentages of Party Identification by Income, with Equal Group Appeal Scores

62 Income: Slight, Steady, and Difference

In 1952, more voters in every income category identified themselves as Democrats than Republicans. In 2020, increases in Independents across all income groups came at the expense of Democrats, who still drew over one-third of the voters in every category. Between 1952 and 2020 Republicans drew increasingly more identifiers from wealthier voters. Meanwhile, Democrats dropped from 56 to 36 percent among voters with the lowest incomes.

Nevertheless, both parties appealed fairly evenly to all income groups. The Democrats Equal Group Appeal scores rose from a high 0.90 in 1952 to an almost perfect 0.98 in 2020. The Republicans drop from a high of 0.91 in 1952 to 0.77 in 2020, reflecting their increased appeal to wealthier voters and decreased appeal to poorer ones.

Party Base Concentration by Income

Figure 5.4 is a horizontal bar chart showing the same income groups as a proportion of all Republican and Democratic identifiers. In 1952, almost half of all Republican identifiers came from the upper third of the income distribution. By 2020, the middle third had increased its share of the Republican base, but most identifiers still came from those whose income ranked in the upper third of the electorate. Whereas in 1952 almost one-third of Republican identifiers represented the lower third of the national income distribution, that proportion had slipped below one-quarter by

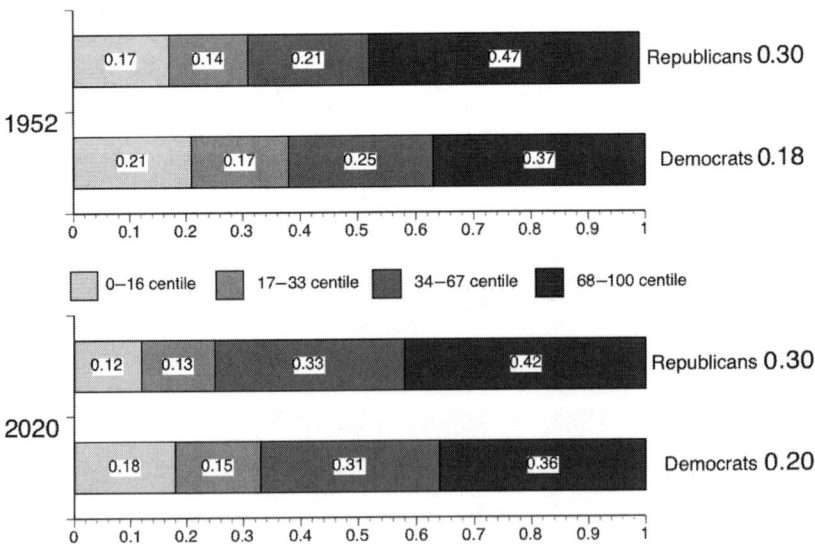

Figure 5.4 Proportions of Party Identifiers by Income Centiles, with Party Base Concentration Scores

Income: Slight, Steady, and Difference 63

2020. Still, Republicans' Base Concentration score of 0.30 was the same as in 1952, and the Democrats' 2020 Base Concentration score was almost the same. These bars evidence little change over seven decades.

Equal Appeal and Base Concentration by Income Since 1952

Taken together, Figures 5.3 and 5.4 demonstrate that the American party system was not sharply divided by income differences among the electorate in either 1952 or in 2020. Figure 5.5, which plots both parties' voter appeal and Base Concentration scores, shows that the 1952 and 2020 scores are fairly typical of all such scores since 1952. Nonetheless, some trends and deviations deserve to be noted.

Generally speaking, and in every year since 1976, Democrats scored higher than Republicans on Group Appeal across income groups. The difference was particularly large in 2008—when Democrat Barack Obama defeated the Republican presidential candidate, John McCain. In that year, only 11 percent of voters in the lowest income centile voted for McCain versus 46 percent of respondents in the top income group. This difference led to Republicans scoring only 0.50 on Equal Group Appeal across the four income groups. The same year also produced the

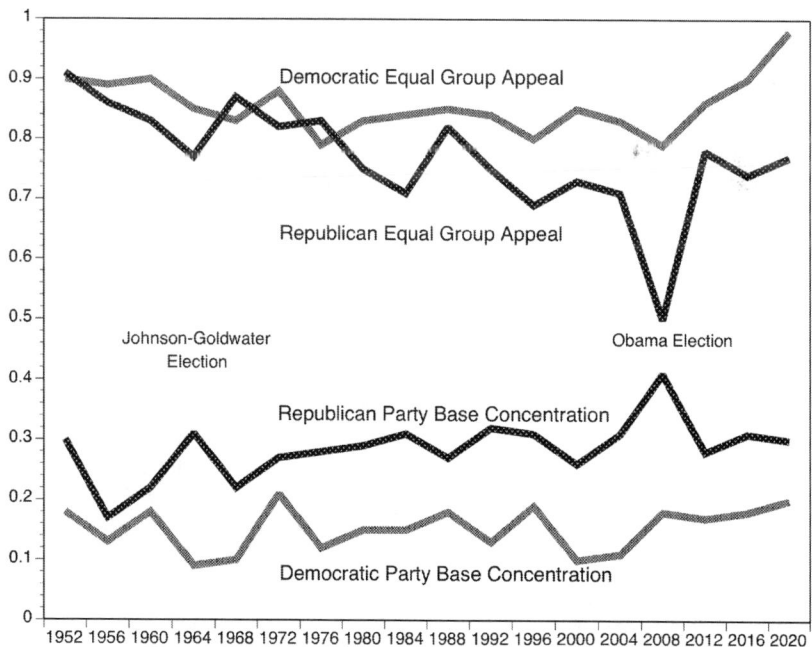

Figure 5.5 Parties' Equal Group Appeal and Party Base Concentration Scores, Income 1952–2020

Republicans' highest Base Concentration score of 0.41, as 0.46 of all Republican identifiers came from the 68–100 percentile versus only 0.06 from the lowest income group.

The 1964 presidential election between Democrat Lyndon Johnson and Republican Barry Goldwater produced the second highest Base Concentration score for Republicans at 0.31—as 0.47 of all Republican identifiers were in the 68–100 percentile. Similar to the pattern of voter appeal scores, Democrats usually ranked lower on Base Concentration in all of the 17 surveys.

Reminiscing, and Summarizing

My father held many jobs—speakeasy piano player, office clerk, bartender, electronic technician—but none paid very well. His last one, as a Nike anti-aircraft missile repairman working out of the Joliet Arsenal, paid the best and carried government benefits. Most political scientists would classify him as a likely Democrat, but I do not recall him saying a good word about any Democratic presidential candidate. He also said little about Democratic or Republican economic policies. I do not recall my parents discussing voting or elections.

James Carville, a Democratic strategist in Bill Clinton's 1992 presidential campaign against incumbent George H.W. Bush, was credited with creating the campaign's catchy slogan, "It's the economy, stupid." Clinton won, cementing the belief that economic concerns drive citizens' voting. However, others have noted that "the economy" affects voters differently. One analyst wrote that "the use of one word to summarize the material, financial and fiscal life" in different regions, industries, and demographics is itself "stupid."[6] Nevertheless, political conflict often swirls about economic concerns, and one expects to find substantial polarization around citizens' socio-economic status. That is, the Democratic and Republican parties "should" appeal to distinctly different income groups in the electorate and demonstrate sharp differences in their bases' composition.

Many readers will be surprised to learn that the Democratic and Republican parties are not sharply divided according to socio-economic status. At least as measured by income percentiles in national election surveys, socio-economic status neither clearly nor consistently separates respondents into Democratic and Republican piles. Perhaps the fault lies in using income as an indicator of economic status. Weakliem's research into social class as a cleavage in voting behavior found that "changes in the effects of income and occupation follow completely different patterns,"[7] but he studied voting, which is more volatile than party identification. Maybe occupation would have differentiated party identifiers better than income—too bad the ANES did not continue to include occupation codes in its election surveys after 2004. However, an earlier study did supplement the 1952–2004 ANES surveys with other surveys for 2008 and 2010 that contained data on occupation. That study concluded, "In essence, Democrats and Republicans differed only marginally in their occupational bases of support."[8]

Today's media characterize American party politics as highly polarized—even hyper-polarized. In an article titled, "It's Not the Economy Anymore, Stupid," a *Wall Street Journal* columnist wrote:

> Polarized politics mean that voters' views of the economy are increasingly shaped by their party preference, rather than the other way around. And for some key voting blocs, noneconomic issues such as immigration, race relations and Mr. Trump himself have superseded economic concerns in determining their vote.[9]

A caveat: The 2020 surveys were taken January 1 through April 30, 2020, before the massive unemployment and sharp drop in economic activity as a consequence of the COVID-19 crisis. Nevertheless, surveys in June, when about 14 percent of the workforce was unemployed, showed no significant change in the distribution of Democratic and Republican identifications.[10] We must look to other social cleavages for strong and enduring differences in party support.

Notes

1 F.S. Chapin, "A Quantitative Scale for Rating the Home and Social Environment of Middle Class Families in an Urban Community: A First Approximation to the Measurement of Socio-economic Status," *Journal of Educational Psychology*, 19 (February, 1928), 99–111 at p. 99.
2 Karl R. White, "The Relation Between Socioeconomic Status and Academic Achievement," *Psychological Bulletin*, 91 (1982), 461–481 at p. 462.
3 David Streitfeld, "Uncertain Payoff in an Apps Boom," *New York Times* (July 18, 2012), 1 and 19.
4 Extended searches of survey archives found no suitable poll that asked about type of occupation and party identification in 2012. The 2008 American National Election Study did ask about type of occupation, but the open-ended responses to the question asked had not been coded into categories by 2012. See http://electionstudies.org/nesguide/toptable/tab1a_5.htm.
5 Many presidential election year surveys had fewer than 100 respondents in the top income category. Nationscape data for 2020 had over 100,000 respondents, which would have allowed for finer distinctions, but keeping the data comparable was more important.
6 David Masciotra, "Anyone Who Says, 'It's the Economy, Stupid' Is Being Stupid," *Salon* (November 9, 2019).
7 David L. Weakliem, "The United States: Still the Politics of Diversity," in Geoffrey Evans and Nan Dirk De Graaf (eds.), *Political Choice Matters: Explaining the Strength of Class and Religious Cleavages in Cross-National Perspective* (Oxford: Oxford University Press, 2013), 114–136 at p. 136.

8 Kenneth Janda, *The Social Bases of Political Parties: Democrats and Republicans, 1952–2012 and 2032* (eBook edition 1.0, February, 2013), p. 25.
9 Greg Ip, "It's Not the Economy Anymore, Stupid," *Wall Street Journal* (November 19, 2019).
10 An NBC News/*Wall Street Journal* Survey, Study #200266 (June, 2020), showed 35 percent Democrat and 26 percent Republican, which is close to the 36 percent Democrat and 30 percent Republican in the January–April, 2020 Netscape poll.

6 Urbanization
Shifting Effects

By definition, urbanization is "a process by which the number of urban dwellers increases in relation to rural dwellers."[1] Some scholars have viewed "urbanization" and "civilization" as two sides of the same coin, seeing urbanization as "the process by which preliterate agriculturalists living in villages and towns first came together to form larger, more complex *civilized* societies."[2] As more people began living next to one another they interacted in new ways and adopted, or conformed to, new values—which meant surrendering old ways and sacrificing old values. So urbanization, regardless of whether it truly advanced civilization, brought cultural changes.

In 1787, when the Constitution was adopted, the United States was estimated to be 95 percent rural. In 1900, more than a century later, 60 percent of the people still lived in rural areas. Not until 1920 did a majority of the population live in urban areas—and just barely, 51 percent urban to 49 percent rural. Today, about a third of the population lives in central cities and another two-fifths in their suburbs.

During the nineteenth century, this inexorable and massive process of urbanization brought cultural change, economic development, and even political conflict as rival cities sought to become regional centers.[3] In the latter half of the 1800s, mass migration from Europe and Black migration from the South altered partisan politics in the nation, as the Democratic Party in major cities welcomed newcomers. European ethnics, Blacks, Catholics, and liberals in the North voted with white southerners in President Roosevelt's New Deal coalition. This ungainly coalition sustained the Democratic Party until the 1960s. Since then, the politics of urbanization has changed significantly.

Changes in Urban-Rural Population Distribution, 1950–2018

According to the Census Bureau, 60 percent of the population resided in urban areas in 1950.[4] However, what the Census counted as an urban area may not match what you think it is, and the definitional issue has vexed research on urbanization. The history of defining what is urban and what is rural prior to 1900 is complicated, and its later history only somewhat

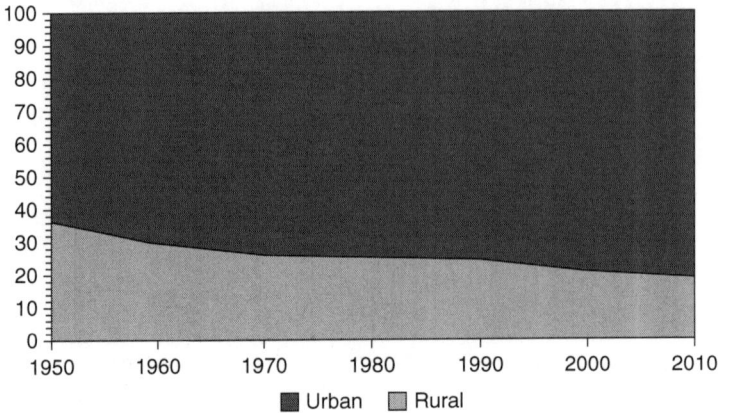

Figure 6.1 U.S. Census Estimate of Percent Urban-Rural Population, 1950–2010

less so. According to the Census's *Geographic Areas Reference Manual*, "In the decennial censuses from 1910 through 1940, *urban* comprised all territory, people, and housing units in incorporated places of 2,500 or more."[5] Finding that many people lived in *un*incorporated places of more than 2,500, the 1950 Census created a Census Designated Place as "a densely settled population center that has a name and community identity, and is not part of any incorporated place."[6] The Census also moved toward recognizing cities by defining an "urbanized area" as "a continuously built-up area with a population of 50,000 or more." Still today, the Census defines "urban" as any incorporated or CDP with at least 2,500 inhabitants. Many people across America living in small towns that size may be surprised to learn that—officially—they are urbanites.

The 1950 Census failed to settle the problem of identifying urban areas. Indeed, the Census Bureau has tweaked its definitions prior to every decennial population count since. Figure 6.1 simply accepts the percentages of inhabitants in urban and rural areas as published in the seven decennial censuses from 1950 to 2010. In 1950, 64 percent of the population lived in urban areas. By 2010, that percentage had climbed to 81 percent. But classifying 81 percent of the U.S. population as urban combines people living in areas that, sociologically speaking, ought to be separated. People who inhabit densely populated cities surely live differently from those residing in less crowded suburbs of those same cities. Unfortunately, the standard Census categories do not break out the suburban population over time.

Changes in Urbanization, 1952–2018

Survey organizations had to struggle with the changing Census categories. The American National Election Studies said, "Definitions describing urbanism categories have continued to change over time," and gamely used respondents' sampling addresses to code its interviews as occurring in "Central cities," in "Suburban areas," or in "Rural, small towns, outlying and adjacent areas."[7] (The ANES codebook ran for 13 pages to fit its interviews into those three categories for interviews from 1952 to 2000.) In 2004, ANES abruptly stated, "Data are not available after 2000," and dropped the geographic variable from later surveys. As pollsters moved away from face-to-face interviews to polling by telephone and internet, they lost track of exactly where respondents reside. Polls that ask respondents to describe "the place where they live" produce percentages that vary substantially from those shown in earlier surveys.[8]

Lacking ANES subsequent data and unable to locate suitable surveys in 2020, I used data for 2004–2018 from the General Social Survey, which has periodically conducted national surveys since 1972.[9] Data from the 2018 General Social Survey will serve for 2020. This "more-than-you-want-to-know" description of difficulties in distinguishing urban from rural (and both from suburban) illustrates the research problem: the urban-rural distinction is undeniably important in society and politics—yet devilishly hard to record using current electronic survey methodology.

Figure 6.2 shows that the decline in rural population did not simply translate into population growth in central cities. About 33 percent of Americans lived in cities in 1952 compared with about 35 percent in 2018. The real population growth occurred in suburban areas, which held about 30 percent of the population in 1952 and over 40 percent in 2018. Indeed, the Great Recession of 2007 generated population decline in some major U.S. cities.[10] People did not shift massively toward small towns and rural areas; they tended to move to city suburbs.

Regardless of whether people moved to cities or suburbs, in every region of the country over the last 60 years they migrated to more urban areas.

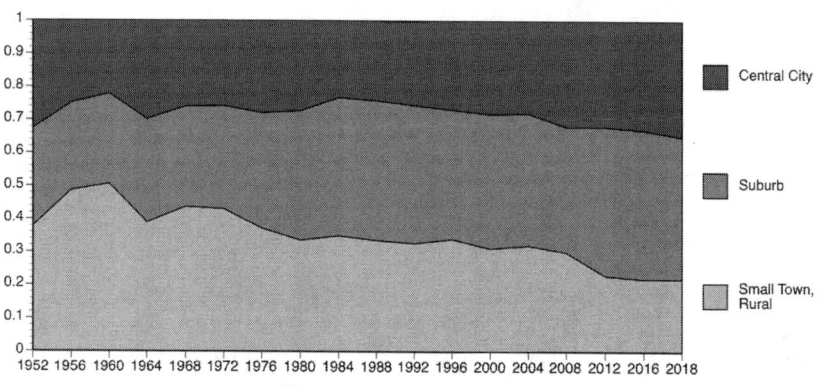

*ANES Surveys 1952-2000; General Social Survey 2004-2018

Figure 6.2 Population in Rural, Suburban, and Urban Areas, 1952–2018*

Many moved primarily to obtain employment in manufacturing. Others were drawn to the luster of bright lights and urban living. In the process, those who moved from rural to urban areas often suffered culture shocks as they encountered people outside their familiar ethnic and religious groups, were constrained by zoning laws, experienced crime and police misconduct, and so on. Moving to the city meant more than just a change of scenery. How did the Democratic and Republican parties appeal to this migrating population?

Group Appeal by Levels of Urbanization

The northern portion of Roosevelt's New Deal voting coalition consisted of European ethnics, Blacks, Catholics, and liberals. They were concentrated in cities and voted overwhelmingly Democratic through the 1930s and into the 1950s. During the 1930s and 1940s the Democratic Party dominated national politics. Franklin Delano Roosevelt was elected president in 1932, winning 57 percent of the popular vote and 89 percent of the electoral vote. He surpassed that huge victory in 1936, re-elected with 61 and 98 percent respectively of the popular and electoral votes. For good measure, FDR was re-elected again in 1940 and 1944 with strong but less spectacular margins. Throughout that time, the Democrats also controlled the House and the Senate by commanding margins. Roosevelt's New Deal coalition lived on after his death in 1945, helping to elect his Vice-President, Harry Truman, to the presidency in 1948. World War II hero General Dwight D. Eisenhower ended Democratic control of the White House with his election and re-election in 1952 and 1956.

Although the urban base of Roosevelt's coalition still supported the Democratic Party, it became severely weakened after World War II as people moved from city centers to suburbs. One scholar attributes its decline to the automobile: "The automobile and the freeway system, the development of which was made possible by the Federal Highway Act of 1956, encouraged a new kind of decentralization that undermined the central city."[11] Electoral politics shifted from an urban-rural tussle to an urban-suburban-rural struggle. The vote-delivering importance of mostly Democratic big-city political machines was lessened both by the growth of suburbs and by new federal welfare programs that bypassed city officials.

Nevertheless, the affinity between cities and the Democratic Party is still evident in Figure 6.3. Remember that most citizens nationally in 1952 identified with the Democratic Party nearly 2 to 1. (See Figure 2.2 in Chapter 2.) Therefore, it is not surprising that most people in cities, suburbs, and less populated areas should favor the Democrats to a similar extent. That the tendency to identify as Democrats varied little across the population groupings can be seen in the Democrats' nearly perfect attraction score of 0.95. That 32 percent of suburbanites were Republican in 1952—even more than the 28 percent of those in towns and rural areas—attests to the early link between the suburbs and the Republican Party.

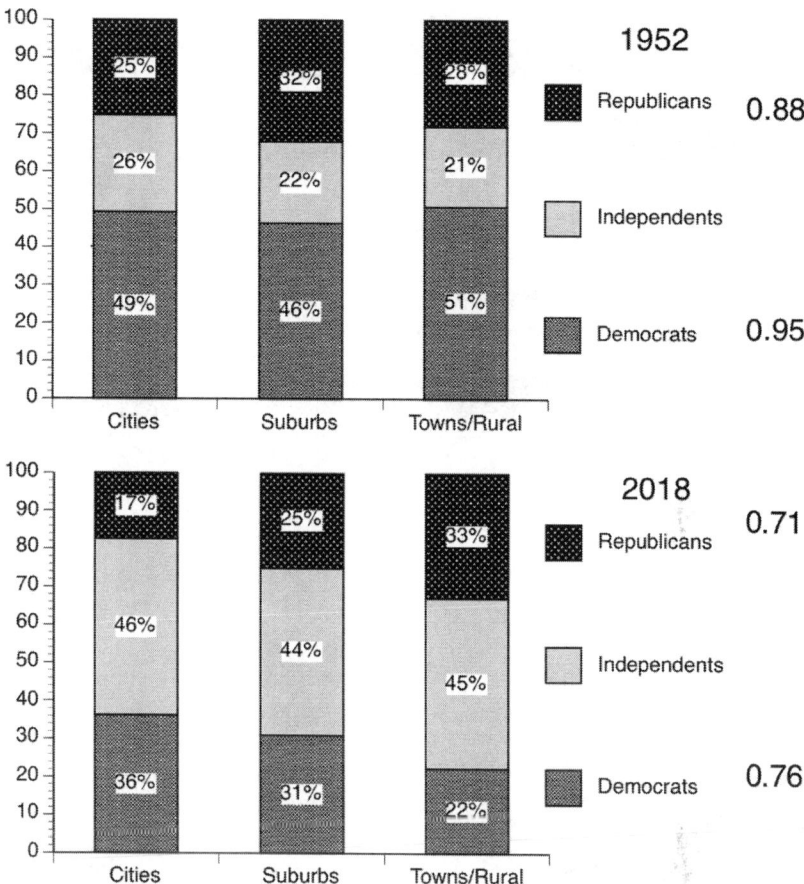

Figure 6.3 Percentages of Party Identification by Urbanization, with Equal Group Appeal Scores

The 2018 General Social Survey shows the two parties drawing very differently from the three population groupings. Democrats retained their roughly 2 to 1 margin over Republicans among city respondents, but their lead over the Republicans in the suburbs decreased and they lost their lead in towns and rural areas. Reflecting the changing patterns of party support, both parties dropped considerably in their Equal Group Appeal scores.

Base Concentration by Urbanization

Sometimes Appeal and Concentration scores tell different stories about patterns of party support, but not in the case of urbanization. Figure 6.4 portrays a similar picture to Figure 6.3. In 1952, both parties were composed almost equally of identifiers from cities, suburbs, and less populated areas.

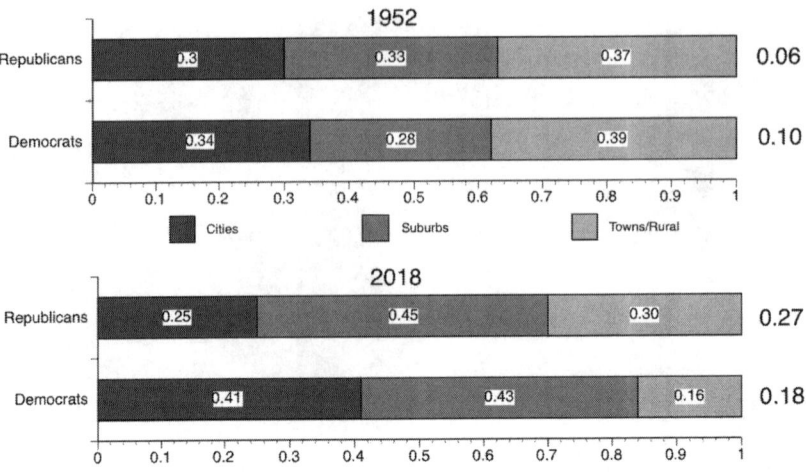

Figure 6.4 Proportions of Party Identifiers by Urbanization, with Base Concentration Scores

By 2018, almost half of Republican identifiers were suburbanites, and only one-quarter lived in cities. With their increased presence in the population, suburbanites also accounted for a larger proportion of Democrats, while people in towns and rural areas dwindled to only 0.16 of all identifiers. Accordingly, both parties increased in their base concentration scores, with Republicans concentrated in the suburbs and Democrats split between cities and suburbs.

Whereas in 1952 both parties' bases were nearly equally composed of party identifiers from every population category, each party's base in 2018 had a different composition. Republican identifiers were more likely to come from towns and rural areas—a shrinking segment of the electorate—than from cities. Democratic identifiers from towns and rural areas were in a small minority, vastly outnumbered by city dwellers and suburbanites, which greatly increased its Party Base Concentration score.

Equal Appeal and Base Concentration by Urbanization Since 1952

Figure 6.5 plots the urbanization attraction and concentration scores over time. It convey three messages:

1. For both parties, the Group Appeal scores are fairly high consistently and the concentration scores fairly low. These scores indicate that, historically, level of urbanization has not been a major differentiator for party support.

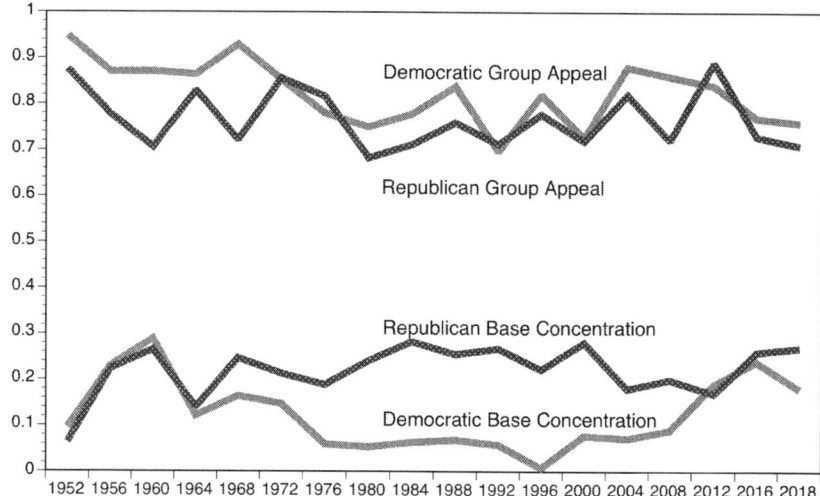

Figure 6.5 Parties' Equal Group Appeal and Base Concentration Scores, Urbanization 1952–2018

2. Both parties show a recent trend toward being less appealing across population groupings and more concentrative of population subgroups. These trends suggest that level of urbanization has become more politically important since 2008.
3. The Republican Party has rated almost consistently above the Democratic Party in concentration scores. In 2018, that reflects the relatively higher proportion of suburbanites over urbanites among Republican identifiers.

Reminiscing, and Summarizing

I had an ideal upbringing, going to grade school in a city of three million people and attending high school in a town of three thousand. I liked Chicago and became a Cubs and Bears fan, but I was happier in Wilmington, which offered everything that teenagers and families needed back then. Like many small towns, it had a vibrant commercial center. Multiple shops lined the main street and sold groceries, toiletries, ice cream, clothing, hardware, appliances, and so on—all within easy walking or cycling distance from home. Today, still three-quarters of almost 20,000 incorporated places in America have fewer than 5,000 people.[12] However, most have lost their retail establishments, and those that remain cluster on the edge of town, leaving the formerly vibrant center with taverns, antique stores, and vacant properties. That describes my hometown today.

The nation's population doubled in size from 1950 to 2020, but most small towns showed little growth or declined in size. Their residents also grew older and suffered economically. As cities and suburbs became more culturally diverse, small towns and rural areas remained ethnically homogeneous—especially in northern and western states. The 2018 General Social Survey found 87 percent or more of respondents in such places classifying themselves as white. Although these small towns and rural areas needed new people, they were uncomfortable with accepting minorities and immigrants willing to work in their communities.

As time passed, white voters in small towns and rural areas became more susceptible to the nostalgic cultural appeals of the Republican Party. Conversely, city voters of all ethnicities became more attracted to policies and politics of the Democratic Party. In 2018, Pew Research documented these demographic and political trends in a major study of the urban-rural divide. Concerning party identification, the report stated:

> Adults in urban counties, long aligned with the Democratic Party, have moved even more to the left in recent years, and today twice as many urban voters identify as Democrats or lean Democratic as affiliate with the Republican Party. For their part, rural adults have moved more firmly into the Republican camp.[13]

Suburban voters, the report noted, became almost equally divided in party loyalties. In commenting on the growing relationship between population density and voting behavior from 1960 to 2018, Wilkinson said, "there is no such thing as a Republican city."[14] While some small towns are still Democratic, their numbers are dwindling.

Notes

1 Thomas Bender, "Urbanization," in Eric Foner and John A. Garraty (eds.), *The Reader's Companion to American History* (Boston: Houghton Mifflin, 1991), 1101–1104 at p. 1101.
2 Robert McC. Adams, "Urban Revolution," in David L. Sills (ed.), *International Encyclopedia of the Social Sciences, Volume 16* (New York: Macmillan, 1968), 201–207 at p. 201.
3 Bender, p. 1101.
4 U.S. Census Bureau, "Table 1. Urban and Rural Population: 1900 to 1990," released October, 1995, available at www.census.gov/population/censusdata/urpop0090.txt.
5 Michael Ratcliffe, Charlynn Burd, Kelly Holder, and Alison Fields, "Defining Rural at the U.S. Census Bureau," *American Community Survey and Geography Brief* (December, 2016). Available at www2.census.gov/geo/pdfs/reference/ua/Defining_Rural.pdf.
6 *Ibid*, p. 2.
7 *American National Election Studies (ANES) Cumulative Data File, 1948–2008 Codebook*, p. 28.
8 For example, the ANES 2019 Pilot Study, conducted over the Internet by YouGov, asked, "Do you currently live in a rural area, small town, suburb, or a

city?" Their responses do not match well against objectively determined population categories.
9 The National Opinion Research Center at the University of Chicago supervises the General Social Survey. See https://gss.norc.org/About-The-GSS. The ten categories in the GENSOC variable, XNORCSIZ, were recoded into three: Central Cities (1 & 2), Suburbs (3, 4, & 5), and Small Towns and Rural (6–10).
10 Haya El Nasser, "Most Major U.S. Cities Show Population Declines," *USA Today*, June 27, 2011.
11 Bender, p. 1104.
12 Amel Toukabri and Lauren Medina, "Latest City and Town Population Estimates of the Decade Show Three-Fourths of the Nation's Incorporated Places Have Fewer Than 5,000 People," U.S. Census at www.census.gov/library/stories/2020/05/america-a-nation-of-small-towns.html.
13 Kim Parker, Juliana Horowitz, Anna Brown, Richard Fry, D'Vera Cohn, and Ruth Igielnik, "What Unites and Divides Urban, Suburban, and Rural Communities," Pew Research Center (May, 2018).
14 Will Wilkinson, "The Density Divide: Urbanization, Polarization, and Populist Backlash," Niskanen Center Research Paper (June, 2019), at www.niskanencenter.org/the-density-divide-urbanization-polarization-and-populist-backlash/, p. 12.

7 Education
Incremental Reversal

In their study of social cleavages and political alignments in presidential elections from 1960 to 1992, Brooks and Manza did not treat education as a social cleavage, only as a control variable to analyze the effects of other cleavages.[1] Nevertheless, differences in levels of education have sparked partisan voting at times in our history. Historians credit the 1828 presidential election of Andrew Jackson to poorly educated voters in western states. Educated eastern elites called Jackson's voters "common" men, "uneducated ruffians" who embodied "mob rule."[2] The 1828 election also marked the founding of the Democratic Party, regarded for many decades as the reputed champion of workers over bosses, of employees over employers, of union over management, and thus of the uneducated over the educated.

Changes in Educational Levels Since 1952

Although 1828 may have marked the high point for education as a social and partisan cleavage, differences in educational levels have always had partisan implications. As the electorate became more highly educated since 1952, the American National Election Studies changed its questions about education. For 20 years after 1952, the ANES only asked respondents how many grades of school they finished. Later the surveys inquired about attending college, eventually asking about the highest degrees completed. Here is a summary of the questions asked.

> *1952–1972: How many grades of school did you finish?*
> *1974 AND LATER: What is highest grade of school or year of college you have completed? Did you get a high school diploma or pass a high school equivalency test?*
> *1974, 1976: Do you have a college degree? (IF YES:) What degree is that?*
> *1978–1984: Do you have a college degree? (IF YES:) What is the highest degree that you have earned?*
> *1986 AND LATER: What is the highest degree that you have earned?*[3]

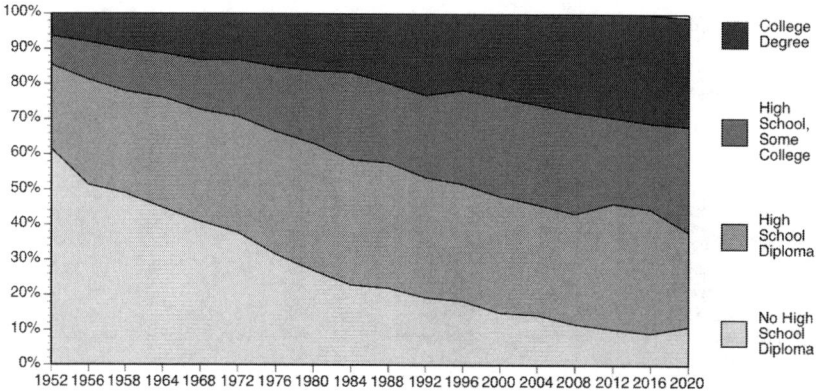

Figure 7.1 Distribution of Educational Levels, 1952–2020

For this chapter, responses to the ANES interview questions over the years and to the 2020 Nationscape survey were organized into four categories:

No High School diploma—in 1952, 62 percent lacked a high school education
High School Diploma—or equivalent; may have had further technical schooling
High School Diploma, Some College—includes community college
College Degree—includes postgraduate work

Over seven decades, the American population shifted from most people lacking a high school education to almost everyone having a high school education. As shown in Figure 7.1, only about 15 percent of respondents had any college at all in 1952. By 2020, over half the population had some college education and almost one-third had college degrees.[4]

Equal Group Appeal by Levels of Urbanization

How did the Democratic and Republican parties absorb these enormous changes? Figure 7.2 displays the percentages of respondents at four educational levels—no high school, high school, some college or other education, and college graduates—who identified with the Democratic or Republican parties or who had no party preference in 1952 and 2020. In 1952, 40 percent of the relatively small segment of society who held college degrees identified with the Republican Party, versus 24 percent who supported the Democrats. In 2020 the college-educated had reversed their party preferences and were more likely to be Democrats than Republicans by 39 to 32 percentage points.

78 Education: Incremental Reversal

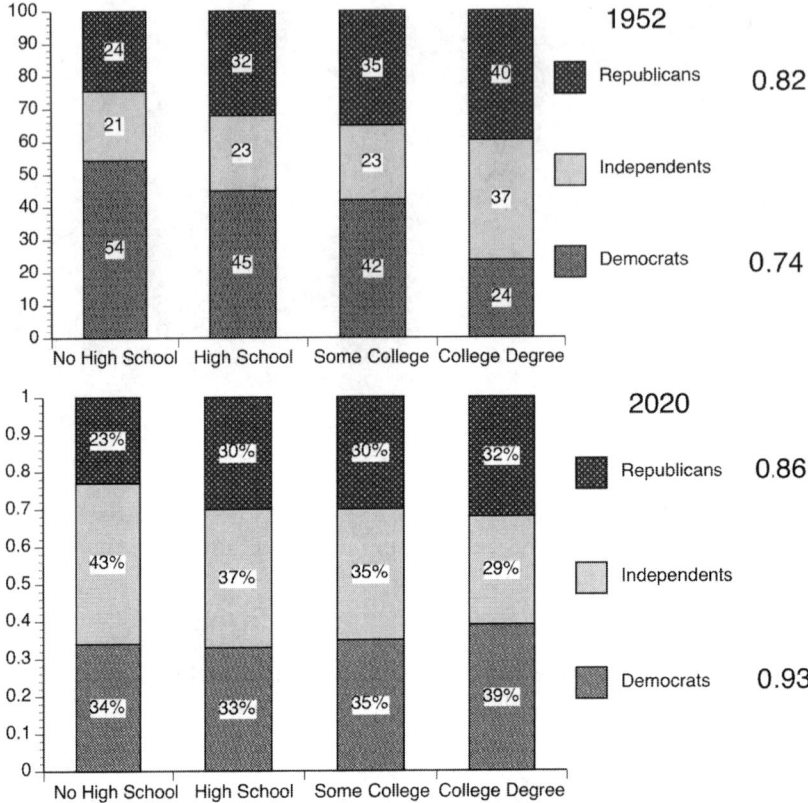

Figure 7.2 Percentages of Party Identification by Education, with Equal Group Appeal Scores

The link between education and independents also changed. In 1952, the least educated were the most partisan, and the most educated the least partisan. This relationship completely reversed in 2020, as the relatively few respondents who had not completed high school were far more likely (43 to 21 percent) to say they were "independents" than in 1952. As time passed and the glow of the Roosevelt era faded, the less educated citizens apparently found little to attract them to either party.

Because Democrats in 1952 fared so well with the least educated group and so poorly with the best educated, they scored lower (0.74) in the Equal Group Appeal scores for education than Republicans (0.82). But in 2020, the parties' Group Appeal scores were reversed. Democrats drew support more evenly across all educational groups than Republicans, so Democrats achieved a higher Equal Group Appeal score in 2012—0.93 versus 0.86.

Base Concentration by Education

The changing composition of educational groups in party politics can be seen even more clearly in Figure 7.3, which portrays the proportion of identifiers in each party who came from each educational level. It paints a different picture of education's impact in 1952 versus 2020. In 1952, citizens who identified with American parties reflected the society's lack of education, as both parties were composed of relatively few people with college education. Nine out of ten Democratic Party identifiers in 1952 had only a high school education at best, whereas about one-fifth of Republican identifiers had some college education. In 2020, one-third of both party identifiers had college degrees.

The most striking difference between both parties' bases in 1952 and 2020 resulted from the overall increase in the American electorate's education. The preponderance of identifiers with less than a college education accounts for the relatively high educational concentration scores for both parties in 1952, when Republicans scored 0.40 in Party Base Concentration and the Democrats a resounding 0.58. Those high scores resulted because over half of all Democratic and Republican party identifiers lacked a high school education in 1952. By 2020, college graduates formed the largest segment of both parties' bases.

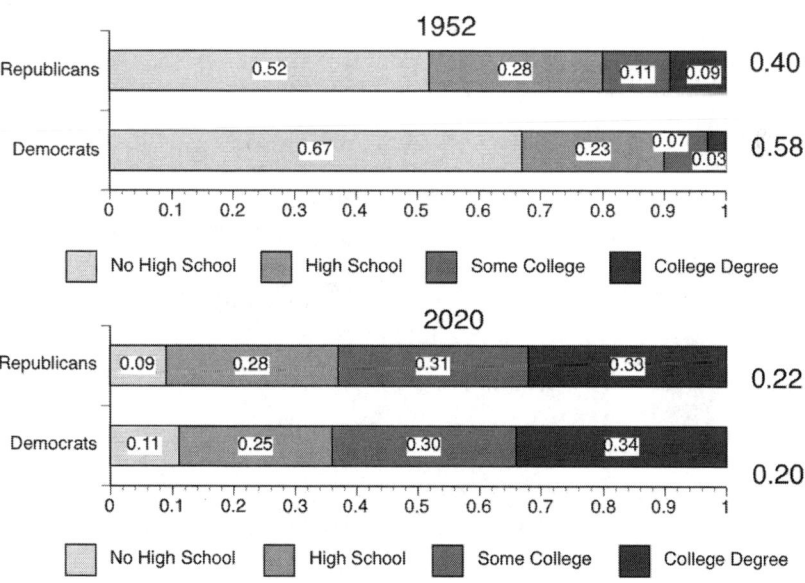

Figure 7.3 Education Groups as Proportion of Party Identifiers, with Party Base Concentration Scores

Group Appeal and Base Concentration by Education Since 1952

Figure 7.4 plots both parties' educational Equal Group Appeal and Base Concentration scores over time. Up to Ronald Reagan's election in 1980, the two parties appealed about equally to all educational categories. Running for re-election in 1984 against Democrat Walter Mondale, Reagan proved so popular that he won 59 percent of the popular vote and 98 percent of the electoral vote, carrying every state but Mondale's own Minnesota. In that year, 31–35 percent of respondents at all educational levels professed to be Republicans, producing a one-year spike in Republican Group Appeal scores. Democrats spiked in Base Concentration as they lost their least and most educated voters to Reagan, leaving half the party with a high school education.

Reminiscing, and Summarizing

In 2020, only about 5 percent of the U.S. population is over 75 years old. So very few readers will recall how uncommon it was to have a college education in 1952, just 68 years ago. My mother was lucky to have two years of high school; my father stopped after the eighth grade. My parents had absolutely no idea of what college entailed, but I won a small state tuition scholarship and they backed me to apply. I enrolled in a teacher's college with 2,000 students to study Industrial Arts, which I thought was close to Engineering, whatever that was.[5] Fortunately, good teachers encouraged me to change my major from Industrial Arts (where I was getting B grades in technical drawing and woodworking) to Social Science (where I was

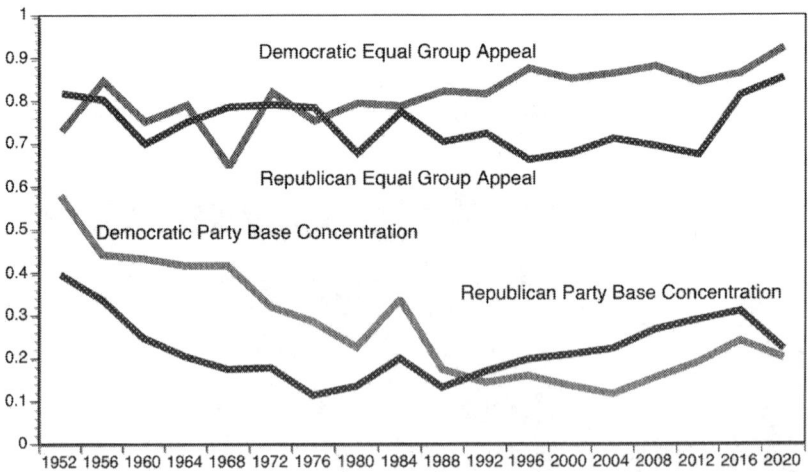

Figure 7.4 Parties' Equal Group Appeal and Party Base Concentration Scores, Education 1952–2020

getting better grades in history and sociology). Others persuaded me to apply to graduate school, which I did not know existed. Like me, most youngsters in the 1950s had no linear track to a college education. Like me, some benefitted from the care and kindness of teachers.

Over seven decades, American society has benefitted from a more highly educated citizenry. In 1950, fewer than two million students were enrolled in all types of institutions of higher education.[6] In 2020, college enrollment grew to over 20 million. Although the nation's population had doubled over that time period, college enrollment increased tenfold. My school, Illinois State Normal University (later Illinois State University), kept pace, growing from 2,000 when I started in 1953 to more than 20,000 students in 2020.

Seven decades ago, going to college was different for children from wealthy families. It was expected, and there was a connection between educational level and party preference. Citizens with college degrees tended to be Republicans and those without a high school education tended to be Democrats. Even then, both parties appealed fairly evenly to all educational groupings. The decline in Base Concentration scores over time occurred as more Americans gained more education. As college education spread more widely, the linkage dissolved between having a college degree and identifying as a Republican.

Not only did the link dissolve in 2020 between having a college degree and identifying as a Republican but so did the connection in the voting booth. Of ANES respondents with college degrees, 62 percent voted for Democrat Hillary Clinton. Republican Donald Trump received his strongest support (59 percent) from respondents without a college education.

So the degree of respondents' education has some relationship to partisanship, but the relationship is not very strong. Let us consider another personal attribute, a respondent's religion or nature of religious belief next.

Notes

1 Clem Brooks and Jeff Manza, "Social Cleavages and Political Alignments: U.S. Presidential Elections, 1960 to 1992," *American Sociological Review*, 62 (December, 1997), 937–946.
2 U.S. History, "The Rise of the Common Man" at www.ushistory.org/us/24a.asp.
3 These questions were extracted from the *American National Election Studies (ANES) Cumulative Data File, 1948–2008 Codebook* (Ann Arbor, MI: Inter-University Consortium for Political and Social Research, undated), p. 27. The codebook is available as a PDF file at http://electionstudies.org/studypages/download/datacenter_all.htm.
4 Why the ANES surveys showed a slight rise in those with high school diplomas in 2012 and 2016 is unclear. The slight rise in proportion of respondents without a high school diploma in 2020 may be due to Nationscape's survey methodology, which relied solely on the Internet.
5 Bloomington *Daily Pantagraph* (February 9, 1953), p. 2.
6 U.S. Census, *Statistical Abstract* (Washington, DC: Government Printing Office, 1950).

8 Religion
Important and in Flux

To avoid persecution in seventeenth-century Europe, religious nonconformists fled across the Atlantic Ocean to settle in the English colonies. True, they sought freedom to practice their own religions, but they also acted to prevent others from practicing theirs.[1] Indeed, 8 of the 13 colonies established official churches, and nonconformists were often persecuted in the colonies as in Europe.[2] Catholics were particularly targeted, but various Protestant sects routinely denounced other Protestants. Freedom to worship as one wished was not generally valued in early colonial America.

In the eighteenth century, the colonists broke away from Britain and were governed from 1774 to 1789 by a Continental Congress under the Articles of Confederation. As explained in a Library of Congress publication, the government promoted "a nondenominational, nonpolemical Christianity."

> Congress appointed chaplains for itself and the armed forces, sponsored the publication of a Bible, imposed Christian morality on the armed forces, and granted public lands to promote Christianity among the Indians. National days of thanksgiving and of "humiliation, fasting, and prayer" were proclaimed by Congress at least twice a year throughout the war. Congress was guided by "covenant theology," a Reformation doctrine especially dear to New England Puritans, which held that God bound himself in an agreement with a nation and its people.[3]

The Articles of Confederation were replaced in 1789 by the United States Constitution, which avoided mentioning religion except to state that "no religious Test shall ever be required as Qualification" for federal office holders. Avoiding religion in the Constitution troubled two opposing groups: those who supported a larger role in government for religion and those who feared that religion would have a larger role.[4] The First Amendment to the Constitution satisfied the second group more. It guaranteed that "Congress shall make no law respecting an establishment of religion, or prohibiting the free exercise thereof."

Nevertheless, religious symbols and references became incorporated in government practices and ceremonies. From their beginnings, both the House and Senate of the Congress created offices of Chaplain; congressional sessions are opened with prayers; "In God We Trust" is imprinted on U.S. coins and dollar bills; the Pledge of Allegiance contains the phrase, "one nation under God"; and presidents today routinely end major addresses saying, "God bless America." Compared with western European publics, Americans place more importance on religion. A 2011 Pew global survey found that half of Americans say that religion is *very* important in their lives, whereas fewer than a quarter in Spain and Germany and only about 15 percent in Britain and France share their view.[5] Because religion is important in American life, religion is important to U.S. politics, where Christianity predominates.

The decennial censuses of the United States never asked about a person's religion, so we lack firm data on the distribution of religious preferences over the first 150 years of American history.[6] However, the Census often asked clergy about the size of their congregations and conducted a separate Census of Religious Bodies from 1906 to 1946.[7] These data documented that Christianity was nearly universal and that Protestantism prevailed over Catholicism. The few Catholics in early America were mostly English. About 1845, famine in Ireland led millions of Catholics to emigrate to the United States. Catholic immigrants from Italy and Austria-Hungary came later. One source estimates that Catholics made up only 5 percent of the population in 1850 but 17 percent in 1906.[8] Still, the United States stayed overwhelmingly Christian. In 1948, a Gallup poll found 91 percent of respondents describing themselves as Christian.

Changes in Religious Composition, 1952–2020

Over the last 60 years, religious characteristics of the American public have changed in several ways: in the distribution of religions by major types, in the rise and decline of denominations within types, and in people's religiosity—the intensity of their faith. For decades after 1952, survey researchers were content to ask whether respondents belonged to the two major variants of Christianity or whether they were Jewish. Those who chose none of the three categories were assigned to the "Other/None" category. Here are the questions asked in the American National Election Studies over time:

> *1952–1964:* "*Is your Church (1962: religious) preference Protestant, Catholic or Jewish?*"
> *1966–1968:* "*Are you Protestant, Catholic or Jewish?*"
> *1970–1988, 2002:* "*Is your religious preference Protestant, Catholic, Jewish, or something else?*"
> *1990 and later (exc. 2002): (IF R ATTENDS RELIGIOUS SERVICES:)* "*Do you mostly attend a place of worship that is*

84 Religion: Important and in Flux

Protestant, Roman Catholic, Jewish or what?" (IF R DOESN'T ATTEND RELIGIOUS SERVICES:) "Regardless of whether you now attend any religious services do you ever think of yourself as part of a particular church or denomination?" (IF YES:) "Do you consider yourself Protestant, Roman Catholic, Jewish or what?"

In 2020, Nationscape asked, *"What is your present religion, if any?"*—with many choices: Protestant, Roman Catholic, Mormon, Orthodox such as Greek or Russian Orthodox, Jewish, Muslim, Buddhist, Hindu, atheist, agnostic, something else, or nothing in particular.

Despite the different wording between the various ANES and Nationscape surveys, the survey results portrayed in Figure 8.1 are clear. Over the last 60 years, the percentage of the population professing Christian beliefs has declined from over 90 percent to under 80 percent. Moreover, this decline occurred primarily among Protestants. Perhaps the most striking feature in Figure 8.1 is the dramatic increase in the "Other/None" category to about 35 percent of the population in 2020. Some responses were "Other" (e.g., Muslim, Buddhist, Hindu, or "something else"), while the rest were "None" (Agnostic, Atheist, or "nothing in particular"). That amounts to an enormous change in religious faith.

During these seven decades, major changes also occurred among denominations regarded as Protestants, primarily dividing Evangelical ("born-again") Christians from Mainline Protestants. Regrettably, the ANES distinguished between the two types of Protestants only from 1960 to 1996, so we cannot generate a graph comparable to Figure 8.1. During those 36 years, however, the percentage of Mainline Protestants was halved (45 to 22 points), while Evangelical Christians grew by 5 points (28 to 33 percentage points). We cannot preserve this distinction in analyzing the bases of party support over the entire time period because we lack the data.

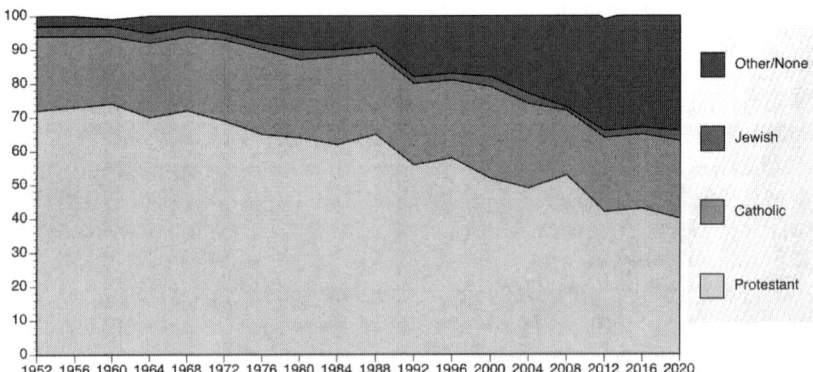

Figure 8.1 Distribution of Religious Affiliations, 1952–2020

Religion: Important and in Flux 85

Finally, religious changes can be assessed according to religiosity—the intensity of faith. The ANES sought to measure respondents' religious intensity by asking about their religious behavior, how often they attended religious services. These are the ANES questions:

1952–1968: (IF ANY RELIGIOUS PREFERENCE) "Would you say you go to church regularly, often, seldom or never?"

1970–1988: (IF ANY RELIGIOUS PREFERENCE) "Would you say you/do you go to (church/synagogue) every week, almost every week, once or twice a month, a few times a year, or never?"

1990 and later: "Lots of things come up that keep people from attending religious services even if they want to. Thinking about your life these days, do you ever attend religious services, apart from occasional weddings, baptisms or funerals?" (IF YES:) "Do you go to religious services every week, almost every week, once or twice a month, a few times a year, or never?"

Data from these ANES surveys to 2016 are graphed in Figure 8.2. It shows a good deal of stability over time in the percentages of respondents who say that they attend regularly or often but great instability in those who say that they attend seldom or never.[9] The substantial increase over time in respondents who say that they never attend religious services corresponds with the increase of those who answer "none" for religion.

One could argue that the religious basis of party support should be based on the intensity of religion rather than on the type of religion. Preliminary analysis, however, revealed that support for the Democratic and Republican parties differed far more on the type of religion practiced than on the frequency of attendance at religious services. Although patterns of party support also differed more when Mainline Protestants were

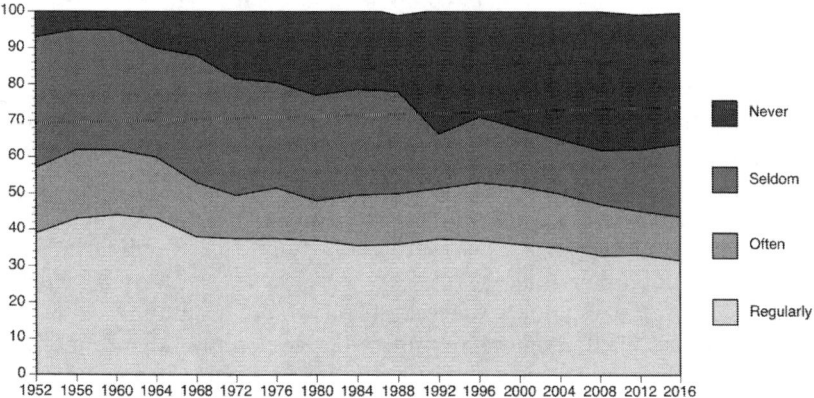

Figure 8.2 Attendance at Religious Services, 1952–2016

distinguished from Evangelical Christians, we did not have enough data to support that analysis over time. The next section concentrates on political party attraction and concentration among religious types, Protestant, Catholic, Jewish, and Other/None.

Group Appeal by Religions

Catholics and Jews were important components of the Democratic voting coalition that Franklin Delano Roosevelt constructed for his first presidential election in 1932. These groups re-elected him to office three times, elected his vice-president, Harry Truman, to the presidency in 1948, and sustained the party in maintaining control of Congress for two decades. During those decades, Catholics and Jews were concentrated in central cities in northern states that held most of the electoral votes needed to elect a president. As population spread out of the central cities to suburban areas and out of the northern states to the South and West, the electoral importance of the Roosevelt coalition declined. However, its existence in 1952 is evident in Figure 8.3.

In 1952, Catholics identified with the Democratic Party over the Republican Party by more than 3 to 1. So few Jews thought of themselves as Republicans that Jewish Republicans did not show up in the 1952 ANES survey. These differences in religious appeal were captured by the 1952 Group Appeal scores: the Democratic score of 0.78 nearly doubled the Republican's 0.44. Sixty years later, Catholics were as likely to be Republicans as Democrats, and Republican Jews surfaced in the survey. The Republican attraction score jumped to 0.70, while the Democrats at 0.80 changed little. Of the old Roosevelt coalition of Catholics and Jews, only Jews remained as loyal Democrats.

Base Concentration by Religions

Turning to the composition of party identifiers, we expect to find Protestants dominating both parties' bases in 1952, when Protestants accounted for more than 70 percent of the public. But as shown in Figure 8.4, Protestants even then were substantially over-represented among Republicans (0.83) and slightly under-represented among Democrats (0.67), leading to Republicans' higher religious concentration score.

In 2020, as the Protestant share of the U.S. population dropped to about 50 percent, the Protestant proportion of Republican identifiers declined accordingly to 0.53, lowering the Republicans' religious Base Concentration. Still, a majority of Republican identifiers were Protestant while Democratic identifiers were about one-third Protestant. Moreover, over one-third of all Democrats professed none of the three traditional American faiths or no faith at all. Data from frequency of attendance at religious services (see Figure 8.2) but not reported here show that half of all Republicans attended regularly in 2020 compared with one-quarter

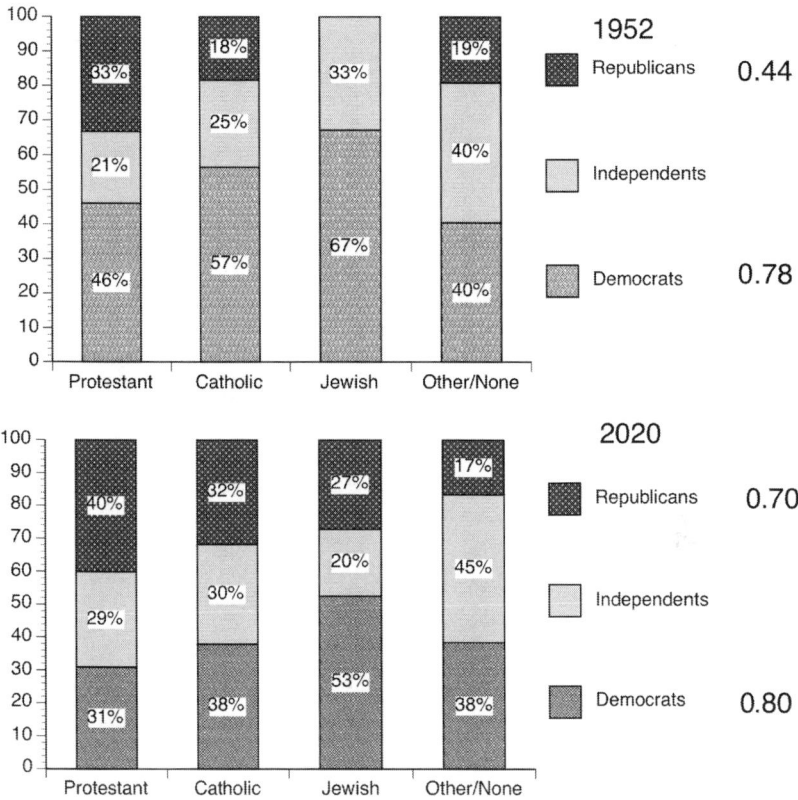

Figure 8.3 Percentages of Party Identifiers by Religion, with Equal Group Appeal Scores

of all Democrats. The Republican Party, it seems, was home for religious believers, especially Protestants.

Equal Appeal and Base Concentration by Religions Since 1952

The pattern of the parties' religious Group Appeal and Base Concentration scores over time is displayed in Figures 8.5 and 8.6. Amidst its ups and downs, the pattern shows two trends: (a) Republicans have tended to increase in appeal across religious groups, and (b) both parties have declined in concentration scores. Although the Democratic Party continues to draw support more evenly from all religious groups than the Republican Party, the Republicans have over time drawn more support from Catholics and Jews, which has caused it to generate increasingly higher appeal scores. As the Protestant share of the electorate has declined over the decades, their capacity to dominate the composition of both parties has declined,

88   *Religion: Important and in Flux*

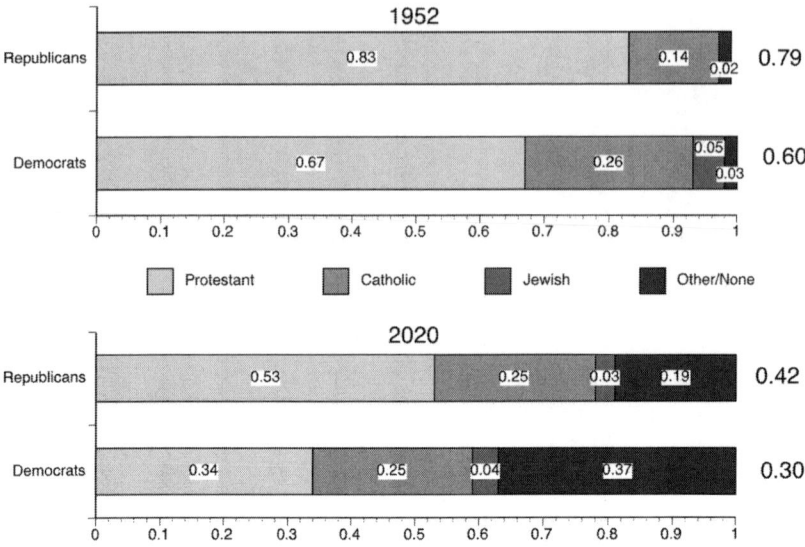

Figure 8.4 Religious Groups as Proportions of Party Identifiers, with Party Base Concentration Scores

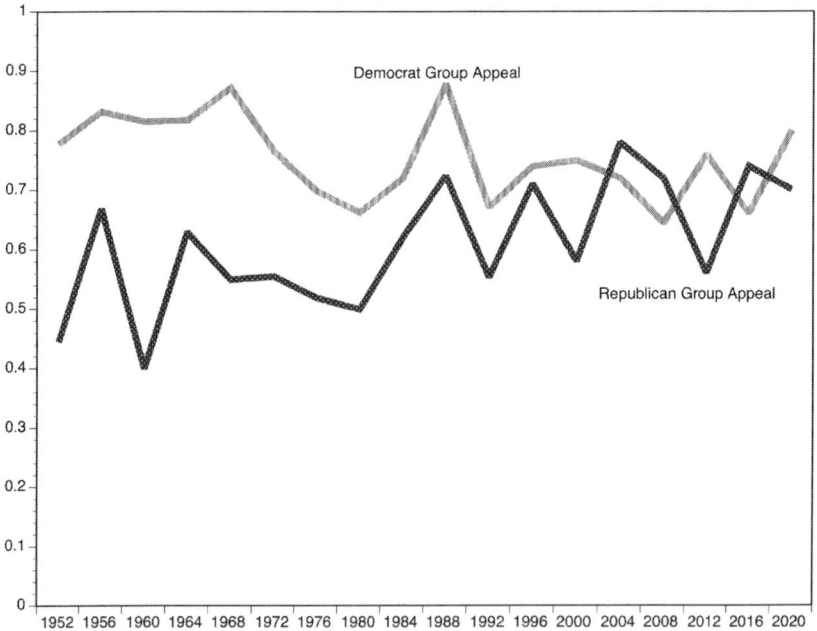

Figure 8.5 Parties' Equal Group Appeal Scores, Religion 1952–2020

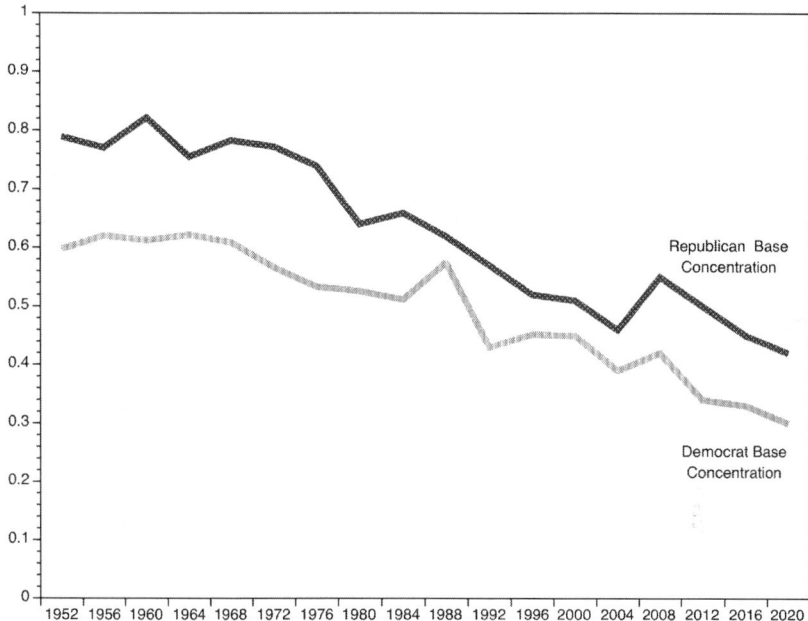

Figure 8.6 Parties' Base Concentration Scores, Religion 1952–2020

resulting in lower concentration scores for Republicans. The Democrats' decline is due to Catholics departing from the party.

If one wonders whether religiosity—as measured by attendance at religious services—matters more in party identification than religious group, consider Figure 8.7, which plots the parties' Group Appeal and Base Concentration scores over time according to whether they attended religious services Regularly, Often, Seldom, or Never. This pattern does not show the strong trends exhibited in Figures 8.5 and 8.6. In general, both parties have appealed more evenly to voters regardless of their participation in religious services and neither party has shown strong changes in the concentration of believers or non-believers in their bases. Republicans, however, have shown some decline in group appeal since Obama's presidency in 2008. In 2016, Republicans claimed loyalty from only 16 percent of those who "Never" attended religious services.

Reminiscing, and Summarizing

In Chicago, we lived in a heavily Jewish neighborhood. On Jewish holidays, my local grammar school gathered the few gentile students in the auditorium to tell us how we would spend our school day. My mother attended a nearby Presbyterian church in Chicago nearly every Sunday and enrolled

90 *Religion: Important and in Flux*

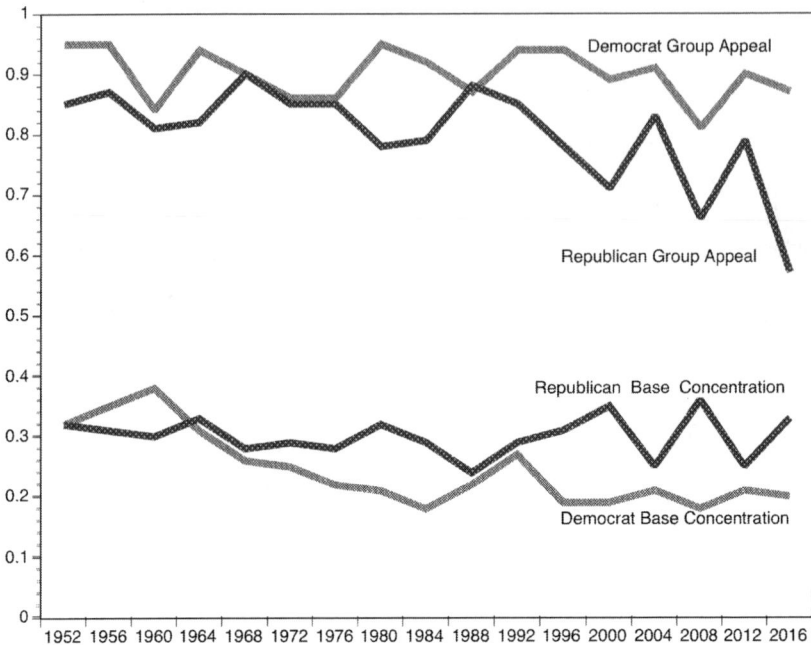

Religiosity measured as attending religious services: Regularly, Often, Seldom, or Never.

Figure 8.7 Parties' Equal Group Appeal and Party Base Concentration Scores, Religiosity* 1952–2016

me in its Sunday school. My father attended church services nearly every Christmas and Easter. Many of my playmates were Jewish. None of my relatives were Catholic, but one boyhood friend was.

Wilmington, to my knowledge, had no Jews but quite a few Catholics. My parents attended the local Presbyterian church. I sang in its choir until I realized that I liked the Methodist girls better and switched to singing in its choir. During my 1971 visit to distant relatives in Czechoslovakia, I found that my ancestors were buried in a Catholic cemetery. I never asked my mother why she was Presbyterian.

In 1947, I saw *Gentlemen's Agreement*, a movie that won three Academy Awards in 1948, including the one for Best Picture. Gregory Peck played a journalist who posed as a Jew to research an exposé on widespread anti-Semitism in New York City. As a 12-year old boy, I was appalled to learn that my Jewish playmates' parents might not be able to rent a hotel room. That movie impacted me like my later experiences in segregated Kentucky.

In 1952, during the last years of the vaunted Roosevelt Democratic coalition, voters' religion was strongly related to their party identification. Most Catholics and virtually all Jews were Democrats. Protestants were and remain mostly Republican. But the strong linkage between religion and party affiliation has changed over time as religion itself has become less salient in society. In 1952, less than 5 percent of respondents failed to claim being Protestant, Catholic, or Jewish. Now almost one-third of respondents choose "None" or "Other" as a religious response, and over a third say that they "Never" attend religious services.

In 1960, people questioned whether a Catholic was fit to serve as president of the United States. Democratic candidate Al Smith in 1928 was the last, and only, Catholic who had run for president, and Smith lost in a landslide to Republican Herbert Hoover. Kennedy won, but only by 0.2 percent of the popular vote.

Journalists routinely identify "evangelical" Christians, who comprise about one-quarter of the U.S. population, as part of President Trump's electoral base. However, data from the University of Chicago's General Social Survey found some moderate Protestants leaving evangelicalism for mainline denominations over Donald Trump's presidency, and that "Evangelicals declined 1.4 percent between 2016 and 2018, while mainline Protestants saw a slight increase."[10] So religion still links to party identification, but the linkage is no longer as strong.

Notes

1 Library of Congress, "Religion and the Founding of the American Republic: I. America as a Religious Refuge: The Seventeenth Century," at www.loc.gov/exhibits/religion/rel01.html.
2 George Washington Institute for Religious Freedom, "Religion in Colonial America: Trends, Regulations and Beliefs," at http://nobigotry.facinghistory.org/content/religion-colonial-america-trends-regulations-and-beliefs.
3 Library of Congress, "Religion and the Founding of the American Republic: IV. Religion and the Congress of the Confederation, 1774–89," at www.loc.gov/exhibits/religion/rel04.html.
4 Library of Congress, "Religion and the Founding of the American Republic: VI. Religion and the Federal Government," at www.loc.gov/exhibits/religion/rel06.html.
5 Pew Research Center, "The American-Western European Values Gap," Pew Global Attitudes Project, November 17, 2011, at www.pewglobal.org/2011/11/17/the-american-western-european-values-gap/.
6 For a comprehensive yet concise description of early Census efforts see Chapter H, "Religions Affiliation," in *Historical Statistics of the United States: Colonial Time to 1957* (Washington, DC: Bureau of the Census, 1960).
7 Pew Research Center, "A Brief History of Religion and the U.S. Census," *The Pew Forum on Religion and Public Life*, January 26, 2010, at www.pewforum.org/Government/A-Brief-History-of-Religion-and-the-U-S--Census.aspx.
8 Julie Byrne, "Roman Catholics and Immigration in Nineteenth-Century America," National Humanities Center at www.nationalhumanitiescenter.org/tserve/nineteen/nkeyinfo/nromcath.htm.
9 Questions about attendance at religious services varied over time, and so did the coding categories. From 1952 to 1968, they were: Regularly, Often, Seldom,

Never, and No religious preference. The last was recoded as Never. From 1972 to 2016, the categories were Every week, Almost every week (both recoded as Regularly), Once or twice a month (became Often), A few times a year (became Seldom), Never, and No religious preference (included with Never).

10 Ryan P. Burge, "Evangelicals Show No Decline, Despite Trump and Nones," *Christianity Today* (March 21, 2019), at www.christianitytoday.com/news/2019/march/evangelical-nones-mainline-us-general-social-survey-gss.html.

9 Ethnicity
Dwindling Whites

The land now known as America was once populated by native inhabitants whom early explorers (thinking they had sailed to India) called Indians. European settlers regarded these indigenous "red men" as biologically distinct and culturally inferior—as they did the enslaved Blacks they forcibly imported from Africa. After waves of immigrants from Europe pushed out the native population and colonized the land, the Europeans treated the Indians brutally, forcing them into reservations and separating them from economic and political life. While the colonists' slaves were also treated brutally, they became an integral part of their economy, unlike Native Americans. Both groups however were excluded from meaningful participation in the new national government, the United States of America.

Although European immigrants had different origins—coming from Britain, Holland, Germany, France, etc.—and often spoke different languages, they were regarded as biologically similar and distinct from American Indians and Africans. In the early 1700s, the eminent botanist and zoologist Carolus Linnaeus defined four types of humans—the white European, the red American, the tawny Asian, and the black African—thus dignifying the concept of race.[1] Essentially, race depends on what outsiders "see"—whether they see people as white or Black. Accordingly, one scholar notes that racial categories "are normally laced with inaccuracies and stereotypes."[2] Today, racial classifications on physical characteristics at birth are suspect. A broader concept is ethnicity, which includes race. Ethnicity depends on the individual's origin—usually where the person (or the person's family) came from. Hispanics, for example, constitute an ethnic group whether they are white or Black.

Throughout most of U.S. history, ethnicity—in the sense of European origin—mattered more than race in party politics. Irish and Italian Catholics and Jews from Germany, Poland, and Russia voted Democratic more often than citizens of British origin and Northern European Protestants. These ethnic differences were consolidated in the voting coalition that Roosevelt built in the 1930s to support his New Deal. However, European ethnicity began to fail in importance with the start of the civil rights movement in the 1950s.

In 1953 during the first term of Eisenhower's administration, many Blacks nationally still favored the Republican Party—President Abraham Lincoln's party. Their allegiance shifted during the 1960s as the Democratic Party and President Lyndon Johnson backed civil rights legislation. Until the late 1960s and early 1970s, the division between Blacks and whites defined the ethnic factor. With increased immigration from other countries, especially Mexico, the racial dichotomy of white/Black—which had always been suspect—was replaced by the broader concept of ethnicity.

Classifying people by either race or ethnicity is difficult to do. And asking people about their race or origin is politically sensitive. According to one report:

> Census forms through the decades have employed a changing list of race categories that reflect their times, and the government did not even attempt to count Hispanics until late in the 20th century. The attempt to classify people by race or origin is by nature an imperfect enterprise. As the Office of Management and Budget acknowledged in 1997, the race categories "represent a social-political construct designed for collecting data on the race and ethnicity of broad population groups in this country, and are not anthropologically or scientifically based."[3]

In the summer of 2012, the U.S. Census Bureau announced a new effort to deal with the problem. In contrast with its 2010 Census form, which asked separate questions about race and Hispanic origin, it created a question that combined the two.[4] The American National Election Studies began asking about ethnicity in the sense of national origin only in 1988. Prior to then, "[I]nformation about Hispanic origin was determined only by interviewer observation."[5] ANES reclassified respondent ethnicity for earlier surveys to 1972.

In 2020, Hispanics constituted about 18 percent of the survey respondents, while Blacks comprised only about 13 percent.[6] Although Asian Americans are the nation's fastest growing ethnic group, they were only about 5 percent of the population in 2020, and sampling them posed special problems for pollsters.[7] National survey data on the changing ethnic distribution of the U.S. population over six decades is reflected in Figure 9.1. Population changes are gradual, so the ups and downs in the graph come from sampling error, question changes, and people answering differently to questions about their ethnicity. Between the 2000 and 2010 censuses, officials found that over 6 percent of the same people changed from multi-racial to single race or vice versa.[8]

Figure 9.1 stops at 2020, but by 2050 the U.S. Census Bureau estimates that Hispanics will account for almost 25 percent of the population, while Blacks are expected to increase to only about 15 percent.[9] The Census Bureau also projects non-Hispanic whites to decline to 50 percent of the population, at the brink of losing their majority status.[10]

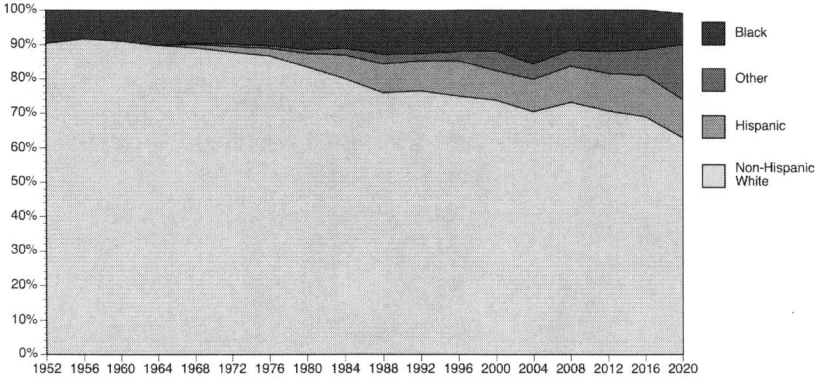

Figure 9.1 Distribution of Ethnic Responses, 1952–2020

Equal Group Appeal by Ethnicity

How have the two major political parties in the United States accommodated these ethnic groups? Back in 1952, American society was essentially monochromatic—Black and white—but overwhelmingly white. Because Blacks constituted only about 10 percent of the population and southern states denied many Blacks the right to vote, both parties concentrated mainly on white voters. As depicted in Figure 9.2, the Democratic Party drew support more evenly from both Blacks and whites nationally, earning an Equal Group Appeal score of 0.73 compared with the Republicans' 0.51. (Hispanics were not sufficiently numerous to be counted.) Locally, urban Blacks were strongly Democratic, but many Blacks elsewhere still owed allegiance to Abraham Lincoln and favored the Republican Party, especially in the South.

By 2020, Blacks shifted substantially in their party preference and fled from the Republican Party. In contrast, non-Hispanic whites cut their support for Democrats almost in half. Hispanics, who by now outnumbered Blacks in the population, split two to one in favor of Democrats. Both parties changed little in their ethnic attraction scores by 2020, and Democrats continued to appeal more evenly to minority groups.

Party Base Concentration by Ethnicity

The concentration of ethnic support within the Democratic Party changed substantially between 1952 and 2020, while that within the Republican Party remained largely unchanged. The data are reported in Figure 9.3. In 1952, both parties were essentially white parties, as reflected in their high concentration scores of 0.94 for Republicans and 0.86 for Democrats. In 2020 Republicans still scored 0.72 for ethnic concentration, as 0.81 of all

96 Ethnicity: Dwindling Whites

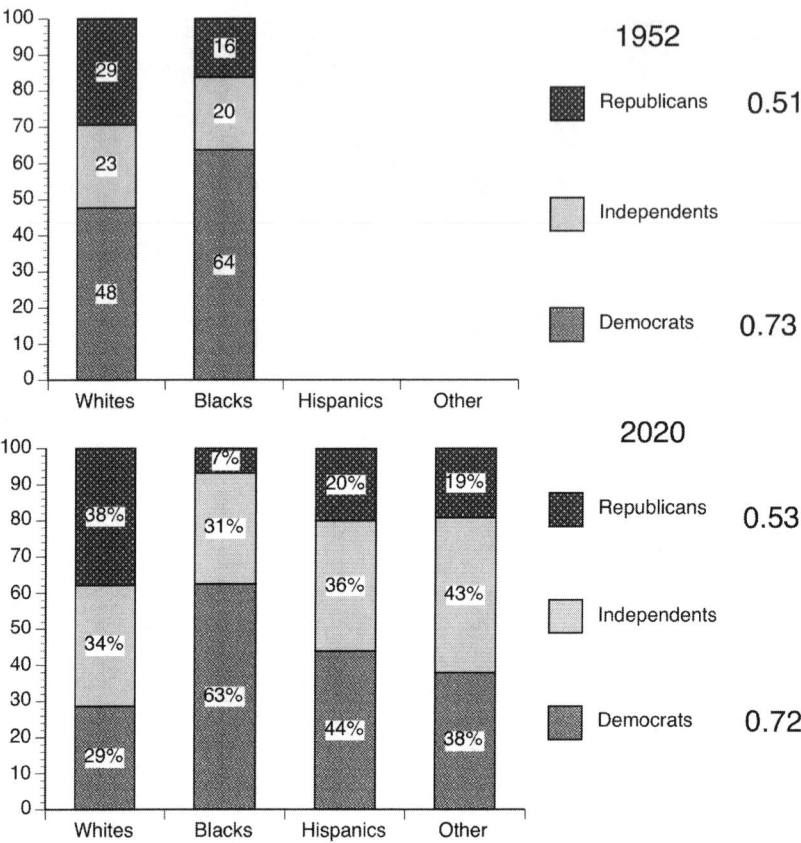

Figure 9.2 Percentages of Party Identification by Ethnicity, with Equal Group Appeal Scores

their identifiers were non-Hispanic whites. However, the Democrats' score dropped to 0.53, with non-Hispanic whites comprising only 0.51 of all Democratic identifiers.

Group Appeal and Base Concentration by Ethnicity Since 1952

Looking at the two election years—1952 and 2020—that serve as bookends to 64 years of American politics tells how much the parties changed over the decades. But looking at only those two years misses important developments between them. Figures 9.4 and 9.5 plot ethnic Equal Group Appeal and Party Base Concentration scores from 1952 to 2020. Recall that prior to 1972 ANES surveys only had two ethnic categories: white and Black. Hispanics were first included in 1972 and only 20 or fewer "Others" appeared in earlier surveys.

Ethnicity: Dwindling Whites 97

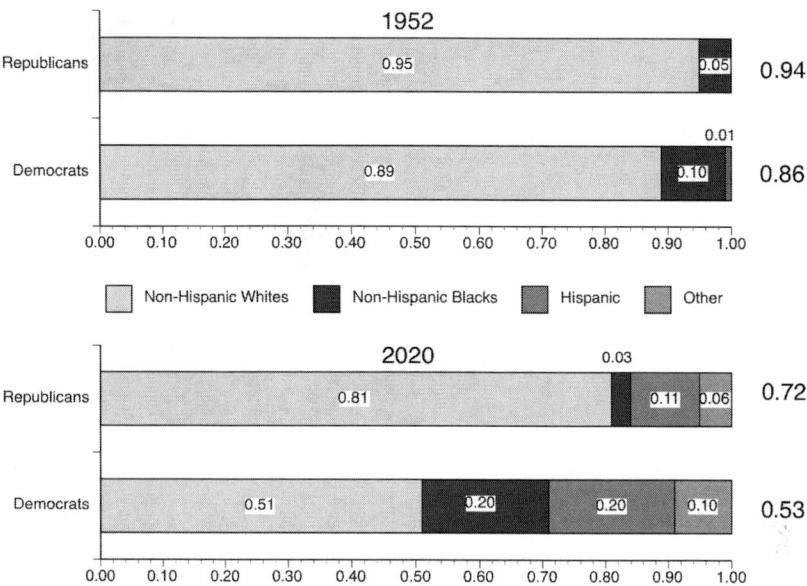

Figure 9.3 Ethnic Groups as Proportion of Party Identifiers, with Party Base Concentration Scores

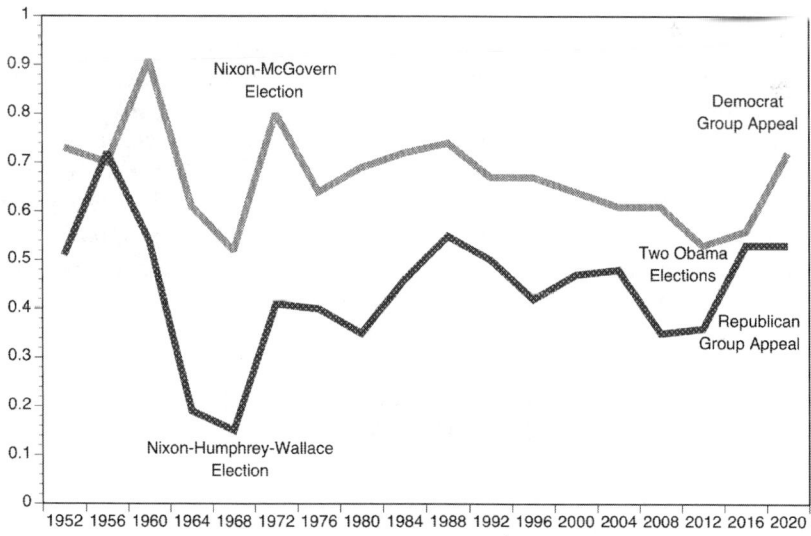

Figure 9.4 Parties' Equal Group Appeal Scores, Ethnicity 1952–2020

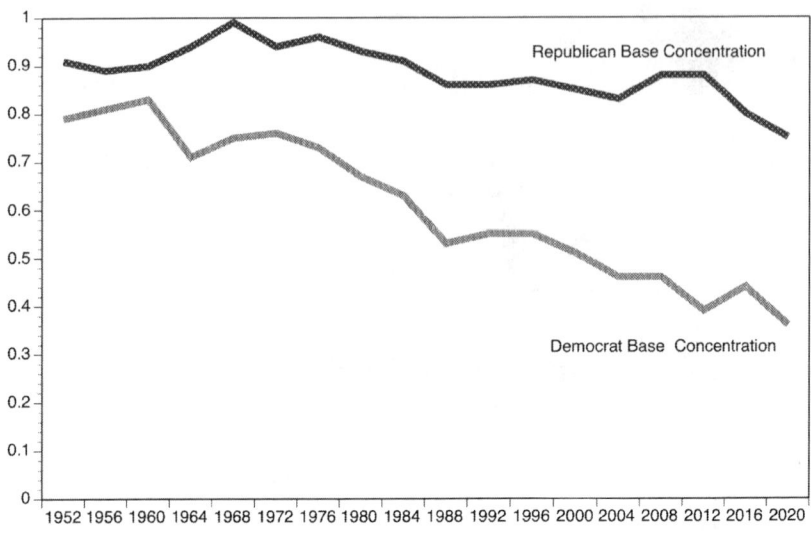

Figure 9.5 Parties' Base Concentration Scores, Ethnicity 1952–2020

In 1952, Dwight Eisenhower was overwhelmingly elected president by an electorate that was almost 95 percent white. It mattered little to the outcome that the few Black voters (about 7 percent) considered themselves Democrats by almost 2 to 1. In 1956, Eisenhower was re-elected by an even larger margin in his rematch with Democrat Adlai Stevenson. Catching the Eisenhower fever, Blacks in 1956 became more likely to describe themselves as Republican: 23 percent in 1956 vs. 16 percent in 1952. The 1956 election marked the high point of the Republican Party's appeal across ethnic groups after World War II.

In 1964, Blacks departed the Republican Party in droves when its presidential candidate, Senator Barry Goldwater, denounced the 1964 Civil Rights Act. Blacks virtually disappeared from the party in 1968, when Republican Richard Nixon ran on his "Southern Strategy" of appealing to white voters' racial grievances. The 1968 ANES survey found only 2 percent of Blacks identifying as Republicans—a drop from 23 percent in 1956. The Republican Party's Party Base Concentration score across ethnic groups in 1968 was 0.99—virtually all party identifiers were white.

Over the past seven decades, the Republican Party generally had lower ethnic Group Appeal scores and higher Base Concentration scores than the Democratic Party.

1. The dark line at the bottom of Figure 9.4 plots the ethnic Equal Group Appeal scores of the Republican Party, which rarely appealed to non-white voters. In 1968, it had almost no non-white party identifiers.

2. The dark line at the top of Figure 9.5 plots the ethnic Base Concentration scores of the Republican Party. Self-identified Republicans were overwhelmingly non-Hispanic whites throughout the period.
3. The two gray lines in both figures plot the ethnic Group Appeal and Base Concentration scores for the Democratic Party. It began as a mostly white party in 1952 but became progressively more diverse over the time period.

The last point above requires some background concerning the changing pattern of ethnic support for the Republican Party from 1956 to 1968. The American National Election Studies estimated the percentages of Blacks who self-identified themselves as Republican in those presidential years as:

Year	Black Republicans
1956	23%
1960	18
1964	7
1968	2

What caused Blacks to flee from the Republican Party—the party of Lincoln—over such a short span of time? The short explanation centers on the Democratic Party's support of the Blacks' struggle for civil rights versus the Republican Party's neglect of—or even opposition to—that struggle.

The 1950s and 1960s were momentous and perilous times in the civil rights movement, and some events before and during those times help provide perspective.

> **1876**: In a dispute over a close presidential election that year, southern politicians supported Republican candidate Rutherford B. Hayes in return for the withdrawal of federal troops and the end of northern Republican efforts to reconstruct the South.[11] Subsequently, the Democratic Party controlled southern politics based on a platform of white supremacy and Black disenfranchisement. For more than 75 years, the phrase "Solid South" referred to the Democratic Party's virtually complete domination of its party politics.[12] The strong connection between southern politics and the Democratic Party began to unravel after World War II, as national Democratic leaders began to support civil rights.
>
> **1948**: At the urging of Hubert Humphrey, then mayor of Minneapolis, the Democratic Convention inserted in its platform a plank that "minorities must have the right to live, the right to work, the right to vote, the full and equal protection of the laws, on a basis of equality with all citizens." In response, many southern delegates walked out of the convention, enraged at this affront to their "way of life." Some quickly formed the States' Rights Democratic Party and nominated their own presidential candidate, South Carolina

Governor Strom Thurmond. These 1948 "Dixiecrats" expected to draw enough electoral votes from the Democratic candidate, Harry Truman, to defeat him, thus regaining their power in the national Democratic Party. Although Thurmond carried four southern states, Truman won in an upset of Thomas Dewey, whose Republican platform said nothing about civil rights for minorities.

1954: The U.S. Supreme Court unanimously declared that segregated schools (which were almost entirely in southern states) were illegal and must integrate Black and white students "with all deliberate speed." This momentous decision launched major developments.

1955: The Montgomery Alabama bus boycott started when a Black woman was arrested for refusing to give her seat to a white woman. The boycott, joined by Dr. Martin Luther King, Jr. (a little known Black minister then), attracted national attention and led in 1956 to a federal ruling that declared segregated transportation unconstitutional.

1957: President Dwight Eisenhower, a Republican, ordered federal troops to enforce the admission of Black students to Central High School in Little Rock, Arkansas, and Blacks praised Eisenhower's decisive action. Although the 1960 Republican platform contained a lengthy and strong section on civil rights, the party did not campaign on the issue of civil rights.

1960: Early in the year, four Black college students refused to leave their seats after being denied service at a lunch counter in Greensboro, North Carolina. Supporting "sit-ins" and protests occurred in more than 65 southern cities in 12 states.[13] Just weeks prior to the 1960 presidential election, Dr. King was arrested in a civil rights protest in Atlanta. Democratic candidate John Kennedy and brother Robert intervened with the judge, leading to King's release and to King's public endorsement of Kennedy for president.

1962: Rioting occurred at the University of Mississippi when James Meredith, a Black Air Force veteran, attempted to register. Two people died and others were injured. In response, President Kennedy took charge of the Mississippi National Guard and sent federal troops to campus to enroll Meredith and end segregation at Ole Miss.[14]

1964: After Kennedy's assassination in November 1963, President Lyndon Johnson continued Kennedy's reforms. Although from Texas, he backed the 1964 Civil Rights Act that outlawed major forms of discrimination against ethnic and religious minorities in schools, at the workplace, and in public accommodations. President Johnson's Republican opponent in the 1964 presidential election was Barry Goldwater, who voted against the Civil Rights Act as an intrusion by the federal government into state affairs.

Goldwater became the first Republican to win the electoral votes of five states in the Deep South since 1877 but suffered a devastating defeat, winning only his home state of Arizona outside the South.

1968: Republican presidential candidate Richard Nixon campaigned to win white votes via a "Southern Strategy"—a term popularized by strategist Kevin Phillips, who said, "The more Negroes who register as Democrats in the South, the sooner the Negrophobe whites will quit the Democrats and become Republicans."[15] African Americans reacted to the Republicans' Southern Strategy by shifting strongly to the Democratic Party. In the 1968 ANES survey, 88 percent of Blacks identified with the Democratic Party while only 2 percent said they were Republicans. Not once since have more than 8 percent of Blacks described themselves as Republican. (Nixon did win the election, but his southern appeal was short-circuited by segregationist George Wallace, former governor of Alabama, who carried six core southern states as the candidate of the American Independence Party.)

2013: After losing two presidential elections to Barack Obama, the Republican National Committee issued a 100-page report, stating in part:

The Republican Party must focus its efforts to earn new supporters and voters in the following demographic communities: Hispanic, Asian and Pacific Islanders, African Americans, Indian Americans, Native Americans, women, and youth. This priority needs to be a continual effort that affects every facet of our Party's activities, including our messaging, strategy, outreach, and budget.

Unless the RNC gets serious about tackling this problem, we will lose future elections; the data demonstrates this. In both 2008 and 2012, President Obama won a combined 80 percent of the votes of all minority voters, including not only African Americans but also Hispanics, Asians, and others. The minority groups that President Obama carried with 80 percent of the vote in 2012 are on track to become a majority of the nation's population by 2050. Today these minority groups make up 37 percent of the population, and they cast a record 28 percent of the votes in the 2012 presidential election, according to the election exit polls, an increase of 2 percentage points from 2008. We have to work harder at engaging demographic partners and allies.[16]

2016: Republican presidential candidate Donald Trump rejected the advice of the RNC's report to welcome voters of all type under a GOP "big tent." Instead, he won election by appealing to ethnocentrism of white voters in midwestern and southern states.

Reminiscing, and Summarizing

I wish I could say that my beloved parents were religiously and racially tolerant, but they were not. In Chicago, they tolerated living in a heavily Jewish neighborhood, but they were quick to join the white flight out of the city in 1947 when Blacks bought homes nearby. We moved permanently to Wilmington, where my father and grandfather had built a summer house in 1938. Rumor had it that Wilmington had a "Sundown Law" requiring Blacks to leave before night. Whether that was true, there were no students of color in our high school of 200 students and no families of color in the town, to the best of my knowledge. I am pleased to report that Wilmington eventually progressed in racial attitudes. In 1997, Afro-American Damien Anderson became the high school's most famous graduate, becoming an All-American running back at Northwestern University in 2000, a Heisman trophy candidate, and a professional football player.

I met my first Black persons at Illinois State Normal University. One was my classmate, Donald McHenry, named by President Jimmy Carter to be U.S. Ambassador and Permanent Representative to the United Nations, from 1979 to 1981. Although my parents did not meet McHenry, they graciously hosted my Korean graduate school roommate whom I brought home for Thanksgiving. Kim Deok later became the first non-military head of the Korean CIA. They also warmly accepted Robert Feldman, my Jewish friend from college who was Best Man at my wedding. So, like Wilmington, my parents progressed too.

From my study of European emigration to the United States in the late nineteenth and early twentieth centuries, I am pinning my hopes that the national electorate will become more tolerant of citizens with different ethnicities. I wrote about the immigrants' experiences in *The Emperor and the Peasant*, an account of my wife's Slovak grandparents who traveled to New York from Austria-Hungary in the 1900s.[17] They came late in the wave, even after my own Czech grandparents. The Irish, who were the first to arrive in great numbers, were called "Micks" (one of the kindlier terms) and met signs saying "No dogs and Irish admitted." Italians were "Dagos" and "Wops," Poles were "dumb Polacks," while Czechs and Slovaks were dismissed as "Bohunks." Very few spoke much English before arriving.

Ironically, children of these immigrants from central and southern Europe often, like my parents, failed to accept Blacks from the South and immigrants from Latin America. Depreciating them as others had once treated their parents. As Blacks and Hispanics proved themselves through work and education, white citizens began to appreciate their efforts. During my eight decades of life, American society has become ethnically and religiously more diverse and more tolerant of different life styles. I trust the trend will continue. Social change takes time.

Unfortunately, I see less progress in American party politics. Partisan polarization and intolerance have increased since 1952.

Notes

1. Staffan Müller-Wille, "Linnaeus and the Four Corners of the World," in K.A. Coles, R. Bauer, Z. Nunes, and C.L. Peterson (eds.), *The Cultural Politics of Blood, 1500–1900* (London: Palgrave Macmillan, 2014) at https://link.springer.com/chapter/10.1057%2F9781137338211_10#citeas.
2. Timothy Bauman, "Defining Ethnicity," *SAA Archaeological Record* (September, 2004), 12–14 at p. 12.
3. D'Vera Cohn, "Census Bureau Considers Changing Its Race/Hispanic Questions," Pew Research Center (August 7, 2012).
4. U.S. Census Bureau, "Census Bureau Releases Results from the 2010 Census Race and Hispanic Origin Alternative Questionnaire Research," *News Release* (August 8, 2012) at http://2010.census.gov/news/releases/operations/cb12-146.html.
5. *ANES Cumulative Data File, 1948–2008 Codebook* (Ann Arbor, MI: Inter-university Consortium for Political and Social Research.
6. U.S. Census, Quick Facts at www.census.gov/quickfacts/fact/table/US/PST045219.
7. Abby Budiman, "Asian Americans Are the Fastest-Growing Racial or Ethnic Group in the U.S. Electorate," Pew FACTTANK (May 7, 2020) at www.pewresearch.org/fact-tank/2020/05/07/asian-americans-are-the-fastest-growing-racial-or-ethnic-group-in-the-u-s-electorate/; and George Gao, "The Challenges of Polling Asian Americans," Pews FACTTANK (May 11, 2016) at www.pewresearch.org/fact-tank/2016/05/11/the-challenges-of-polling-asian-americans/.
8. Jo Craven McGinty, "Documenting Race Proves Tricky for Census," *Wall Street Journal* (July 25, 2020), p. A2.
9. U.S. Census Bureau, International Data Base, at www.census.gov/population/www/projections/usinterimproj/.
10. Ibid.
11. Richard B. Morris (ed.), *Encyclopedia of American History, Bicentennial Edition* (New York: Harper & Row, 1976), p. 301.
12. The completion of the Democratic Party domination is apparent in the map showing the vote in the 1948 congressional election, 72 years after the disputed 1876 presidential election at www.umich.edu/~lawrace/votetour8.htm.
13. John F. Kennedy Presidential Library and Museum, "Civil Rights Movement," at www.jfklibrary.org/JFK/JFK-in-History/Civil-Rights-Movement.aspx.
14. Ibid.
15. Quoted in James Boyd, "Nixon's Southern Strategy 'It's All In the Charts,'" *New York Times Magazine* (May 17, 1970), p. 105ff.
16. Henry Barbour et al., "The Growth and Opportunity Project" (Washington, DC: Republican National Committee, 2013). The report is no longer available at GOP.com.
17. Kenneth Janda, *The Emperor and the Peasant: Two Men at the Start of the Great War and the End of the Habsburg Empire* (Jefferson, NC: McFarland, 2018).

10 Ideology
Partisan Cause or Partisan Effect?

A political ideology can be defined as a coherent and consistent set of values and beliefs about the proper purpose and scope of government.[1] "Coherent" means that the values and beliefs are organized and logically constrain one another. "Consistent" means a person's opinion of the proper role of government on one issue matches the person's opinion on a different but similar issue. Although the term ideology has been used historically in other ways,[2] Frances Lee's research finds that in contemporary political science research it "denotes interrelated political beliefs, values, and policy positions."[3] Studying congressional politics, Lee counted references to ideology and to closely related terms—liberal and conservative—in professional journals and in the *New York Times* from 1900 to 2003. "Prior to the 1950s," she wrote, "scholars generally spoke only of particular liberal or conservative coalitions or legislators"; not until the 1960s were the terms commonly applied to "individual legislators' policy orientations."[4]

Steeped in contemporary politics of ideological conflict, today's readers may be surprised—even astounded—by Lee's finding that not until the 1960s were legislators commonly described as liberal or conservative. In today's politics politicians are routinely painted as spendthrift liberals or backward conservatives. In the past, the words "liberal" and "conservative" were not so negatively colored.

Moreover, the further one goes back in history, the less the terms correspond to what we today would recognize as either liberal or conservative. Verlan Lewis's comprehensive analysis of party positions since the republic's founding convincingly demonstrates the changing meaning of the terms and the parties' switches in positions "on virtually every enduring public policy issue in American history."[5] Lewis wrote: "For the past eight decades or so, virtually whatever the Democratic Party does is termed 'liberal' and whatever the Republican Party does is termed 'conservative.'"[6] Nevertheless, this terminology—at a given time—differentiates the parties for their followers, but the terms' political valence has changed notably over history.

Ideological Terms in Democratic and Republican Party Platforms over Time

The Democratic Party has promulgated 45 election platforms since its first one in 1840 to 2016. The Republican Party announced 41 platforms since its first in 1856. (Because the COVID-19 pandemic prevented both parties from holding a full national convention in 2020, each party's national committee simply adopted its 2016 platform for the 2020 election campaign.) This analysis is based on all the parties' platforms to 2016.

Once upon a time—indeed, for over a hundred years—the Republican Party used the word "liberal" positively in its platforms, and Republican activists proudly wore the liberal mantle. Beginning with the second term of Reagan's presidency in 1984, however, the Republican platforms' usage of the root "liberal" dramatically shifted to the dark side.[7] Meanwhile, the 44 Democratic Party platforms since 1840 staunchly—but not consistently—embraced the liberal label. Concerning "conservative" as a term, neither party mentioned it either frequently or prominently in any of their platforms. Whereas both parties' platforms together alluded to "liberal" in some form a total of 126 times, they used "conservative" only 14 times in all. This analysis focuses only on the term, liberal.

Liberal rhetoric in the platforms of the Democratic and Republican parties over time can be divided into three eras, as shown in Figure 10.1. The first era, which extends from the parties' first platforms to 1956, might be called *A Century of Consensus*. During 116 years from 1840 to 1956, the Democratic Party's platforms used liberal 30 times. During the 100 years from 1856 to 1956, the Republican platforms mentioned liberal 14 times. Both parties throughout this period virtually always used liberal in a positive way—in the sense of "free in giving; generous; open-minded"—as listed in the *Oxford University English Dictionary* of 1937.

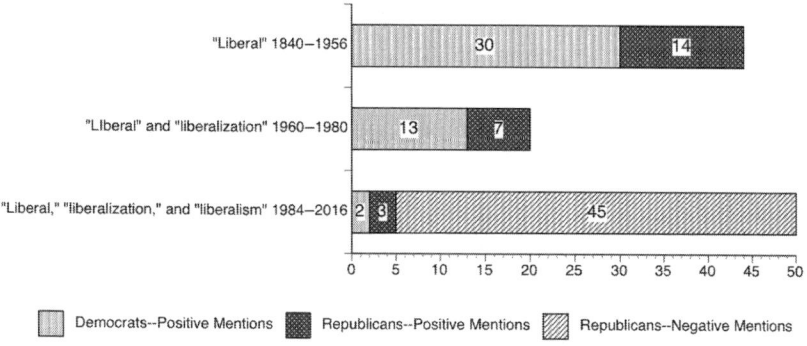

Figure 10.1 Number of Mentions of "Liberal" and Its Forms in Party Platforms Since 1840

The second era, which lasted the 20 years from 1960 to 1980, might be deemed *A Period of Adjustment*. During this time, both parties shifted to talking about *liberalization* instead of liberal. Whereas "liberalization" had previously appeared only once (Democrats, 1952) in 56 party platforms up to 1956, during the 20 years from 1960 to 1980 Democratic platforms mentioned it 13 times and Republicans 7. Following the Republican Party's earlier practice, not once during the *Period of Adjustment* did a Republican platform use liberal in a negative way.

The third era, which has lasted a third of a century, began in 1984 and continued through 2016. It might be labeled *The Age of Attack and Avoidance*. For the first time in history, the 1984 Republican platform attacked Democratic opponents for being liberals. Since then, Republican platforms repeatedly used the term to deride Democrats. Examples include referring to "liberal experimenters" who "destroyed the sense of community" in 1984; "liberal attacks on everything the American people cherished" in 1988; "the liberal philosophy" that "assaulted the family" in 1992; and "the liberal agenda of litigious lawyers" in 1996. By word count, Republican platform attacks quadrupled from two to eight in 1988 and then almost doubled to 15 in 1992.

In response, Democrats—who like Republicans had proudly claimed the liberal label before—now avoided it almost entirely in their party platforms, using it only once from 1980 to 2016. After Republicans began attacking all signs of liberalism, Democrats unilaterally removed their own. Neither liberal nor liberalism appeared in the 2016 platform of the Democratic Party. Both terms were used sparingly in the Republican Party's 2016 platform, which invoked "liberal" pejoratively only twice and "conservative" approvingly only twice.

The point of this analysis is to demonstrate that employing ideological labels in contentious discussions of politics is relatively new in American history. Frances Lee's extensive historical analysis of scholarly articles and news stories about congressional politics found that individual members of Congress were not portrayed as liberals or conservatives until the 1960s. This inquiry into the terms' usage in Democratic and Republican Party platforms found that Republicans did not castigate Democrats as "dirty rotten liberals" until 1984, when Democrats also began avoiding the term in their own platforms. Because the rhetoric of political ideology has permeated recent decades of discussion about American politics, we may think that the world of politics has always revolved about liberal vs. conservative arguments, thought, and positions. That is not true. In fact, asking people in opinion polls to describe themselves as liberal or conservative is also surprisingly recent.

Changes in Ideological Self-Placement, 1952–2020

Few polls prior to the 1970s asked people whether they considered themselves politically liberal or conservative. Proof of that comes from searching the extensive archives of the Roper Center for Public Opinion Research at the University of Connecticut, which—according to its website—"holds data from the 1930s, when survey research was in its infancy, to the present."[8] The Roper Center's iPoll search engine finds questions asked in these surveys by searching for keywords. Searching for "liberal and conservative" reveals all Roper's poll questions that asked people whether they considered themselves liberals or conservatives.[9]

An iPoll search found only 52 polls out of 1,195 U.S. national surveys from the 1930s through the 1960s that even mentioned the keywords "liberal" and "conservative," and most of the 52 used the terms in ways that did not ask respondents to classify themselves. For example, a November 6, 1936 Gallup Poll asked, "*Should President Roosevelt's second Administration be more liberal, more conservative, or about the same as his first?*" A series of questions in an August 1938 Fortune survey named 11 different people (e.g., Henry Ford) and then asked whether respondents would describe each "*as—reactionary, conservative, liberal or radical?*" In April 1944 an Office of Public Opinion Research Survey asked, "*How important do you think it is that the next President be liberal/conservative? ... Very important, moderately important.*"

Of the 240 questions about liberal and conservative in these surveys from 1935 through 1969, only 16 polls asked people about their *own* ideological orientations. Because the questions differed in wording, moreover, poll results from 1930 to 1970 are difficult to compare. Consider the question in a 1936 Gallup Poll (the earliest question turned up in the iPoll search), "*If there were only two political parties in this country—Conservative and Liberal—which would you join?*" Two years later, Gallup asked, "*In politics, do you regard yourself as a liberal or conservative?*" Six years later, a 1944 Gallup Poll asked something close, but slightly different, "*Do you regard yourself as a conservative, or a liberal, or somewhere in between?*" As late as 1967, a Harris poll threw "radical" into the options by asking, "*What do you consider yourself—conservative, middle of the road, liberal or radical?*" (See Appendix C for the text of all 16 questions.)

Not until 1972 did a survey organization, ANES, design an interview question that was used subsequently over an extended time period.[10] Here is the interview instrument in full:

> *We hear a lot of talk these days about liberals and conservatives. I'm going to show you a 7-point scale on which the political views that people might hold are arranged from extremely liberal to extremely conservative. Where would you place yourself on this scale, or haven't you thought much about this?* (7-POINT SCALE SHOWN TO R).[11]

Note that the last portion of the question asks, "*or haven't you thought much about this?*" Regularly since 1972 from 25 to 35 percent of respondents say that they "haven't thought much about it." That important finding confirms that many citizens do not think much about politics generally or about political ideology in particular. Lacking the chance to admit that they "haven't thought much about it," many respondents would probably choose the safe "moderate" category instead of either "liberal" or "conservative," making it appear that many citizens knowingly opted for "moderate" when they did not quite understand their ideological choices. Nationscape's 2020 survey question simply asked, "*In general, how would you describe your own political viewpoint?*" Even then, more than 10 percent replied that they were "not sure."

Although the original ANES question allowed respondents to rank themselves across seven positions from "extremely liberal" to "extremely conservative," most research collapses their responses to the three categories of "liberal," "moderate," and "conservative"—which corresponds to the ideological options in polls prior to 1972. Figure 10.2 reports the results of various surveys that asked reasonably suitable questions about liberal-conservative self-placement prior to 1972.[12] The many respondents who declined classification were excluded from the tally.

According to surveys available prior to 1972 and to the more comparable surveys since, the percentages of self-identified conservatives and liberals have not changed much over time. Recalling that approximately a third of respondents admit that they "haven't thought much" about these terms, we might wonder who does think about the ideological options and what they think the terms mean. In his searching analysis of respondents' verbatim responses to political questions in the 1950s, Philip Converse concluded that only about 17 percent of the public understood the liberal-conservative dimension then in a way "that captures much of its breadth."[13] Most of the "best" responses indicated "that the Democratic Party was liberal because it spent public money freely and that the Republican Party was more conservative because it stood for economy in government or pinched pennies."[14]

More than a decade later, Gallup in 1970 asked this pair of questions: (a) "*What is the first thing that comes to your mind when you think of someone*

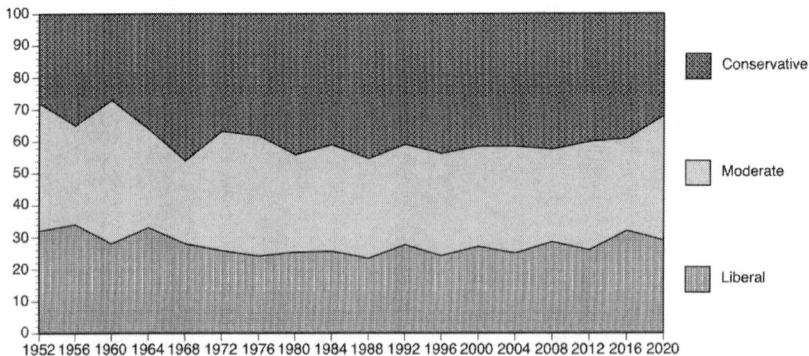

Figure 10.2 Ideological Distribution, 1952–2020

Ideology: Partisan Cause or Effect? 109

Table 10.1 1970 Gallup Poll on Meaning of "Liberal" and "Conservative"

	Poll Question: *What Is the First Thing That Comes to Your Mind ...*
	... When you think of someone who is a liberal?
Count	
182	free thinker, open-minded, fair, lenient: "a person who; is a free thinker," "listens to both sides," "fair in making decisions," "someone who can look at and see all sides to a problem"
126	gives things away, spends money: "giving away a lot of things," "determination to spend other people's money," "urges gov't spending," "someone who is eager to spend money"
110	names specific person: "Hubert Humphrey," "Eugene McCarthy," "Roosevelt," "Rockefeller"
102	mentions general political position, political party: "like an independent," "neither conservative nor reactionary," "little left of center," "not middle of road," "middle of road," "a political party," "Democratic Party"
93	free, kind, generous, good-hearted, giving: "somebody freer," "be free," "kind and good—free hearted," "someone concerned about people in general," "person who is generous or giving"
	... When you think of someone who is a conservative?
265	saves, doesn't throw things away, doesn't spend money: "someone who doesn't throw things away," "want to conserve the money of the public," "keep things," "penny pincher," "tight money," "someone who is stingy," "not wasteful," "a person who plans and saves"
186	do not change, does not take a chance: "people who are not so broad minded or go along with the young people with these new changes," "one who is more satisfied with allowing things to be as they are," "stick to the old beaten path and don't like to change too much," "doesn't like to change too much"
161	cautious, careful, sensible, reserved: "a more reserved person," "level headed people," "sensible people," "a person who thinks and considers every aspect," "thinks more before deciding"
132	close minded, strict, square, intolerant, self-centered: (general negative responses) "someone who is not open to new things," "straight or square," "one point of view," "of one opinion," "very self-centered"
88	Nixon, Republican, current administration: "President Nixon's policy," "the ones in the White House now," "Nixon is a conservative"

who is a liberal?" and (b) "*What is the first thing that comes to your mind when you think of someone who is a conservative?*" About 35 percent of the sample offered what Gallup classified as 12 different answers to "liberal," and about 33 percent offered 8 different views of "conservative." Table 10.1 reports the "top five" types of replies to each question.

A quarter of a century later, a 2006 CBS News poll asked a related question: "*We hear a lot of talk these days about people being liberals, moderates, or conservatives, and we'd like to know what those terms mean to you. What do you think is the biggest difference between liberal views and conservative views?*"[15] Once again, 38 percent didn't know or gave no answer. The overwhelming response given (32 percent) was that "liberal" and "conservative" referred to "personal characteristics and traits." Only

7 percent replied that the terms referred to "general attitude toward money and economics," and a paltry 4 percent suggested that they reflected a "general attitude toward government." However, 8 percent said that liberals and conservatives differed on "values," often mentioning "abortion."

So what can we draw from this inquiry into the public's understanding of liberal" and "conservative" over six decades?

1. Approximately one-quarter of survey respondents hadn't "thought much" about these terms.
2. Those who attempt to define the terms offer wide-ranging definitions, mostly unrelated to politics or economics.
3. A small but substantial minority of citizens (perhaps hovering around 15 percent) does draw politically relevant differences between liberals and conservatives.

Although distinguishing political differences between liberals and conservatives exceeds the comprehension of most citizens in the twenty-first century as in the twentieth, both parties today use ideological language in talking politics—whether or not voters understand what they are talking about.

Equal Group Appeal by Ideology

Given that the 1952 ANES survey did not ask respondents about their ideology, I chose a 1950 Gallup poll to stand in for the missing data.[16] Over the seven decades since 1950, American voters have sorted themselves into partisan ideological camps. In 1950, as shown in Figure 10.3, about half of all self-identified liberals considered themselves Democrats and about half of all conservatives were Republicans. Democrats scored higher in Equal Group Appeal on ideology (0.71) than Republicans (0.56).

By 2020, only 10 percent of liberals described themselves as Republicans, and about the same percentage of conservatives felt they were Democrats. The Equal Group Appeal dropped to 0.39 for Democrats and only 0.22 for Republicans.

Party Base Concentration by Ideology

The Base Concentration of ideological groupings within both parties also changed dramatically between 1950 and 2020, as shown in Figure 10.4. In 1950, conservatives accounted for 0.45 of Republican identifiers but for 0.67 in 2020. Over the same period, Democratic identifiers became more liberal—increasing from just under a third in 1950 to over a half of all identifiers in 2020. These changes resulted in higher ideological Base Concentration scores for both parties. Democrats increased from 0.22 in 1950 to 0.51 in 2020, and Republicans jumped from 0.20 to 0.62.

Ideology: Partisan Cause or Effect? 111

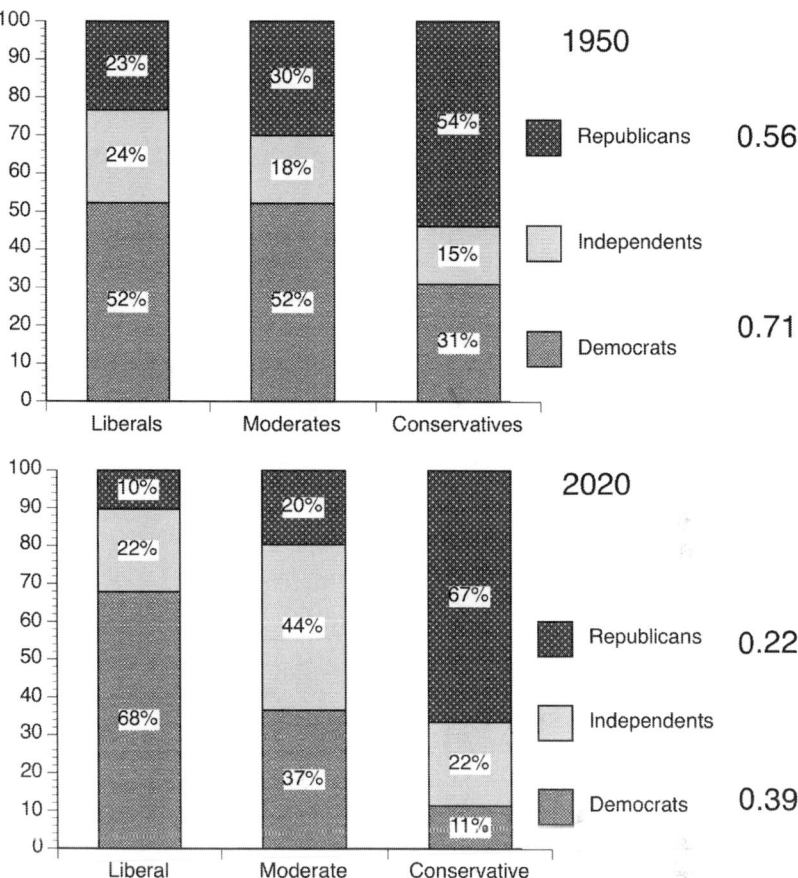

Figure 10.3 Percentages of Party Identification by Ideology, with Equal Group Appeal Scores

Group Appeal and Base Concentration by Ideology Since 1952

Almost continuously since 1952, Democrats and Republicans have, respectively, appealed more strongly to liberal and conservative ideological groups, which also grew increasingly dominant within their parties. These trends are clearly demonstrated in Figure 10.5, which shows a steady decline in both parties' Equal Group Appeal scores of ideology, and Figure 10.6, which shows a steady increase in their Party Base Concentration scores.[17]

The sharp jump for 2020 in both parties' Equal Group Appeal scores and the corresponding sharp drop in their Party Base Concentration scores may result from a change in data sources. All scores from 1972 to 2016

112 *Ideology: Partisan Cause or Effect?*

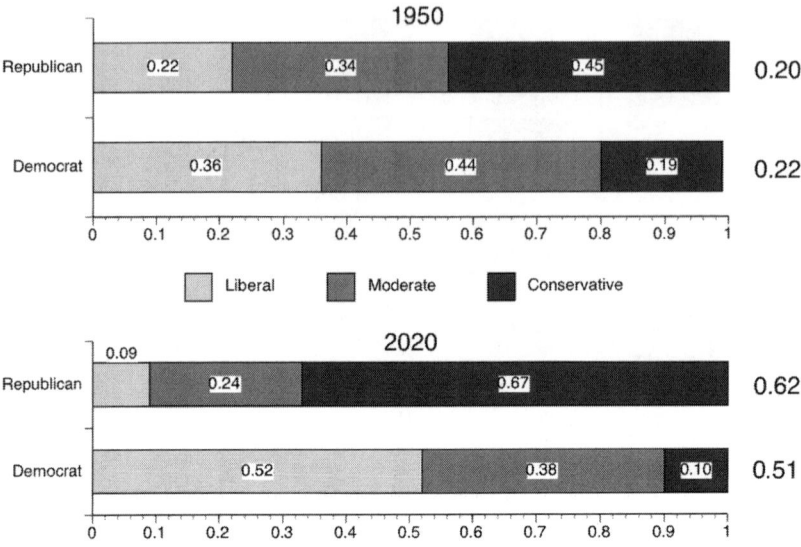

Figure 10.4 Ideology Groups as Proportion of Party Identifiers, with Party Base Concentration Scores

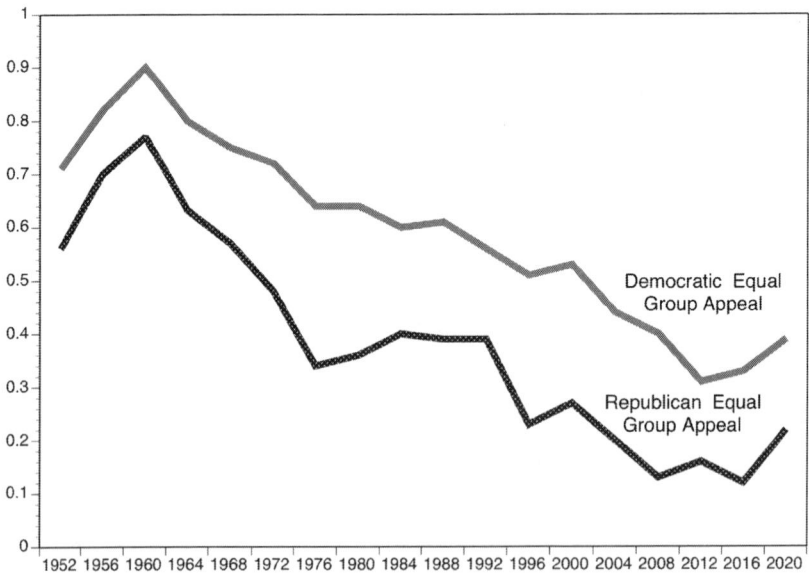

Figure 10.5 Parties' Equal Group Appeal Scores, Ideology 1952–2020

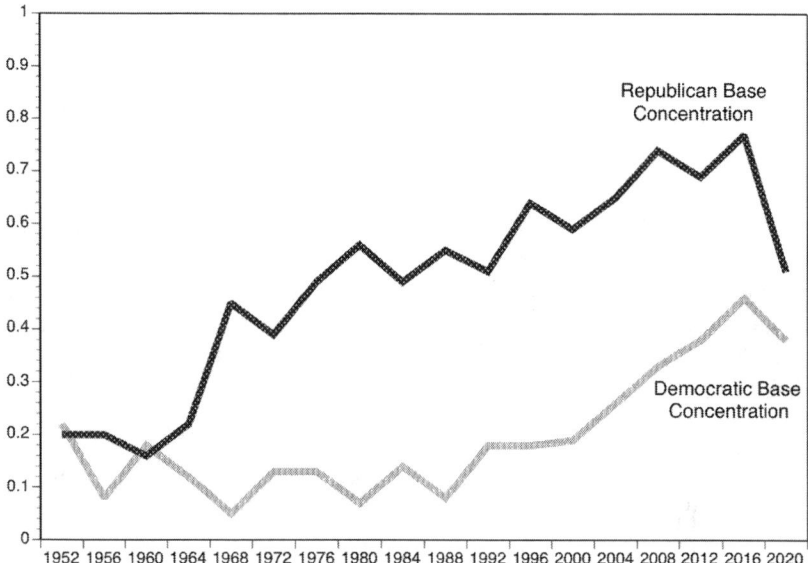

Figure 10.6 Parties' Base Concentration Scores, Ideology 1952–2020

came from ANES surveys. The 2020 scores came from the Nationscape survey from January to April that asked a simple question, "*In general, how would you describe your own political viewpoint?*" So these sharp jumps may be methodological artifacts.

Cause or Effect?

It is time to point out an important difference between ideology as a base of party support and the six social bases considered earlier. That difference is causality. Social factors such as income, education, region, urbanization, religion, and ethnicity may "cause" people to become Democrats or Republicans. Being a banker nudges a person to become a Republican. Being a college professor pushes one to be Democratic. Living in the South (today) inclines one to be Republican. Living in a city encourages being Democratic. Being Protestant favors being Republican, and being Black promotes being Democratic. Certainly no one can credibly argue the reverse: Being a Republican does not nudge a person to become wealthier. Being Democratic does not push one to have a low education, nor does it encourage living in a city nor being Black. Being Republican does not incline one to live in the South nor to be Protestant.

The direction of causality cannot be argued so convincingly for ideology. Certainly, citizens who understand how political ideology relates to partisan politics may choose parties to fit to their ideologies: liberals gravitate to the Democratic Party and conservatives to the Republican Party. To the extent that causality runs in that direction, ideology functions like a social force. But causality can run in the opposite direction. Recall the third of the electorate that regularly admits not having "thought much about" the meaning of liberal or conservatives, and remember the multitudes who show fuzzy thinking about the terms' meanings. Those substantial segments of the electorate are not likely to choose their parties for ideological reasons but may classify themselves as liberals or conservatives if asked. Egan's research shows that, when asked about their social identities, voters sometimes "switch their identities to align with political group prototypes."[18]

Democrats who are unclear about ideology are likely to describe themselves as liberals simply because the media—and the Republican Party—describe the Democratic Party as the liberal party. In turn, Republicans are apt to regard themselves as conservatives because the media portrays their party as conservative. Moreover, Republican leaders and activists have managed to transform "liberal" into a term of scorn, a black tag to pin on Democrats. Knowing that they are not "despicable liberals," self-described Republicans who are unclear about ideology see themselves as the other guys—the good guys, the un-liberals—the conservatives. Because Democrats have not been as successful in converting "conservative" into a negative label, many self-described have not been blackened with the ideological brush.

In short, the terms "liberal and "conservative" function in two very different ways. They serve as labels for citizens who differ in their political ideologies—in their values and beliefs about government. The terms also serve as badges for partisans who may not understand what the terms mean but who want to dress appropriately for the political parade. Conservative columnist David Brooks mourned:

> Thinking was no longer for understanding. Thinking was for belonging. Right-wing talk radio is the endless repetition of familiar mantras to reassure listeners that they are on the right team. Thinking was for conquest: Those liberals think they're better than us, but we own the libs.[19]

Republicans became proud to march as conservatives, while Democrats—negatively branded as liberals—avoided embracing that ideological label.[20] The "ideology gap" between Democratic and Republican identifiers in 1950 and 2016 is portrayed in the parties' ideological attraction and concentration scores in Figures 10.3 and 10.4. Figures 10.5 and 10.6 trace the same scores over time throughout the seven decades. Three points emerge clearly from these graphs:

1. Both parties' ideological attraction scores have tended to decline over time, indicating that both parties increasingly were attracting support unequally from liberal and conservative voters.

2. The Republicans' ideological attraction scores declined more sharply than the Democrats, indicating that Republicans were attracting more support from conservatives and less from liberals.
3. The Republicans' ideological concentration scores increased fairly consistently over the period, indicating that Republican support became concentrated among conservatives.
4. Democratic identifiers tended to be spread among liberals, moderates, and conservatives fairly evenly over the period.

Summary and Conclusion: Ideology and Tribal Politics

Early on, this chapter cited Verlan Lewis's research showing that the "liberal-conservative" ideological continuum does not travel well over centuries of American history. Because the meaning of both terms has changed over time, scholars have difficulty fitting acts of past politicians and parties on that continuum. The founding of the Libertarian Party in 1971 illustrated the inadequacies of a one-dimensional left-right, liberal-conservative continuum for classifying political parties. Seeing no place for themselves on a one-dimensional continuum, libertarians proposed a two-dimensional typology that gave them a space of their own.[21]

The libertarians' two-dimensional typology can be viewed as involving tradeoffs among three core political values—freedom, order, and equality—that generate four ideological groups:

> **Libertarians** are opposed to sacrificing freedom for either order or equality.
> **Liberals** are willing to trade some freedoms to promote equality.
> **Conservatives** are inclined to trade freedoms to maintain order.
> **Communitarians** will restrict freedom to advance either equality or order.[22]

Although the liberal-Democrat and conservative-Republican linkage has structured American party politics, the Republican Party harbors strong libertarian elements, which sometimes erupt in Libertarian Party challengers.

The Libertarian Party has run presidential candidates in every election since 1972, the most prominent being Ron Paul, who had been elected to the House of Representatives as a Republican before he ran as a Libertarian in 1988. The party has also run candidates for Congress every year since 1972—including over 100 candidates in both 2016 and 2018—but failed to win a single seat and never even 2 percent of the total vote. Nevertheless, politicians with libertarian values are prominent within the Republican Party.

Rand Paul, son of Libertarian Party presidential candidate Ron Paul, was elected to the U.S. Senate as a Republican, representing Kentucky. Senator Paul describes himself as a Constitutional conservative and supporter of the Tea Party movement. By opposing government spending and government intervention in the private sector, the Tea Party promoted libertarian economic values within the Republican Party while downplaying socially conservative values. In "Whatever Happened to the Tea Party," an article in *The Hill* (which covers Capitol Hill) noted that its members were unhappy that, under Republican President Donald Trump, "the federal debt has swelled to astronomic proportions."[23] Despite President Trump's flaunting of traditional conservative economic principles, self-identified conservatives intensified their self-identifications with the Republican Party.

Although it significantly departs from political reality, the one-dimensional, liberal-conservative, left-right terminology still dominates American political discussion. Verlan Lewis helps explain this, saying:

> Notably, when a new party takes control of government, the members of the party in government will often exercise the powers at their disposal by enacting interventionist policies—even if their party's ideology during the campaign and in the early years of their control of government calls for limited government power and limited intervention.[24]

He continues:

> In 2017–2018, with unified control of government, Republican politicians passed legislation that set records for federal spending: topping 1 trillion for the first time in American history. Despite the fact that the US economy had pulled out of the Great Recession, Republicans in control of government decided to increase national government spending levels in real terms and as a percentage of GDP. Based simply on the ideas and attitudes articulated by the Republican Party before assuming control of unified government in 2017, we would have expected federal spending and deficits to decrease. But, knowing what we do about the tendency of almost all politicians to exercise and expand the powers at their disposal, the behavior of President Trump and his Republican Congress was perfectly predictable.[25]

In effect, Lewis contends that a dominant president—be it Abraham Lincoln, Teddy Roosevelt, Franklin Delano Roosevelt, Ronald Reagan, or Donald Trump—determines party ideology. They succeed if "partisans want to change their party ideology in ways that justify the actions of their partisans and vilify the actions of their opponents."[26]

In that sense, the social bases that underlie a political party's identifiers are more stable than the ideologies espoused by its supporters. As reported above at length, national surveys find that voters—and thus party identifiers—do not share common understandings of the meanings of "liberal" and "conservative." Yet party identifiers are ready to align themselves with their party's perceived ideologies. Verlan Lewis wrote:

Whatever the Republican Party does (even if it is the opposite of what Republicans did previously) is described as "conservative," and whatever the Democratic Party does (even if it is the opposite of what Democrats did previously) is described as "liberal." Thus, claims that the Democratic Party moved to the "left," or that the Republican Party moved to the "right" are not helpful because they are tautological.[27]

A return to ANES finds that from one-quarter to one-third of respondents, when asked whether they are liberal or conservative, admit that they "haven't thought much about it." Analyzing over 19,000 ANES interviews since 1972 when the question was first asked, we learn that "thinking about" political ideology is strongly related to education, as shown in Figure 10.7. Ideological self-placement had little meaning to half of all voters without a high school diploma and to one-third of those with high school.

So perhaps some voters do not become Republicans because they are conservative or favor Democrats because they are liberal. Instead, some may say they are conservative because they identify with Republicans, or say they are liberal because they identify with Democrats. Ideological self-classification might not be a cause of party affiliation but also an effect of partisanship. Adopting your party's perceived ideology is part of belonging to the tribe.[28]

Identifying with a political party and becoming part of its tribe might seem like an act of free will, but it is often socially determined. Political scientists frequently draw an analogy between religions and partisanship. Green, Palmquist, and Schickler write, "like party identification, religious identification is often acquired early in life as a product of one's family environment or early adult socialization."[29] Just as Muslim children are

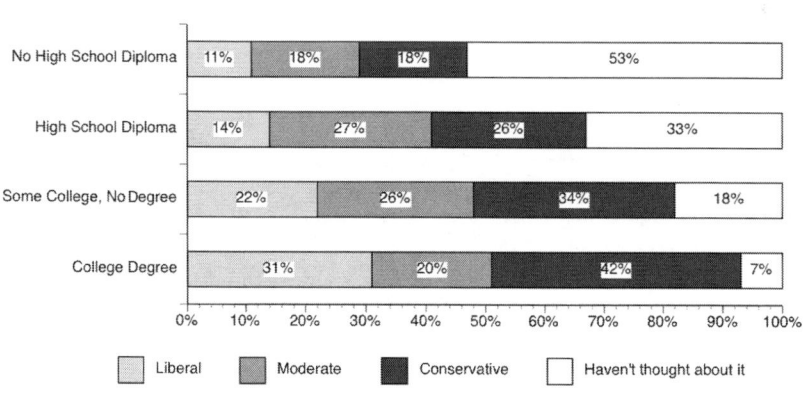

*Based on 19,252 responses consolidated from ANES surveys 1972 to 2008. Questions for 2012 and 2016 were not comparable.

Figure 10.7 1972–2008: "Are you Liberal, Conservative, or Haven't Thought Much About It?"*

born to Muslim parents, Jewish children to Jewish parents and so on, children are born into potential political tribes, albeit ones far more nebulous than religions. Children are born to parents living in an urban or rural area in a state located in a region of the country whose parents have a given ethnic background, economic status, religion, and educational level often shared by other members in their community. In effect, this concatenation of social factors frames a person's party identification. Some individuals can enter a different social milieu through physical and social mobility, but few abandon the religion of their birth and virtually none fully escape their ethnicity. Throughout life, most voters bear the social markings into which they were born.

Chapter 11, which reviews the Democratic and Republican parties' Equal Group Appeal and Party Base Concentration scores for region, economic status, urbanization, education, religion, and ethnicity, also includes ideological orientation.

Notes

1 Philip E. Converse thoroughly explores the importance of coherence to ideology in "The Nature of Belief Systems in Mass Publics," in David E. Apter (ed.), *Ideology and Discontent* (New York: Free Press, 1964), 206–261.
2 Kathleen Knight traces the history of the term in "Transformations of the Concept of Ideology in the Twentieth Century," *American Political Science Review*, 100 (November, 2006), 619–626. Also see Terence Ball and Richard Dagger, "Ideologies, Political," in George Thomas Kurian, *The Encyclopedia of Political Science, Volume 3* (Washington, DC: CQ Press), 759–762.
3 Frances E. Lee, *Beyond Ideology: Politics, Principles, and Partisanship in the U.S. Senate* (Chicago: University of Chicago Press, 2009), at p. 27.
4 *Ibid.*, pp. 31–32.
5 Verlan Lewis, *Ideas of Power: The Politics of American Party Ideological Development* (Cambridge: Cambridge University Press, 2019), p. 2.
6 *Ibid.*, pp. 5–7.
7 The observed shift to attack mode in Republican platform rhetoric in 1984 is consistent with the analysis of Walter J. Stone, Ronald B. Rapoport, and Alan I. Abramowitz, "The Reagan Revolution and Party Polarization in the 1980s," in L. Sandy Maisel (ed.), *The Parties Respond: Changes in the American Party System* (Boulder, CO: Westview Press, 1990), 67–93.
8 The Roper Center website is at www.ropercenter.uconn.edu/about_roper.html.
9 Terminating a search term in iPoll allows for truncated searching, which finds liberal, liberals, liberalism, liberalize, and so on. Both liberal% and conserve% were used as search terms.
10 Consider the treatment of ideology in 1960 in Angus Campbell, Philip E. Converse, Warren E. Miller, and Donald E. Stokes, *The American Voter* (New York: John Wiley, 1960), the landmark book on voting behavior, which was based primarily on their 1952 and 1956 national election surveys conducted by the Survey Research Center at the University of Michigan, where they taught. On page 193, the authors write: "Perhaps no abstraction … has been used more frequently in the past century for political analysis than the

concept of a liberal-conservative continuum—the 'right' and the 'left' of a political spectrum." Indeed, the authors analyzed open-ended questions to probe respondents' understanding of ideology, finding that: "Some people clearly perceived a fundamental liberal-conservative continuum" (p. 227). However, they asked no question in either 1952 or 1956 as to whether respondents thought of themselves as liberals or conservatives. Despite the fact that ideology was a central concept in their analysis of public opinion and voting behavior, subsequent national surveys in 1960, 1964, and 1968 also failed to ask that question. When Philip Converse, the only surviving author of *The American Voter* and a key participant in the Survey Research Center's later surveys, was asked via email, "Why did ANES not ask the ideological self-placement question prior to 1972?" He replied:

> I am in my mid-80s and getting very forgetful, so I have no real answer whatever! Nonetheless, it occurs to me that possibly such a way of grading people was more or less unknown until 1972, and we helped give it some publicity that since has taken off!

And take off it did.

11 In fact, the self-placement interview instrument changed over time. Here is the "Note" from the Cumulative File Codebook:

> 1972–1982: If self-placement was "DK," NA or "haven't thought much" R was not asked for party placements on this scale. 1984–1996: If R responded "DK," NA or "haven't thought much about it" to self-placement AND if R responded "DK" or NA (1996: or "refused to choose") to the self-placement follow-up ("If you had to choose would you consider yourself a liberal or a conservative?" [VCF0849]), then R was not asked for party placements on this scale.

12 Five polls taken prior to 1972 were chosen to include in Figure 10.2. The March 26–31, 1950 Gallup Poll # 1950-0454 was used for 1952. The February 25–March 2, 1954 Gallup Poll #527 represented 1956. The January 17–22, 1957 Gallup Poll #1957-0577 stood for 1960. The July 23–28, 1964 Gallup Poll #695 was used for 1964. The January 1967 Harris Poll, Study No. 1702, represented 1968. Survey interview data for all five polls were provided by the Roper Center for Public Opinion Research. The data from 1972 through 2016 came from the American National Election Studies. The 2020 data from Nationscape departs from the ANES data by showing more than 12 percentage points more Moderates than in 2016, 10 points fewer Conservatives, and almost 3 points fewer Liberals. These differences may be genuine changes in the distribution of ideological types, or they may be due to methodological differences between the ANES and Nationscape surveys.

13 Converse, p. 223.
14 *Ibid.*, p. 222.
15 This CBS News poll occurred February 22–26, 2006. It was turned up in an iPoll search for "liberal and conservative" (which turned up over 3,000 questions) and then by searching for "mean" within the set.
16 The March 26–31, 1950 Gallup Poll # 1950-0454 was used for 1952.
17 The sharp drop in 2020 for both parties' Base Concentration scores was unexpected, but the 2020 Nationscape survey reported significantly fewer conservatives and somewhat fewer liberals in the electorate. See note 12.

18 Patrick J. Egan, "Identity as Dependent Variable: How Americans Shift Their Identities to Align with Their Politics," *American Journal of Political Science*, 64 (July, 2020), 699–716, at p. 708.
19 David Brooks, "The Future of Nonconformity," *New York Times* (July 24, 2020), p. A23.
20 "Negative branding" is an established term in advertising. See Maxwell Winchester, Jenni Romaniuk, and Svetlana Bogomolova, "Positive and Negative Brand Beliefs and Brand Defection/Uptake," *European Journal of Marketing*, 42 (2008), 553–570.
21 The libertarian typology is succinctly represented in the "World's Smallest Political Quiz." Answers to its ten questions place a person in one of four corners within a square: Libertarian, Liberal (left), Conservative (right), or Statist. See www.theadvocates.org/quiz/.
22 Kenneth Janda, Jeffrey M. Berry, Jerry Goldman, Deborah Schildkraut, and Paul Manna, *The Challenge of Democracy: American Government in Global Politics* (Boston: Cengage, 2020), chapter 1. A supporting quiz of 20 questions exists at www.idealog.org/.
23 Brad Bannon, "Whatever Happened to the Tea Party," *The Hill* (August 13, 2018).
24 Lewis, p. 29.
25 *Ibid.*, p. 126.
26 *Ibid.*, p. 36.
27 *Ibid.*, p. 8.
28 Matt Lewis, "America's Political Parties Are Just Tribes Now," *Daily Beast* (April 13, 2017) at www.thedailybeast.com/americas-political-parties-are-just-tribes-now; George Packer, "A New Report Offers Insight into Tribalism in the Age of Trump," *New Yorker* (October 13, 2018) at www.newyorker.com/news/daily-comment/a-new-report-offers-insights-into-tribalism-in-the-age-of-trump; and Zack Beauchamp, "'Hidden Tribes,' the New Report Centrists Are Using to Explain Away Polarization, Explained," *Vox* (October 22, 2018) at www.vox.com/policy-and-politics/2018/10/22/17991928/hidden-tribes-more-in-common-david-brooks.
29 Donald Green, Bradley Palmquist, and Eric Schickler, *Partisan Hearts and Minds: Political Parties and the Social Identities of Voter*s (New Haven, CT: Yale University Press, 2002) at p. 7.

11 Reviewing the Survey Data

From election to election, voters are more likely to change their choices of presidential candidates than to change their party identifications. Because partisanship, as a form of group loyalty, tends to be stable across time, changes in the Democrats' and Republicans' group appeal and base composition inform us about the course of American party politics.

Preceding chapters on the parties' social identities reported a great deal of data in many figures. Chapters 4 through 9 recounted statistics on the Equal Group Appeal and Party Base Concentration of Democratic and Republican identifiers since 1952 on six social factors—region, economic status, urbanization, education, religion, and ethnicity. Chapter 10 reported similar data for ideological self-placement. This chapter reviews and summarizes those findings.

My review relies on a graphical display of statistical data called a "box plot." The "box" itself embraces 50 percent of all cases for a given data distribution. A bar across the middle marks the distribution's median value—the point that divides the cases into two equal halves. The highest and lowest values in the distribution are shown by lines (called "whiskers") extending beyond the end of the box, except for extreme values that lie outside 1.5 and 3 box-lengths from the box's edge. Such extreme observations are considered "outliers" and marked by ○.[1] If this sounds complicated, studying Figure 11.1 should clarify understanding.

Figures in Chapters 4 through 10 plotted the Democrats' and Republicans' Equal Group Appeal and Party Base Concentration scores over all six social factors and ideology over time. They portrayed the scores' ups and downs across all presidential election years. Because box plots do not include presidential years, they succinctly summarize both sets of scores, emphasizing their main features. The first four figures below report Democratic and Republican box plots for Equal Group Appeal and then for Party Base Concentration.

Reviewing Equal Group Appeal Scores

A party's Equal Group Appeal score reflects the extent to which the party draws support equally from all groupings in a social cleavage. The closer

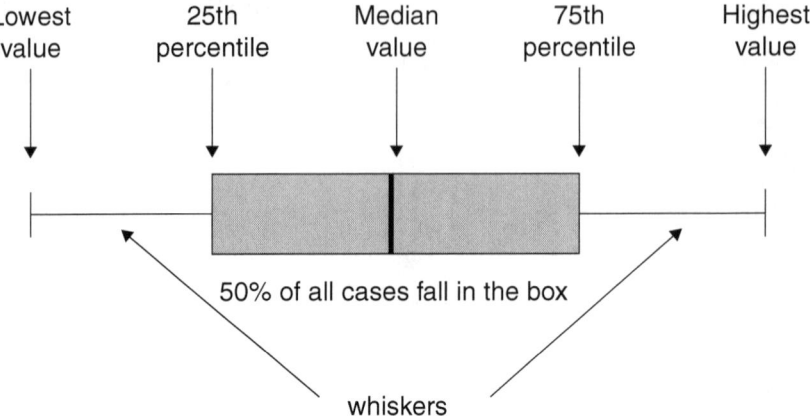

Figure 11.1 A Box Plot

the score to 1.0, the more evenly the party appeals to all groupings. The box plots in Figure 11.2 summarize all Democratic Equal Group Appeal scores since 1952. The heavy black line in the middle of each box marks the median score (half above and half below) for each social cleavage, next to the median value. The cleavages are ordered from highest to lowest Equal Group Appeal.

Figure 11.2 shows that Democrats appealed almost equally to voters from different regions, with different incomes, and with different levels of urbanization and education. The figure shows two outliers in this set of four social cleavages. In 2020, the Democrats' Equal Group Appeal score stood out as voters from all four income levels identified as Democrats almost equally. The tumultuous election year 1968 was an outlier in education for unusual reasons. On March 31, 1968, President Johnson, consumed by the Vietnam War, chose not to run for re-election. In August, the party nominated his vice-president, Hubert Humphrey, for president—despite not having run in any party primaries. Students led riotous protests against Humphrey's nomination at the Chicago convention and in favor of outspoken anti-war candidates like Eugene McCarthy and George McGovern, who had vigorously challenged President Johnson. Afterward, only 28 percent of college educated voters identified as Democrats, compared with 40 percent in 1964.

Compared with region, income, levels of urbanization, and educational level, Figure 11.2 also shows that Democrats appealed less equally to religious, ethnic, and ideological groupings. Concerning religious groups, the party's Equal Appeal scores dropped by losing Protestant support while gaining support from Jews. Its ethnic Equal Appeal scores suffered because it appealed less to the white majority and more to minorities. Its high outlier for ethnicity in 1960 occurred for a surprising reason: fewer Blacks

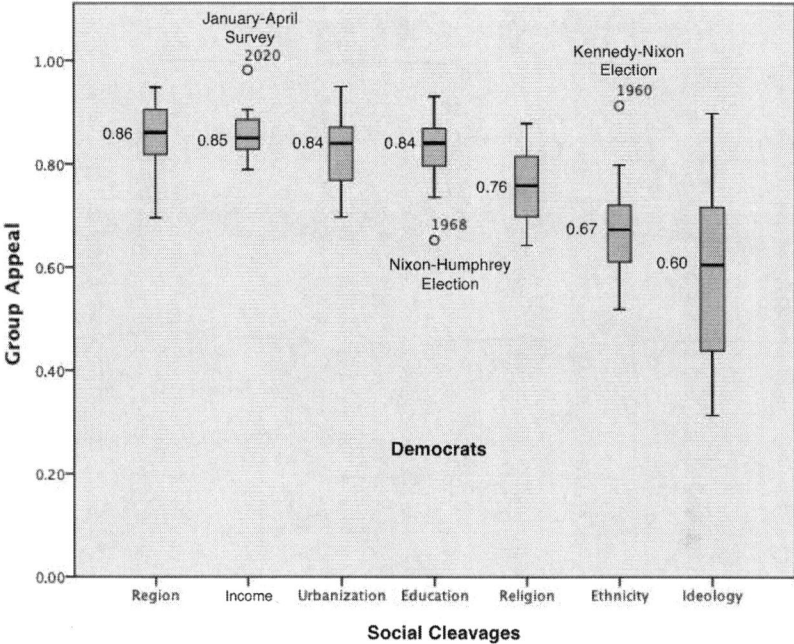

Figure 11.2 Democrats' Group Appeal Box Plots Since 1952, with Median Values

that year identified as Democrats. In 1960, only 50 percent of Blacks claimed to be Democrats, compared with 61 percent in 1956 and 77 percent in 1964. Perhaps that was because Kennedy was Catholic, and Blacks were 95 percent Protestant. The reduction in Black identification in 1960 caused an odd surge in the party's Equal Group Appeal score. Blacks may have voted for Kennedy because of his call to jailed Martin Luther King, Jr.,[2] but fewer became Democratic identifiers. Concerning ideology, the Democrats' Equal Group Appeal scores were the lowest of all seven social cleavages, but they ranged widely from a high of 0.90 in 1960 (Kennedy's election, which attracted conservatives) to a low of 0.31 in 2012 (Obama's re-election, which heavily attracted liberals).

The box plots for Republicans in Figure 11.3 conform perfectly to the above pattern of box plots for Democrats. The median values obediently march down from left to right in the same order. The main difference is that the Republican Equal Group Appeal scores are lower than the Democrats' for all seven social cleavages. Once again, Republican Equal Group Appeal scores for region, income, urbanization, and education differed little from one another and were substantially higher than scores for religion, ethnicity, and ideology. The Republicans' Equal Group Appeal score for economic status score for 2008 was a low outlier, as only 11 percent of voters in the lowest income quintile professed to be Republican.

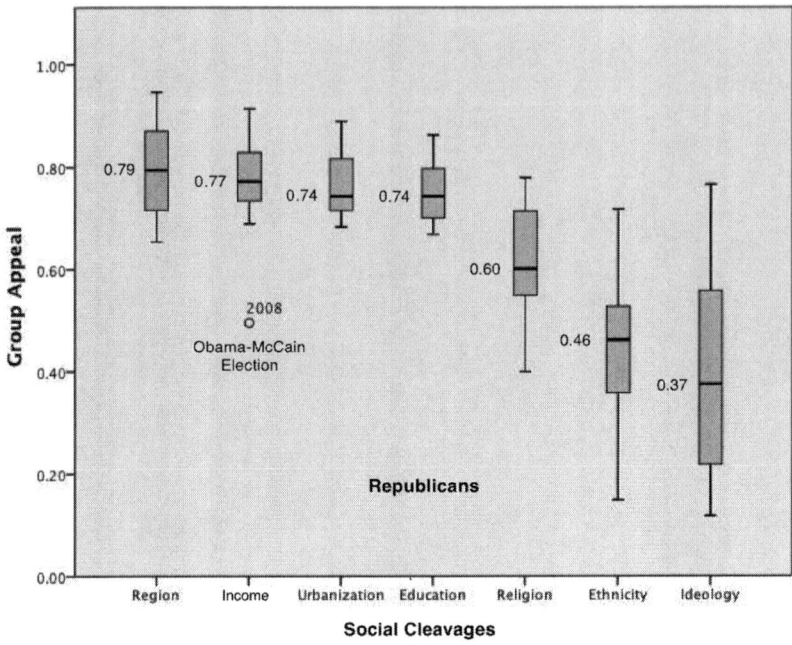

Figure 11.3 Republicans' Group Appeal Box Plots Since 1952, with Median Values

Like Democrats, Republicans had difficulty attracting party identifiers from all religious, ethnic, and ideological groups. They also scored noticeably lower than Democrats on Equal Group Appeal for all three social cleavages: 0.60 on religion vs. 0.76; 0.46 on ethnicity vs. 0.67; and 0.37 on ideology vs. 0.60.

Although Republicans won 10 of 17 presidential elections from 1952 to 2016, Democrats managed to draw party identifiers more equally from different groups in all seven social cleavages. If Democrats appealed more equally to different groups, why did they lose elections to Republicans? As stated in Chapter 3, the Equal Group Appeal score is a measure of evenness not strength. Republicans tended to draw strong support from groups with a large share of the population (i.e., whites and Protestants) but little from groups with small shares (e.g., Blacks and Jews). Consequently, Republicans generated more votes in elections than Democrats, who drew large shares of the vote from smaller electorates. As the Democrats' electorates grow in size, Republicans will face a problem.

As mentioned in Chapter 3, the Republican National Committee in 2013 recognized that the electorate was becoming less white and less Protestant over time. Confronting this problem, RNC chair Reince Priebus launched the Growth and Opportunity Project, which urged the party to recognize "the nation's demographic changes." Candidate Donald Trump

Reviewing Base Concentration Scores

Party Base Concentration scores measure the extent to which a group in a social cleavage dominates the party composition. The closer to 1.0, the greater the concentration of party identifiers in a single group. Let us review the components of the Equal Group Appeal and Party Base Concentration scores. Group Appeal scores are built from three ingredients: the percentages of each group in a social cleavage that identifies as Democrat, Independent, or Republican. Group size is disregarded in computing percentages. Given that the Independents' percentages always fall between those of Democrats and Republicans, variation in Equal Group Appeal scores is limited.

Base Concentration scores depend on only two ingredients: the proportions of Democrats and Republicans coming from each group in the social cleavage. Those proportions do reflect the groups' sizes in the social cleavage. The practical consequence is that Base Concentration scores demonstrate more variation than Group Appeal scores. Base Concentration and Group Appeal scores also tend to be negatively correlated; the higher a party's Equal Group Appeal score, the lower its Party Base Concentration score.[3] Calculated for 126 observations over all 18 surveys and all seven cultural differentiators, the negative correlations are stronger for Republicans (−0.76) than for Democrats (−0.32).

Because Group Appeal and Base Concentration scores are negatively correlated, the box plots in Figure 11.4 for the Democrats' Base Concentration scores contrast with their Group Appeal scores in Figure 11.2. There, the Democrats' Group Appeal boxes start high at the upper left and then descend to the lower right. The Democrats' Base Concentration scores are not so easily described. Three observations invite mention.

First, the Democrats' Base Concentration scores are low for region, income, urbanization, and education. These low scores, ranging between 0.09 and 0.21, correspond to the party's high Equal Group Appeal. The two sets of scores document the Democrats' broad social appeal and inclusive partisanship.

Second, the Democrats' higher Base Concentration scores for religion (0.52) and ethnicity (0.69) reflect the plurality status of Protestants and whites in the society, which makes them the largest groups among party identifiers. Third, the Democrats' low Base Concentration score for ideology (0.21) indicates that liberals do not dominate the party, although they account for most party identifiers. For the most part, those who identify with the Democratic Party reflect the social composition of society.

The box plots for Republicans in Figure 11.5 resemble the display for Democrats. Like the Democrats' Base Concentration scores, the

126 *Reviewing the Survey Data*

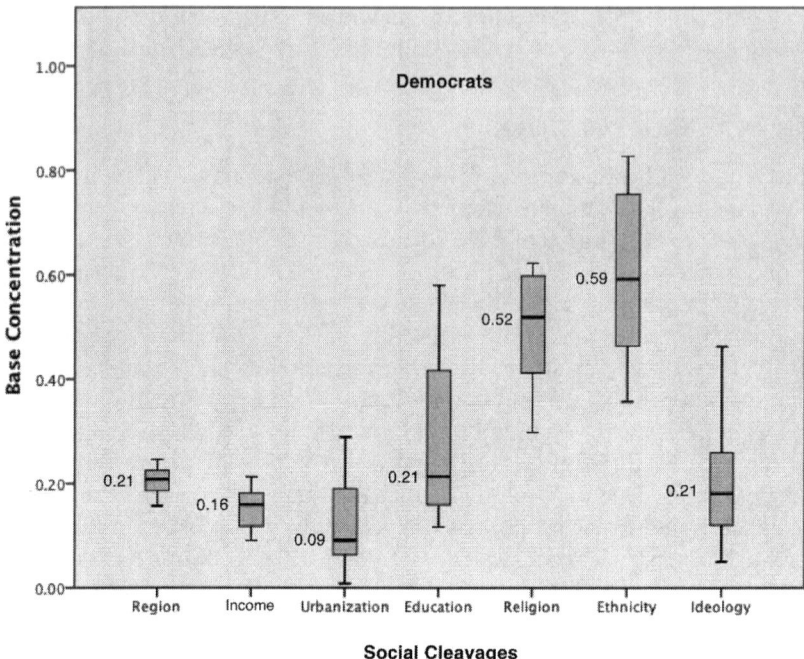

Figure 11.4 Democrats' Base Concentration Box Plots Since 1952, with Median Values

Republicans' scores for region, income, urbanization, and education are relatively low, ranging from 0.18 to 0.29. However, this group of scores has three outliers, two of which dealt with income. In 1956, Eisenhower won re-election with over 57 percent of the vote and claimed party identifiers from the lowest income group; that produced an abnormally low Republican Base Concentration score. In 2008, voters in the lowest economic group flocked to the Democrats and Barack Obama; that produced an abnormally high Republican Base Concentration score (very few low income identifiers). The urbanization outlier for 1952 came from a Republican high point of city identifiers (30 percent), compared with 20 percent in 1956.

Like the Democrats' Base Concentration scores, the Republican scores jumped sharply for the last three social cleavages, religion (0.63), ethnicity (0.89), and ideology (0.51). Moreover, the Republicans' scores were respectively higher by 0.11, 0.30, and 0.30 points. Like the Democrats, the Republicans' higher scores for religion and ethnicity reflected the plurality status of Protestants and whites in America, but unlike the Democrats, these groups were more heavily represented within the party than within society.

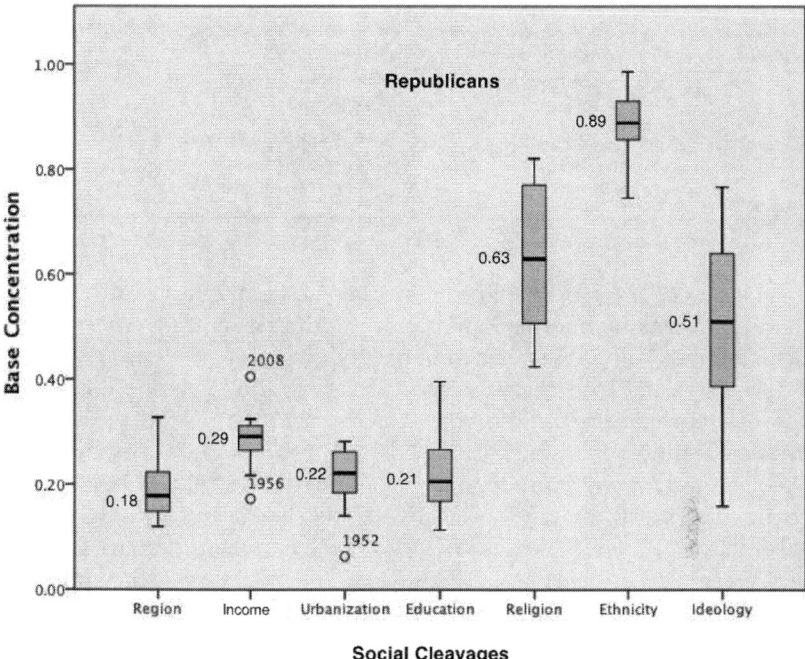

Figure 11.5 Republicans' Base Concentration Box Plots Since 1952, with Median Values

Reinforcing Social Cleavages

Up to now, I have reported only on the distribution of party identifiers among groups within individual social cleavages. Lilliana Mason observes that "single social identities not only have effects on politics in isolation but they have significantly different effects when understood in relation to each other."[4] Suppose we considered the subset of white Protestants with only high school or less education who lived in small towns and rural areas. How likely would they be to identify as Republicans compared with non-white, non-Protestant voters with some college education who did not live in small towns or rural areas? Forming subsets from these combinations mimics the "social milieu" discussed in Chapter 2 as influencing party identification.[5]

In principle, this question can be studied through survey research, but in practice that raises some problems. The first problem, and perhaps the most serious, is finding a sample of adequate size to divide into homogeneous groups of adequate size. A second problem is determining the appropriate "cutting points" for sorting the social groups into categories to maximize partisan predictions. Unable to solve these problems here, I hope

128 Reviewing the Survey Data

Table 11.1 Partisan Assignments of Four Social Cleavages

Percent of Sample	Assigned as Pro-Republican	Assigned as Pro-Democrat	Percent of Sample
65	white	non-white	35
35	Protestant	other religion/none	65
32	small town, rural	city, suburb	68
38	no college	some college/degree	62

to illustrate what a proper study might reveal by analyzing a relatively large survey and making informed guesses of appropriate cutting points. Other cutting points will produce different results.

The data came from the 2019 VOTER survey of 6,779 adults conducted between November 17, 2018 and January 7, 2019 by the survey firm YouGov for the Voter Study Group.[6] It occurred two years after President Trump's election and more than a year prior to the 2020 COVID-19 pandemic. The social cleavages were divided as shown in Table 11.1. Their percentages of the 6,779 cases are given in the marginal columns. Because the percentages in Table 11.1 come from a different survey, they may not match with percentages in figures from earlier chapters.

Evidence previously reviewed found that many voters who are white, Protestant, live in small towns or rural areas, and have only a high school education tend to identify as Republicans. Conversely, many who are non-white, are not Protestant, live in a city or suburb, or have some education beyond high school tend to be Democrats. What happens if these traits are combined? Do reinforced cleavages of ethnicity, religion, urbanization, and education materially improve prediction of party identification?

These four dichotomized social cleavages produce 16 combinations of respondents. Some combinations yield few respondents. For example, in a sample of almost 7,000, only 29 were non-white Protestants with no college education living in a small town. The largest group (1,410) consisted of white non-Protestants living in cities or suburbs with some college. Figure 11.6 tallies the percentage of respondents in all 16 combinations ordered by percentage of respondents in each combination and providing the percentages in each group that identified with the Republican and Democratic parties.

The 16 rows of bars in Figure 11.6 gush with information—too much to process without dissection. First, let us ignore the bottom five rows of bars, which together embrace less than 5 percent of the electorate. Then, let us concentrate on the top five rows, which embrace over 63 percent of the electorate. Each row deserves discussing.

1. **White, not Protestant, not small town, some college** respondents are 21 percent of the sample.

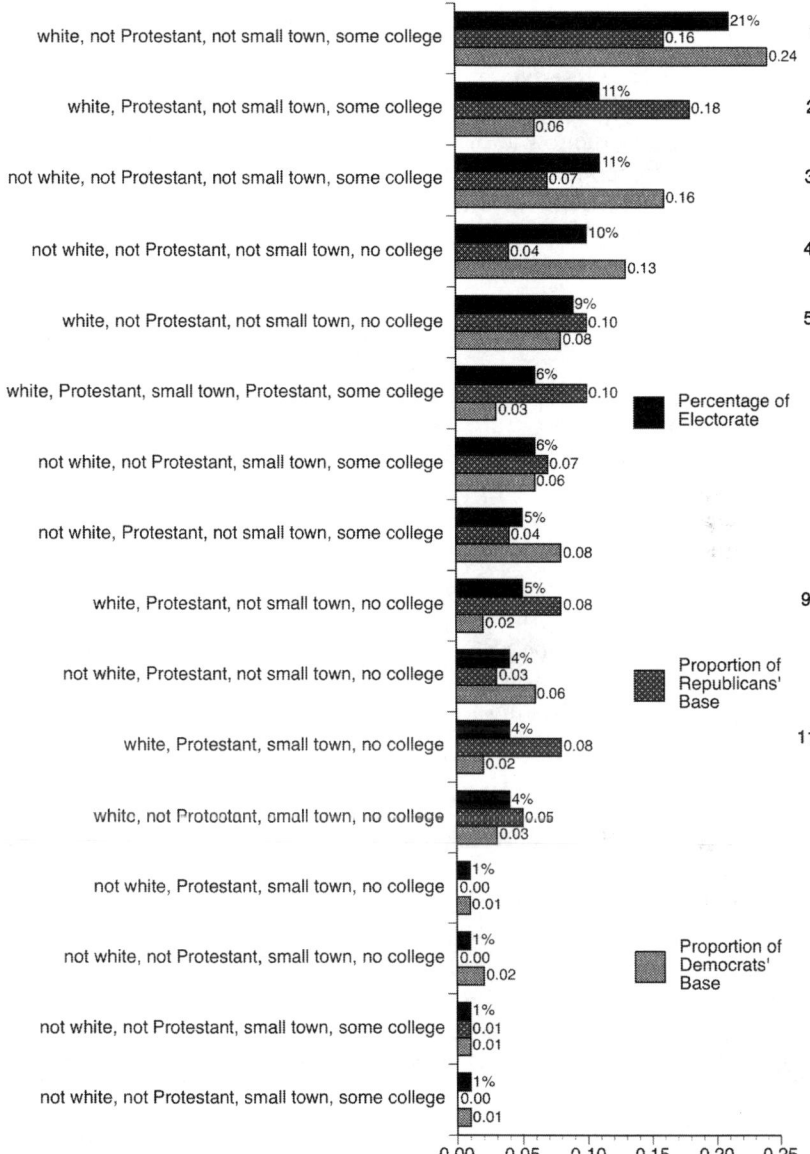

Figure 11.6 Percentages of 2019 Electorate and Proportions of Party Bases by Ethnicity, Religion, Urban, and Education

As expected this combination contributes 0.24 of the Democrats' base, but only 0.16 of the Republicans. This discrepancy (0.08) is far short of that appearing in the next row.

2. **White, Protestant, not small town, some college** respondents are 11 percent of the sample.

This combination differs only in religion, and religion makes a big difference. These Protestants make up 0.18 of Republican identifiers but only 0.06 of Democratic identifiers, a difference of 0.12.

3. **Not white, not Protestant, not small town, some college** respondents are 11 percent of the sample.

    In contrast to the row above, this combination of ethnic minorities is heavily Democratic, making up 0.16 of the party's base, compared to only 0.07 of the Republicans. Adding race is significant.

4. **Not white, not Protestant, not small town, no college** respondents are 10 percent of the sample.

    This combination of minorities differs from the row above only by lacking some college. It also contributed heavily to the Democratic base (0.13) as opposed to the Republican base (0.04). Level of education hardly affects the partisanship of non-Protestant minorities in small towns.

5. **White, not Protestant, not small town, no college** respondents are 9 percent of the sample.

    This combination of minorities differs from the row above only by being white. There is no major discrepancy in their contribution to the two parties' bases.

Perusing further down the rows, one can spot some interesting information tidbits, especially in rows 9 and 11. For white Protestants who live in small towns or cities, lacking a college education substantially increases their contribution to the Republican base over the Democratic base—0.08 compared with 0.02.

While Figure 11.6 shows that some combinations of social groups can reinforce social cleavages to enhance Democrat and Republican party identifications, no alignment of these four social groups completely account for respondents' party identifications. Although white Protestants living in a small town or rural area and lacking any college education are four times more likely to identify as Republicans, one-fifth claims to be Democrats. More can be learned through further research about the effects of reinforced cleavages on partisanship, but this illustrative effort suggests that this line of analysis is worth pursuing.

Summary and Conclusion: Group Appeal vs. Base Concentration

Equal Group Appeal and Party Base Concentration scores tell us different things about political parties, some things not typically discussed in the media. When newspapers, television, and the Internet cite percentages of a group who claim to be Democrats, Republicans, or Independents, they are reporting data used to calculate Equal Group Appeal scores. This is useful information. Social groups are a party's "customers" and learning how much people in a given social group "like" each party indicates its prospective "buyers" (voters) in the next election.

For some reason, however, the media decline to report on the proportions of Democratic and Republican party identifiers from each social group—proportions used in calculating the parties' Base Concentration scores. This alternative information is useful too, for party identifiers, in effect, "own" their party. Knowing who owns a company is as important as knowing who buys its products.

Chapter 3 disclosed two assumptions about the relationship of Equal Group Appeal and Party Base Concentration to interest aggregation and articulation:

> Assumption 1: *Parties that appeal equally to all groups in a social cleavage tend to aggregate the interests of all groups.*
> Assumption 2: *Parties whose base is dominated by any group in a social cleavage tend to articulate the interests of that group.*

The box plots in Figures 11.2 and 11.3 indicate that both parties appealed reasonably equally to voters in all regions, income levels, urban and rural areas, and levels of education, but the Democrats appealed more equally to groups in these cleavages than Republicans. So Democrats probably aggregate their interests better than Republicans. Both parties appeal less equally to religious, ethnic, and ideological groups, but again Democrats also appealed to them more equally than Republicans and probably aggregate their interests better.

The last two box plots (Figure 11.4 and 11.5) reveal that both parties have relatively low Party Base Concentration scores for regions, income levels, urban and rural areas, and levels of education, but again Democrats tend to be lower than Republicans. None of these groups seem to dominate the bases of either party, so neither party can be said to articulate the interests of selected groups in these social cleavages.

However, the box plots in Figures 11.4 and 11.5 show both parties with higher Party Base Concentration scores for religion, ethnicity, and ideology, with Republicans scoring markedly higher. Protestants constitute the dominant religious group in the Republican Party and whites command its ethnic makeup. Both groups are positioned to have the party articulate their interests.

Notes

1 Maria I. Norusiš, *SPSS Introductory Statistics Student Guide* (Chicago: SPSS, 1990), p. 97.
2 Taylor Hiegel, "Remembering Kennedy's Micro-targeting in the 1960 Election," *NBC News* (November 22, 2013) at www.nbcnews.com/news/world/remembering-kennedys-micro-targeting-1960-election-flna2D11641336.
3 The two sets of scores are not only calculated using different formulae, but Independents are included in the Group Appeal scores but not in the Base Concentration scores.

4 Lilliana Mason, *Uncivil Agreement: How Politics Became Our Identity* (Chicago: University of Chicago Press, 2018), p. 19.
5 Christopher Ojeda and Peter K. Hatemia, "Accounting for the Child in the Transmission of Party Identification," *American Sociological Review*, 80 (2015), 1150–1174.
6 Voter Study Group, "@019 VOTER Survey Full Data Set," (January, 2020) at www.voterstudygroup.org/publication/2019-voter-survey-full-data-set.

12 Baneful Effects

Elected in 1789 and re-elected in 1792, President George Washington declined to run for a third term. On September 19, about ten weeks before the 1796 election, *The American Daily Advertiser* published what came to be known as his "Farewell Address." Washington stressed the importance of unity among states and the common interests of all regions. He spoke against foreign influences and entanglements. Most relevantly to this book, he warned about loyalties to parties over the state:

> I have already intimated to you the danger of parties in the State, with particular reference to founding them on geographical discriminations. Let me now take a more comprehensive view, and warn you, in the most solemn manner, against the baneful effects of the spirit of party, generally.[1]

The adjective "baneful" has fallen into disuse over the centuries. Almost a hundred years ago, the 1937 multi-volume edition of *The Oxford Universal English Dictionary* defined baneful as "life-destroying, poisonous" and "pernicious." Dictionaries today define it as something harmful or hurtful. Washington certainly viewed parties that way. Most party scholars simply cite his warnings of parties' "baneful effects" but do not discuss what else he said that relates to contemporary party politics. Washington continued:

> This spirit, unfortunately, is inseparable from our nature, having its root in the strongest passions of the human mind. It exists under different shapes in all governments, more or less stifled, controlled, or repressed; but, in those of the popular form, it is seen in its greatest rankness and is truly their worst enemy.
> ...
> There is an opinion that parties in free countries are useful checks upon the administration of the government and serve to keep alive the spirit of liberty. This within certain limits is probably true—and in governments of a monarchical cast patriotism may look with indulgence, if not with favor, upon the spirit of party. But in those of the popular character, in governments purely elective, it is a spirit not to

be encouraged. From their natural tendency, it is certain there will always be enough of that spirit for every salutary purpose. And there being constant danger of excess, the effort ought to be, by force of public opinion, to mitigate and assuage it. A fire not to be quenched, it demands a uniform vigilance to prevent its bursting into a flame, lest instead of warming it should consume.

As a life-long student of party politics and believer that democratic government in a nation-state cannot function without strong, competitive political parties, I had discounted Washington's warning. Elected president without serious opposition, he wrote before candidates competed for votes across the country. In Chapter 1, I wrote that parties were needed because winning a majority of votes from a large number of voters requires organized collective action from a set of individuals. I then quoted John Aldrich's succinct explanation of why parties were necessary and inevitable.[2] Political scientist Ralph M. Goldman valued parties for affording a peaceful way to transfer government power in a democracy, arguing that "a stable political party system is the most effective institutional alternative to warfare."[3]

While still holding to these ideas, I now harbor doubts about my abiding faith in party politics. John Maynard Keynes reportedly (and disputably) said something to the effect: "When the facts change, I change my opinions." Well, the facts have changed. The Democratic and Republican parties in 2020 are not like they were in 1952.

Parties or Tribes?

In the early 1950s, European scholars denigrated the two American parties as pragmatic "catch-all" parties, whose "aim was to catch all categories of voters, not just traditional constituencies based on societal cleavages."[4] Compared with the major "mass" parties that contested elections in Western democracies, ours lacked distinct social roots and looked to maximize votes from any corner of society. They were sociologically muddled. Today, however, the Democrats' and Republicans' social identities are defined sharply enough that political scholars and journalists refer to them as "tribes."[5] That is a controversial term to many anthropologists. Reviewing its usage in anthropology, Lobban and Fluehr-Lobban say, "[T]he term carries negative and derogatory connotations, as relics of an historical era, colonialism, now formally passed, there are no contemporary grounds for the continued use of 'tribe.'"[6] Probably not for anthropologists, but political scientists have found grounds to use the term.

In truth, contemporary political analysts do not equate political party organizations with tribes. More fairly, they compare those who identify with parties as exhibiting features of a "tribal society," such as "consciously recognized social and cultural identity."[7] Concerning party politics, Mason and Wronski say, "The cumulative effects of party-group alignment reveal a psychologically durable partisan social identity that can be singular in nature—in essence, a tribe that binds all other identities together."[8] Sports researchers also see tribal behavior among sports fans in "the reemergence of quasi-archaic values: a local sense of identification, religiousness, syncretism, group narcissism."[9]

While analysts do not equate party organizations with tribes, they often use tribal terminology in discussing contemporary political partisanship. One journalist wrote about "Tribalism in the Age of Trump."[10] A team of independent researchers issued a long report on *Hidden Tribes* in America's polarized landscape.[11] Ghere's review of Mason's 2018 book, *Uncivil Agreement*, finds "convincing evidence that the two party 'tribes' in the United States are much less concerned with the substance of policy issues than of triumphant victory or, alternatively, staving off the humiliation of defeat."[12] Then there are political uses of tribal markings.

The COVID-19 pandemic in 2020 made facial masks political symbols. Early on, the national government did not advise the public to wear masks to combat infection. When health experts decided that wearing masks in public places was helpful to avoid spreading the virus, Republican President Donald Trump failed to encourage people to do so. He only deigned to wear one himself after the pandemic spread. Not wearing a mask became a social and political statement for some Republican identifiers. A national survey in mid-June found Republicans "much more likely than Democrats to say that masks should rarely or never be worn (23% vs. 4%)."[13] Partisan mask-wearing reached the level of absurdity on the last day of the Minnesota state legislature's special session in June. As the Minneapolis *StarTribune* reported, "Every Democrat entered the room with a face covering, but not one Republican wore a mask."[14] How did party politics evolve to such a sorry state of tribal symbolism?

Blaming Technology

Technological advances had profoundly changed society here and abroad long before I was born. Many significant advances came from ingenious uses of electricity and electronics. The telegraph (1844), telephone (1876), and electric lights (1879) all came in the nineteenth century.[15] The twentieth century brought us radio (1901), television (1927), and early computers (1937), all before World War II. Because automobiles relied on spark plugs to ignite fuel in internal combustion engines and on electric lights for driving at night, one could add them to the list. These technological advances dramatically transformed how people lived, worked, and traveled. Before the twentieth century, people lived much as they lived in previous centuries; afterward, they lived very differently.

In many respects, American life in 2020 is not much different from the immediate post-World War II era. People then and now live in centrally heated, air-conditioned houses. They have indoor plumbing with hot and cold running water, benefit from electric lights and appliances, and enjoy freedom of travel by car over a nation-wide network of highways. There is one huge difference between 1952 and 2020. Technology has wrought irreversible changes in how people communicate.

Chapter 2 noted the growth of television news networks from only three in 1952 to five today plus innumerable cable outlets. It also noted that news gatekeepers—those who select and edit the news—have declined in importance and almost disappeared. Although network radio as a source of information about national news has greatly decreased, talk radio as an alternative source of political opinions has greatly increased. As a result, citizens have access to more choices in political news and in opinions about politics than citizens had after World War II. Technology evolved over time to give politicians more ways to broadcast to citizens.

In 2007, information technology experienced a revolutionary change with release of the first iPhone. Politicians soon learned that they could communicate directly with citizens, and some—like Donald Trump—capitalized on the opportunity by Tweeting his momentary thoughts directly to receptive listeners. Political partisans—both Democrats and Republicans—quickly found that they could talk politics with other like-minded individuals, reinforcing and escalating their partisan beliefs and prejudices. This exchange of messages fed partisans' social identity.

The partisan consequences appeared less than a decade after the iPhone appeared. In 2015, Tamburrini, Cinnirella, Jansen, and Bryden, a team of London researchers in biological sciences and psychology, viewed "Twitter," a software application for cell phones, as "a micro-blogging web-site" through which users share their opinions and thoughts in brief messages called "tweets."[16] Group members could discuss (and share) their behavior, social values, and political thoughts. They wrote: "Consequently, social identity can be heightened which explains why some group phenomena, such as polarisation of attitudes, and stereotyping, can seem enhanced in some online environments."[17]

While that team of authors did not mention political parties or even politics, one team member subsequently analyzed a sample of approximately 250,000 Twitter accounts in connection with the 2016 U.S. presidential election. Bryden and Silverman employed advanced computer techniques to identify Alt-right, Republican, and Trump groups whose members tended to follow one another and characterized each group using biographical information on member profiles.[18] They found various Alt-right and Republican groups following the Trump group composed "of real, highly-engaged supporters."[19]

Political partisans soon learned how to harness the power of newer social media tools, like Twitter, and older ones, like Facebook, to build social groups of like-minded individuals. Neuroscientists Meshi, Tamir, and Heekeren note that social media's reach is unlimited: "No longer constrained by spatial, social, and temporal distance, social media allows people to interact with audiences that are essentially limitless in size." The authors continue:

social media can elicit behaviors that significantly diverge from those elicited in face-to-face interactions. For example, by releasing us from the norm of reciprocity, social media may allow our desire to self-disclose to run wild. ... Further, politeness norms dictate that we should behave cordially to one another in face-to-face interactions. By contrast, the social distance provided by certain social media platforms, such as YouTube and Twitter, can result in the repeated violation of these norms.[20]

For years, social media platforms refused to serve as gatekeepers, censoring messages that users posted on their sites (except sexual content and illegal drugs). Media reporter Mike Isaac writes, "While Facebook, Twitter, YouTube, Reddit and others originally positioned themselves as neutral sites that simply hosted people's posts and videos, users are now pushing them to take steps against hateful, abusive and false speech on their platforms."[21]

In the summer of 2020, Reddit—a social news aggregation, web content rating, and discussion website—banned "The_Donald," a community (called a subreddit) whose more than 790,000 users posted memes, viral videos, and supportive messages about Mr. Trump.[22] Uninitiated outsiders soon learned how extensively political groups used social media. *The New York Times* said that Reddit

> was also banning roughly 2,000 other communities from across the political spectrum, including one devoted to the leftist podcasting group "Chapo Trap House," which has about 160,000 regular users. The vast majority of the forums that are being banned are inactive.
>
> "The_Donald," which has been a digital foundation for Mr. Trump's supporters, is by far the most active and prominent community that Reddit decided to act against.[23]

Reddit's C.E.O. acknowledged that "The_Donald" was

> a very large political community that, at one point in time, represented the views of many Americans. Political speech is sacred in this country, ... At the same time, that community had rule-breaking content—content that was harassing or violence or bullying.[24]

The_Donald did not come into line with Reddit's policies. Its clampdown "fueled a backlash from the White House and its defenders."[25]

While liberals and Democrats also effectively use information technology in politicking, Schradie's 2019 book claims that "digital activism favors conservatives,"[26] and it

> provides strong evidence that conservative groups focused more on "informationalizing," while the liberal groups tended more toward

organizing. Conservative activists ... were more focused on spreading the "Truth" about the liberal assault on freedom, whereas progressive activists were focused on organizing campaigns around principles of fairness that demanded real concessions from corporate and political leaders.[27]

When partisans exploit information technology to manipulate news sources, citizens find it hard to distinguish genuine reports of public affairs from "fake news." A survey of news audiences in the United States, the United Kingdom, and France found more American respondents (36 percent) saying they have been exposed to "fake news" than in France (under 30 percent) and Britain (19 percent). The researchers also found that:

> disbelief in news is correlated with candidate support in the United States. The Trump effect on news belief constitutes an unbalancing of the information flywheel in politics. The capacity of Trump supporters to believe information about outcomes unfavorable to them is limited.[28]

One study considered the effect of "incivility" in partisan news sources, defining personal-level incivility as "violations of politeness that include slurs, threats of harm, and disrespect" by the reporters. It found:

> when partisan media comes from an in-party source (e.g., a Republican watches Fox News), incivility *depolarizes*: partisans feel less close to and trusting of their party (relative to those watching a more civil program). When individuals watch out-party sources (e.g., a Democrat watches Fox News), the opposite happens, and incivility polarizes respondents.[29]

The researchers said their "most intriguing finding" was that "exposure to in-party incivility (relative to exposure to in-party civility) works to move people away from their party." Presumably, partisans can be turned off by incivility to the other side, which does promise something.

Blaming Electoral Politics

Clearly, the twenty-first century brought technological changes that facilitated creating, expanding, and sustaining the social identity of highly partisan voters. Social media helped cultivate tribal tendencies among party identifiers. So to some extent we can blame today's affective, emotional, polarization of politics on relatively abrupt technological innovation over the last two decades. However, incremental changes in politics can be blamed, too.

As documented in Chapter 2, most voters (over three-quarters) in 1952 readily identified themselves as Democrats or Republicans and nearly half (41 percent) saw no differences between the parties. In fact, the parties truly had no "colors."[30] The parties' 1952 bumper stickers showed both candidates' names in red on a blue background. In white, the ads urged, "Vote Democratic" or "Vote Republican." In 2020, fewer voters (one-third) are Democrats or Republicans, and both candidates' websites flaunt their parties' colors (blue for Democrats, red for Republicans). However, the official website of the Democratic presidential candidate, Joe Biden, does not urge visitors to "Vote Democratic" nor does Republican President Trump's official site urge visitors to "Vote Republican"—in recognition of partisan toxicity.

By past actions of their presidents and presidential candidates, both parties have helped escalate the polarization since 1952. Democrats and Republicans did not start with a blank slate; history weighed heavily on both parties. In the mid-1860s, they were on opposite sides in a Civil War. For decades afterward, southern Democrats kept former enslaved Blacks from equal treatment in social, political, and legal affairs. By default, Republicans benefitted both morally and politically, until Democratic President Harry Truman desegregated the armed forces by executive order in 1948. Roughly speaking, that remained the situation in 1952.

In 1951, the National Association for the Advancement of Colored People (NAACP) began filing lawsuits to end segregation of schools. Despite Truman's bold action in desegregating the military, the Democratic Party failed to support the NAACP. Given the Democrats' strong base in segregated states, its position was understandable. As the "party of Lincoln," the Republican's failure to help is less so. In 1952, 48 percent of whites identified as Democrats, versus only 29 percent Republican. Republicans may have had a chance then to reclaim Lincoln's moral legacy. After the Supreme Court in 1954 ordered school desegregation "with all deliberate speed" and Republican President Dwight Eisenhower sent federal troops to Little Rock to enforce the order in 1957, Republicans had another opportunity to take a stand for racial equality.

For whatever reasons in 1960, Republicans took the other fork in the road. As Republican Richard Nixon faced off against Democrat John F. Kennedy in the 1960 presidential election, many Black leaders initially supported Nixon. After Dr. King was jailed for participating in a sit-in, Kennedy suddenly attracted Black support in October by phoning Martin Luther King's wife. In contrast, Nixon's strategists concluded that he should be silent about the jailing.[31] Of Nixon, King said, "When this moment came, it was like he had never heard of me."[32] Kennedy's victory by less than 1 percent of the popular vote has been credited to his phone call.

After President Kennedy's assassination in 1963, new President Lyndon Johnson pressed to enact Kennedy's Civil Right legislation that banned discrimination on the basis of race (and sex) in public facilities, interstate commerce, the workplace and housing, and promoted Black voter registration. Whether he actually said, "We have lost the South for a generation," Johnson realized that he opened the door to Republican victories.[33]

In 1964, Republican presidential candidate Barry Goldwater launched "Operation Dixie" and campaigned against the new Civil Rights Act. He did win five states in the deep South but only his home state of Arizona elsewhere. In 1968, Nixon followed a different version of a "Southern Strategy," making coded appeals to "law and order" to end marches and protests and implying "benign neglect" of civil rights enforcement. Facing a deeply divided Democratic party over Hubert Humphrey's nomination, Nixon eked out a narrow victory.

In 1980, Republican Ronald Reagan embarked on a "Nationwide Strategy" of appealing to white voters by picturing "welfare queens" living off public funds and painting minorities as "takers' of government services.[34] Thus, Republican presidents and presidential candidates had scrapped the party's historic identification as the "Negro's friend" long before 2020, when it appealed to only 7 percent of Blacks.

In 2008, the Democratic Party also contributed to the racial divide. It audaciously nominated an Afro-American as its presidential candidate. Then Democrats elected Barack Obama president of the United States, and whites took notice.

Blaming Congressional Politics

Certainly electoral politics at the presidential level affected the distribution of party identifiers among American voters. But some key developments in Congress drove wedges between the parties. Concerning the House, historian Julian Zeilzer points to the period between January 1987 and March 1989, when Republican congressman Newt Gingrich used "no-holds-barred partisan warfare" to oust Democratic Speaker Jim Wright over ethics violations.[35] That event changed the tone of chamber conversation and marked Newt Gingrich as an uncompromising partisan.

In September 1994 as Minority Whip, Gingrich staged a mass signing of "The Contract with America" by 367 Republican House candidates. They all pledged to pass ten major legislative items within the first 100 days of Congress if Republicans won control of the chamber. Unexpectedly, they won a small majority, made Gingrich Speaker, and with strong party discipline passed nine of the ten items in the Contract, only failing to pass a constitutional amendment for term limits that required a two-thirds majority.

As Speaker of the House, Gingrich followed the informal rule that he would only bring up to vote a bill supported by a majority of Republican members. In 1999, Republican House Speaker Dennis Hastert embraced that practice by naming it the "Hastert Rule"—legislation would be brought to vote only if it had a majority of the majority. Legislation that might be backed by a majority coalition of Republicans and Democrats in the House would never come to a vote. When Mitch McConnell became Majority Leader of the Senate Republican Party, he followed an informal rule not to bring up a bill that Republican President Donald Trump would not sign.

Responsible Party Government

Although scholars widely regard political parties as essential to democratic government, they recognize that parties play different roles in multi-party systems versus two-party systems. In multi-party systems, the largest party often fails to win a majority of legislative seats and must govern in coalition in one or more other parties. That situation occurs often in Western Europe. Historically, Britain stood out as the exception, as only the Conservatives and Labour parties competed for parliamentary majorities in a basically two-party system. Also having two major parties, American political scientists admired British party government and called it the "responsible party model."[36]

In fact, the American Political Science Association (APSA) in 1950 issued a report, "Toward a More Responsible Two-Party System," which urged that American parties show more discipline, like British parties.[37] The responsible party model embodied four principles:

1. Parties should present clear and coherent programs to voters.
2. Voters should choose candidates on the basis of party programs.
3. The winning party should carry out its program once in office.
4. Voters should hold the governing party responsible at the next election for executing its program.

How well do these principles describe American politics? The Democratic and Republican platforms do differ and are much more ideologically consistent and distinct than many people believe. So the first principle has been met fairly well.[38] Less evidence supports the second principle: that voters should choose candidates on the basis of party platforms. Party platforms are usually absent from campaigning and from voters' minds when they cast their ballots, but platforms do reflect party ideology, which influences many voters' choice of presidential candidates.[39]

Authors of the APSA report were most concerned about the third principle: the winning party should carry out its program. American parties, the authors felt, were insufficiently disciplined to carry out their parties' programs. If party members in Congress did not vote cohesively for party programs, there was little chance to fulfill the fourth principle: voters should hold the governing party responsible at the next election.

In the 1950s, neither party showed much party unity. In 1956, a majority of Democrats voted against a majority of Republicans only 44 percent of the time in the House and 53 percent in the Senate.[40] On those votes, only 70 percent of Democrats and Republicans in both chambers voted with their parties. Nearly one-third often voted with the opposition. In contrast, six decades later in 2017, a majority of Democrats voted against a majority of Republicans 70 percent of the time in the House and 69 percent in the Senate. On those votes, over 90 percent of Democrats and over 90 percent of Republicans voted with their parties in both chambers.[41] Few members in either party, in either chamber, voted against their party majority.

In the 1950s, political scientists viewed the lack of party discipline and cohesiveness as a problem for effective government. Today, analysts widely regard the presence of rigid party discipline in the House and Senate as a serious problem. Democrats and Republicans in Congress may be behaving "responsibly" by voting cohesively according to their party leaders, but they may not be voting responsibly concerning the public. Disciplined "responsible" parties can also produce stalemate in policy making. If the presidency and one chamber of Congress are controlled by different parties, strict party discipline—each pushing their constituents' clashing interests—reduces government's ability to pass legislation. Hence, party polarization in 2020 has undermined the model of responsible party government proposed in 1950.

In retrospect, the 1950 APSA report can be viewed as calling for more party discipline, not complete party discipline. Greek philosopher Socrates is credited for the saying, "Everything in moderation. Nothing in excess." Perhaps both parties are "excessively" cohesive today, and the two parties would function better in our federal system of divided government by allowing room for moderation, more bipartisan legislation. Other scholars, younger ones, need to address this question, for Democrats and Republicans are here to stay.

Former speechwriter for President Reagan, Peggy Noonan wrote in August 2020, "it's true that the two-party system is a mess":

> But in the end, together and in spite of themselves, both parties still function as a force for unity in that when an election comes, whatever your disparate stands, you have to choose whether you align more with Party A or Party B. This encourages coalitions and compromise. It won't work if there are four parties or six; things will splinter, the system buckle. The Democratic Party needs the Republican Party, needs it to restrain its excesses and repair what it does that proves injurious. The Republicans need the Democrats, too, for the same reasons.[42]

At the start of this book, I evoked Charles Dickens' famous opening in his *A Tale of Two Cities*, by writing: "Since its beginning, the American polity has been very stable, but it has greatly changed." My tale of two parties has told how they changed since 1952. Peggy Noonan reminds us of our polity's stability. Since the Civil War, our two-party system has contained the competition for political power by ambitious politicians, thus resulting in peaceful transition between presidential administrations. Ralph Goldman's multination study, *From Warfare to Party Politics*, ended his chapter on the United States with these sentences:

By the 1880s, the party system also stabilized and provided the principal channel of leadership recruitment and elite competition in the nation. The United States appears to have completed its critical transition.[43]

Assuming that this "critical transition" continues, we must also insure that the two-party system also governs effectively for all of its citizens.

Reminiscing, and Summarizing

Chapter 2 reported that only 23 percent of respondents in the 1952 ANES survey said they were Independent. It also said that the 2020 January-April Nationscape survey found 34 percent Independents, which grew to 40 percent in a June 2020 Gallup poll.

Chapter 10 stated that 40 percent of respondents said they were ideologically "moderate" in 1952. It also said that the percentage of moderates dropped substantially to 29 percent in the 2016 ANES survey, and that the 2020 Nationscape survey recorded a rise to 39 percent moderate—almost the same as in 1952.

Taken together, these data suggest both a decline in partisan identifiers in 2020 and more ideological moderation. Scanty as they are, these data fit with recent findings by Klar, Krupnikov, and Ryan that "The majority of individuals are not 'affectively polarized'; rather, many are averse to partisan politics."[44] The findings also fit with new research that "a great deal of measured partisan animosity reflects disagreement about contentious issues and not simply teamism."[45] To the extent that voters reduce the "social identity" component of their party identification and vote according to their understanding of candidates' policy positions, parties might be behaving less like tribes.

Notes

1 The U.S. Senate published Washington's full address at www.senate.gov/artandhistory/history/resources/pdf/Washingtons_Farewell_Address.pdf.
2 John Aldrich, *Why Parties?* (Chicago: University of Chicago Press, 1995), p. 23. See also *Why Parties? A Second Look* (Chicago: University of Chicago Press, 2011), p. 21.
3 Ralph M. Goldman, *From Warfare to Party Politics: The Critical Transition to Civilian Control* (Syracuse, NY: Syracuse University Press, 1990), p. 1.
4 Alexandra Cole, "Comparative Political Parties Systems and Organizations," in John T. Ishiyama and Marijke Breuning (eds.), *21st Century Political Science: A Reference Handbook* (Thousand Oaks, CA: SAGE, 2011), 150–158, at p. 153. Otto Kirchheimer is credited to popularizing this term. See Andre Krouwel, "Otto Kirchheimer and the Catch-All Party," *West European Politics*, 26 (April, 2003), 23–40.
5 George Packer "A New Report Offers Insights into Tribalism in the Age of Trump," *New Yorker* (October 13, 2018), at www.newyorker.com/news/daily-comment/a-new-report-offers-insights-into-tribalism-in-the-age-of-trump;

Stephen Hawkins, Daniel Yudkin, Míriam Juan-Torres, and Tim Dixon, *Hidden Tribes: A Study of America's Polarized Landscape* (New York: More in Common, 2019) at https://static1.squarespace.com/static/5a70a7c3010027736a22740f/t/5bbcea6b7817f7bf7342b718/1539107467397/hidden_tribes_report-2.pdf; Richard K. Ghere, "Review: *Uncivil Agreement: How Politics Became Our Identity*," *Public Integrity*, 21 (2019), 214–219; Lilliana Mason and Julie Wronski, "One Tribe to Bind Them All: How Our Social Group Attachments Strengthen Partisanship," *Advances in Political Psychology*, 39 (Suppl. 1, 2018), 257–277.

6 Richard A. Lobban Jr. and Carolyn Fluehr-Lobban, " 'Tribe': A Socio-Political Analysis," *Issues* (Rhode Island College Digital Commons, 1976), 143–165 at p. 161.
7 I.M. Lewis, "Tribal Society," in David L. Sills (ed.), *International Encyclopedia of the Social Sciences, Volume 16* (New York: Macmillan and Free Press, 1968), 146–152 at p. 148.
8 Mason and Wronski, p. 274.
9 Pedro Dionisio and Carmo Leal, "Fandom Affiliation and Tribal Behaviour: A Sports Marketing Application," *Qualitative Market Research: An International Journal*, 11, No. 1 (2008), 17–39 at p. 22.
10 Packer.
11 Hawkins et al.
12 Ghere, p. 214.
13 Pew Survey, "Republicans, Democrats Move Even Further Apart in Coronavirus Concerns," (June 25, 2020) at www.pewresearch.org/politics/2020/06/25/republicans-democrats-move-even-further-apart-in-coronavirus-concerns/.
14 Jesse Van Berkel, "Rift Grows as Walz Weighs Mask Rule," Minneapolis *StarTribune* (July 13, 2020), p. 1.
15 Erik Gregersen, "History of Technology Timeline," *Encyclopaedia Britannica* at www.britannica.com/story/history-of-technology-timeline.
16 Nadine Tamburrini, Marco Cinnirella, Vincent A.A. Jansen, and John Bryden, "Twitter Users Change Word Usage According to Conversation-Partner Social Identity," *Social Networks*, 40 (2015), 84–89 at p. 84.
17 *Ibid.*, p. 85.
18 John Bryden and Eric Silverman, "Underlying Socio-political Processes Behind the 2016 US Election," *PLoS ONE*, 14(4): e0214854 at https://doi.org/10.1371/journal.pone.0214854.
19 *Ibid.*, p. 4.
20 Dar Meshi, Diana I. Tamir, and Hauke R. Heekeren, "The Emerging Neuroscience of Social Media," *Trends in Cognitive Sciences*, 19 (December, 2015), 771–782 at http://dx.doi.org/10.1016/j.tics.2015.09.004.
21 Mike Isaac, "Reddit Bans User Group Devoted to Trump," *New York Times* (June 30, 2020), p. B1.
22 *Ibid.*
23 *Ibid.*
24 Kevin Roose, "Reddit's C.E.O. on Why He Banned 'The_Donald' Subreddit," *New York Times* (July 1, 2020), p. B5.
25 Robert McMillan and Deepa Seetharaman, "Platforms Halt Forums for Trump Supporters," *Wall Street Journal* (June 30, 2020), p. B3.

26 Jen Schradie, *The Revolution That Wasn't: How Digital Activism Favors Conservatives* (Cambridge, MA: Harvard University Press, 2019).
27 David Karpf, "Review: *The Revolution That Wasn't: How Digital Activism Favors Conservatives*," *The International Journal of Press/Politics*, 25 (2020), 538–544 at p. 539.
28 Karolina Koc-Michalska, Bruce Bimber, Daniel Gomez, Matthew Jenkins, and Shelley Boulianne, "Public Beliefs About Falsehoods in News," *The International Journal of Press/Politics*, 25 (2020), 447–468 at 461.
29 James N. Druckman, S.R. Gubitz, Ashley M. Lloyd, and Matthew S. Levendusky, "How Incivility on Partisan Media (De)Polarizes the Electorate," *The Journal of Politics*, 81 (December 3, 2018), 291–295 at 291–292.
30 Most analysts used red for Democrats and blue for Republicans, but television networks switched the color scheme in reporting the 2000 presidential election, and the switch stuck. See Philip Bump, "Red vs. Blue: A History of How We Use Political Colors," *Washington Post* (November 8, 2016) at www.washingtonpost.com/news/the-fix/wp/2016/11/08/red-vs-blue-a-brief-history-of-how-we-use-political-colors/.
31 Steven Levingston, "John F. Kennedy, Martin Luther King Jr., and the Phone Call That Changed History," *Time* (June 20, 2017) at https://time.com/4817240/martin-luther-king-john-kennedy-phone-call/.
32 "Nixon, Richard Milhous," The Martin Luther King, Jr. Research and Education Institute, Stanford University, at https://kinginstitute.stanford.edu/encyclopedia/nixon-richard-milhous.
33 Steven J. Allen, "'We Have Lost the South for a Generation': What Lyndon Johnson Said, or Would Have Said if Only He Had Said It," *Capital Research Center* (October 7, 2014) at https://capitalresearch.org/article/we-have-lost-the-south-for-a-generation-what-lyndon-johnson-said-or-would-have-said-if-only-he-had-said-it/.
34 This account draws heavily on Angie Maxwell, "What We Get Wrong About the Southern Strategy," *Washington Post* (July 26, 2019) at www.washingtonpost.com/outlook/2019/07/26/what-we-get-wrong-about-southern-strategy/.
35 Julian E. Zelizer, *Burning Down the House: Newt Gingrich, the Fall of a Speaker, and the Rise of the New Republican Party* (New York: Penguin, 2020); reviewed by Geoffrey Kabaservice, "When American Politics Turned Toxic," *New York Times* (July, 2020) at www.nytimes.com/2020/07/07/books/review/burning-down-the-house-julian-zelizer.html. Citations are to the review.
36 See Frances McCall Rosenbluth and Ian Shapiro, *Responsible Parties: Saving Democracy from Itself* (New Haven, CT: Yale University Press, 2018) for a comprehensive defense of the model. The definitive treatment of the model's origin is Mark Wickham-Jones, *Whatever Happened to Party Government?* (Ann Arbor: University of Michigan Press, 2018).
37 American Political Science Association, "Toward a More Responsible Two-Party System," *American Political Science Review*, 44, II (September, 1950), 1–99. Some scholars questioned whether American parties were able to be reformed to behave like British parties. See Robert Harmel and Kenneth Janda, *Parties and Their Environments: Limits to Reform?* (New York: Longman, 1982).
38 Jeffrey M. Jones, "Americans Lack Consensus on Desirability of Divided Gov't," *Gallup Poll Report*, 10 June 2010.

39 Some research finds that voters do differentiate between policies backed by the president and by congressional candidates. See David R. Jones and Monika L. McDermott, "The Responsible Party Government Model in House and Senate Elections," *American Journal of Political Science*, 48 (January, 2004), 1–12.
40 *Roll Call*, "Party Unity on Congressional Votes Takes a Dive: CQ Vote Studies" at www.rollcall.com/2019/02/28/party-unity-on-congressional-votes-takes-a-dive-cq-vote-studies/.
41 The percentages of party votes in both chambers dropped somewhat in 2018, but the percentages of Democrats and Republicans who voted with their parties changed only slightly. Data were not available for 2019.
42 Peggy Noonan, "Burn the Republican Party Down?" *Wall Street Journal* (August 1, 2020), p. A13.
43 Goldman, p. 111.
44 Samara Klar, Yanna Krupnikov, and John Barry Ryan, "Affective Polarization or Partisan Disdain? Untangling a Dislike for the Opposing Party from a Dislike of Partisanship," *Public Opinion Quarterly*, 82 (Summer, 2018), 379–390 at p. 380.
45 Lilla V. Orr and Gregory A. Huber, "The Policy Basis of Measured Partisan Animosity in the United States," *American Journal of Political Science*, 64 (July, 2020), 569–586 at p. 584.

13 Donald Trump's Last Hurrah

The phrase, "the last hurrah," applies to Donald Trump's 2020 election campaign. It comes from the title of Edwin O'Connor's 1956 prize-winning novel, made into an award-winning film in 1958.[1] O'Connor wrote about a veteran Democratic Party big city politician who relied on re-election by the old formula of urban politics—dispensing jobs and money—after government programs had replaced political handouts. The old-style boss lost to a challenger who recognized social change and ran television ads. O'Connor's phrase became known as "a swan song; or the ballyhoo of old-time politics."[2] Republican speechwriter, William Safire, defined "the last hurrah" as the "exit of a politician especially one who has had a boisterous career: more generally, the final, losing campaign."[3]

Losing future elections was what the Republican National Committee feared after Democrat Barack Obama won in 2008 and 2012. Chapter 3 tells that the RNC funded a study to respond in future elections to a changing electorate. In 2013, the RNC's Growth and Opportunity Project urged the party to recognize "the nation's demographic changes," saying: "If we want ethnic minority voters to support Republicans, we have to engage them and show them our sincerity."[4] After Donald Trump won the 2016 Republican nomination for president, he decided to go in a different direction. Trump would cater instead to the remaining dwindling white Christian plurality, and the RNC dumped its own report. Many observers said that Trump launched an avowedly conservative campaign to woo his conservative base.

Problems arise when trying to classify Trump, other politicians, and the electorate on the liberal-conservative continuum.[5] The ideological concepts of liberal and conservative definitely have useful meanings, but—as described in Chapter 10—their meanings are neither widely understood nor shared. Prominent conservatives opposed Trump's election, and the list of conservative opponents grew during his administration.[6] While striving to defend conservatism against Trump, many struggled to explain conservatism itself.[7] Even Barry Goldwater's 1960 book, *The Conscience of a Conservative*, lacked a formal definition, only stating, "the Conservative looks upon politics as the art of achieving the maximum amount of freedom for individuals that is consistent with the maintenance of social order."[8] John Dean's *Conservatives Without Conscience* (dedicated to Goldwater) devoted a chapter to defining conservatism, eventually invoking Goldwater's concern with balancing freedom and order in contemporary society.[9]

Conservatism is not a simple philosophy. Conservatives do not simply seek to return to the past. Conservative thought generally respects learning from the past to apply in the present and future. Those who do strive to recover an idealized past, says political theorist Mark Lilla, are reactionaries. They "are not conservatives."[10]

Donald Trump ran in 2016 not as a conservative but as a reactionary, "one who believes in returning to governmental and economic conditions of an earlier time."[11] He based his election campaign not on abstract values in political philosophy but on certain voters' recollections of social history. By evoking voters' nostalgic and imperfect memories of the past, Trump shrewdly appealed to emotions of two social groups that had once dominated American politics. In 1952, whites composed over 90 percent of the electorate, with white Christians (Protestants and Catholics) accounting for almost 80 percent. As shown in Figure 13.1, white Christians dropped to under 40 percent by 2019. By promising to "Make America Great Again," Trump ostensibly spoke to voters who had suffered economically from government policies that increased profits for global corporations by outsourcing manufacturing abroad. More ominously, he spoke to those who had lost their superior social positions in society.

Were there enough voters in these dwindling groups to produce a Trump victory? The Republican National Committee's own research in 2013 did not think so, but Donald J. Trump surprised his party, the opposition party, legions of political analysts, and perhaps himself by winning enough popular votes in strategic states to capture a majority of the electoral vote and the presidency in 2016. Could he pull off a last hurrah in 2020?

Early in 2020, Donald Trump appeared to be confident about his re-election. Unemployment was very low, and the stock market was very

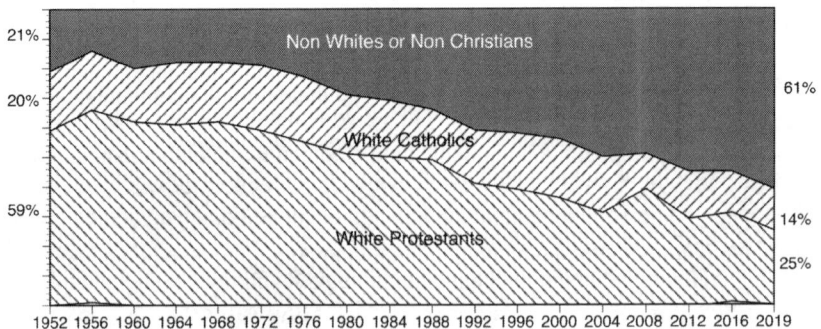

*American National Election Studies, 1952-2016, and Democracy Fund Voter Study Group Data Release No.1, Published January, 2020.

Figure 13.1 Changes in the American Electorate, 1952–2019*

high. Since 1952, only two presidents who sought re-election had lost (Carter in 1980 and G.H.W. Bush in 1992). Nevertheless, the process of demographic change that worried the Republican National Committee had continued inexorably from 2016 to 2020. Whites had declined below 65 percent of the electorate and Christians below 40 percent. Given that Donald Trump lost the popular vote in 2016, pundits expected a close race—with the outcome again hinging on strategic states and their electoral votes.

The COVID-19 pandemic that struck in January 2020 killed over 200,000 people by autumn, led to massive unemployment, and generally wrecked the economy. While most voters disapproved of President Trump's handling of the pandemic, many other voters backed him to restore "law and order" after police killings of Black citizens in the spring and summer produced nationwide protests against racial justice sometimes accompanied by wanton rioting, looting, and burning. Gallup polls from February to August reported an uncommonly large swing in voters' identification away from Republicans (from 33 to 26 percent) and toward Democrats (from 26 to 31 percent).[12] Although a series of polls in August showed Democratic candidate Joe Biden with double-digit leads over Donald Trump in presidential preference, reporters noted that summer leads in polls often disappear by the November election.[13] Hillary Clinton had regularly led Trump in 2016 summer polls only to lose to him in November. Other pundits wrote that some Trump voters "hid" from polls but would loyally turn out to vote for him in the election.[14]

The 2020 Presidential Election

Technically speaking, the president of the United States is not elected by voters in a national election. The president is chosen through a *federal* election, in which states cast the votes. The 50 states, plus the District of Columbia, possess numbers of electoral votes equal to their congressional representation. The candidate who wins a majority (270) of the total number of electoral votes (538) wins the presidency. All but two states grant all their electoral votes to the candidate with a plurality of the popular votes in their states. Maine (4 votes) and Nebraska (5 votes) apportion their electoral votes to how candidates perform in their congressional districts and the state overall.

Before the election, most national polls predicted that Democratic challenger Joe Biden would defeat President Donald Trump by about 8 percentage points of the popular vote. Polls also predicted that he would capture a substantial majority of the nation's electoral votes, that he would increase Democratic representation in the House, and that the Democrats might wrest control of the Senate from the Republicans. The presidential election turned out to be much closer than predicted by the polls. Four additional days were required to tabulate popular votes in enough states to declare who had won the required 270 majority of state votes.

Joe Biden was eventually credited with 306 electoral votes—ironically, the same number that Donald Trump won in 2016 in defeating Hillary Clinton. Like Clinton, Biden won more popular votes in 2020 than Trump took in 2016, but unlike Clinton, Biden won an absolute majority: 51 to 47 percent of over 150 million votes, which marked the highest turnout since 1900. Although pluralities in 45 of the 50 states in 2020 favored the same parties' presidential candidates as in 2016, Biden managed to "flip" the outcome in five states—Wisconsin, Michigan, and Pennsylvania in the upper Midwest, Georgia in the South, Arizona in the West. He also won a single electoral vote in Nebraska, taking the congressional district that includes Omaha. Biden collected his 306 electoral votes by winning 25 of the 50 states, Washington, DC, and one vote representing a Nebraska congressional district.

A poll of 15,000 voters exiting the booths found that nearly all Democrats (94 percent) cast ballots for Biden while nearly all Republicans (93 percent) chose Trump.[15] Democratic identifiers (37 percent) and Republicans (35 percent) were almost equally divided among exit poll respondents, putting Independents (28 percent) in command of the outcome. Independents voted mainly for Biden (54 to 40 percent), contributing largely to Biden's margin of 4 percentage points in the popular vote. Exit polls found that 11 percent of 2020 voters did not vote in 2016. These new voters split for Biden by 61 to 37 percent. A much larger survey of 110,000 respondents immediately before and on election day showed similar findings: the 15 percent of 2016 non-voters split 56 to 41 for Biden.[16]

Both polls agreed that white Evangelical voters divided about 80 to 40 percent for Trump. However, white Evangelicals comprised only about 25 percent of the electorate. The other 75 percent of the electorate voted about 60 percent for Biden. White Christians (a larger groups including Catholics and Evangelicals) voted over 60 percent for Trump, but that group was smaller than the non-white non-Christians who strongly favored Biden.

In the end, Trump's electoral strategy of explicitly appealing to a dwindling segment of the electorate—which won him election in 2016—failed him in 2020. Not only did the white Christian share of the electorate dwindle further, but larger percentage of non-white non-Christians turned out to vote against Trump. Intriguingly, Republican congressional candidates ran ahead of him in many places, gaining seats in the House and retaining control of the Senate. Given the electorate's changing demographics, the Republican Party might wish to reconsider Trump's strategy of appealing to white Christians when competing in the 2024 presidential election.

Were it not for the COVID-19 pandemic, could Donald Trump have pulled off a final "hurrah"? We will never know, but the Republican National Committee will surely create another committee to consider how party candidates can appeal to an increasingly diverse electorate in 2024. The Lincoln Project, formed in 2019 by prominent Republicans to oppose

President Trump's re-election, reminded their fellow Republicans that after the northern states won the Civil War, "Lincoln's thoughts turned to how the nation would 'bind up its wounds' and move forward together."[17]

Reminiscing, and Summarizing

Citizens in monarchies do not choose the kings, queens, emperors, and empresses who govern them. Because citizens in democracies do choose their leaders, prospective leaders must appeal to large numbers of voters. Most candidates tout policies in their election campaigns, but a few appeal more to voters' emotions. Demagogues may vow to rectify national humiliation, or to restore former glory. Hitler promised voters that he would redress the cost and shame inflicted on Germany by a "stab in the back" that kept it from winning World War I. Mussolini promised voters to return Italy to the "glory of Rome." Both Hitler and Mussolini were freely elected to leadership, a fact that many people forget.

We need not go back that far for less militaristic examples of nostalgia's appeal to voters and politicians. For centuries, British citizens took pride that "the sun never sets on the British Empire," and British politicians tried after World War II to bolster that pride. But as Brian Lapping recounted in *End of Empire*, "The right to self-determination had since 1776 inspired nationalist leaders through the world and muzzled the direct assertion of imperial power."[18] Lapping told how revered statesmen, most notably Winston Churchill, fought to keep Britain great against unstoppable demographic and political change.

Those reactionaries lost in Britain, but another was more successful in Russia. Elected president in 2000, Vladimir Putin publicly vowed to restore Russia to its glorious past. He returned the Russian Orthodox Church to prominence after decades of suppression under atheistic communism, strengthened the military, and annexed Crimea. He and his party repeatedly won re-election, and Putin himself engineered constitutional changes that could keep him in office until 2036.

When Donald Trump exhorted his followers to help "Make America Great Again," I wondered when it had been greater during my lifetime. Was it greater before the 1952 Supreme Court decision that ended school desegregation? ... Before the 1964 Civil Rights Act that guaranteed voting to Blacks in southern states and banned discrimination in public accommodations and employment based on race, color, religion, and sex? ... Before the 1965 Medicare and Medicaid legislation that provide health care to older and poorer citizens? ... Before the Clean Air Act of 1970 and the Clean Water Act of 1972 that reduced pollution in our air and water? ... Before the 1990 Americans with Disabilities Act that helped millions of handicapped citizens improve their lives? ... Before the 2015 Supreme Court decision to legalize same sex marriages? Trump is ten years younger than I am. How had I missed seeing America's apex of greatness?

Then I realized, Trump was harkening back to the early 1950s, when whites made up 90 percent of the electorate. Of course! "Make America Great Again" was not a call to action but to reaction. It was akin to saying, "Return a White Man to the White House." All would be well in America by turning back the calendar, to when the United States was a white Christian nation. Trump's fanciful slogan appealed to enough voters in enough states to make him president in 2016. That appeal fell short in 2020.

Looking back over the eight decades of my life, I think that America is greater today than it was in 1952. I am also confident that it will become greater in the future, much greater than it was in the past.

Notes

1 Edwin O'Connor, *The Last Hurrah* (Boston: Little, Brown, 1956); the film, by Columbia Pictures, starred Spencer Tracy as the old time city boss, Frank Skeffington.
2 Martin F. Nolan, "Larger Than Life," *Boston Globe* (October 24, 1999), p. 254.
3 William Safire, *Safire's Political Dictionary* (Oxford: Oxford University Press, 2008), p. 380.
4 Henry Barbour et al., *Growth and Opportunity Project* (Washington, DC: Republican National Committee, 2013), p. 7.
5 Verlan Lewis, "The Problem of Donald Trump and the Static Spectrum Fallacy," *Party Politics* (July, 2019).
6 Mariam Morshedi, "Prominent Conservative Voices Against Trump," *Subscript Law* (June 8, 2020) at www.subscriptlaw.com/blog/conservative-voices-against-trump.
7 George F. Will left the Republican Party soon after Trump's election and disassociated Trump from conservatism in *The Conservative Sensibility* (New York: Hachette, 2019).
8 Barry M. Goldwater, *The Conscience of a Conservative* (Princeton, NJ: Princeton University Press, 1960), p. 20.
9 John W. Dean, *Conservatives Without Conscience* (New York: Viking, 2006), pp. 34–37.
10 John Banville, "*The Shipwrecked Mind: On Political Reaction* by Mark Lilla Review—How Reactionaries Have Ruined Our World," *The Guardian* (December 14, 2016) at www.theguardian.com/books/2016/dec/14/the-shipwrecked-mind-on-political-reaction-by-mark-lilla-review.
11 Safire, p. 605.
12 Gallup Poll, "Party Affiliation," Gallup at https://news.gallup.com/poll/15370/party-affiliation.aspx on July 21, 2020.
13 Nate Cohen, "Large Polling Leads Tend to Erode. Is 2020 Different?" *New York Times* (July 21, 2020), p. A14.
14 Gerald F. Seib, "Trump—and Biden—Hunt for Hidden Voters," *Wall Street Journal* (July 21, 2010), p. A4.
15 "National Exit Polls: How Different Groups Voted," *New York Times* (November 3, 2020) at www.nytimes.com/interactive/2020/11/03/us/elections/exit-polls-president.html.

16 "Fox News Voter Analysis," in cooperation with Associate Press and the National Opinion Research Center at www.foxnews.com/elections/2020/general-results/voter-analysis.
17 The Lincoln Project, "Dedicated Americans Protecting Democracy" at https://lincolnproject.us.
18 Brian Lapping, *End of Empire* (New York: St. Martin's, 1985), p. xiii.

Appendix A: Equal Group Appeal Formula

Political parties appeal to different groups for their support. Parties that draw support equally from different groups within the same potential social cleavage rate high in "Equal Group Appeal." The evenness of the support is important, not the amount of support. Relying on evenness and not amount differentiates a party's Equal Group Appeal from a party's "strength."

A party that draws support equally from each significant group within a potential social cleavage earns a score of 1.0 on Equal Group Appeal. The more variation in the groups' support for a party, the lower the party's Equal Group Appeal. These several concerns are included in our Equal Group Appeal formula:

$$\text{Equal Group Appeal} = \left(1 - \frac{\frac{\sum_{i=1}^{k}|X_i - \bar{X}|}{k} / \bar{X}}{\frac{2(k-1)}{k}}\right)^2$$

where k is the number of subgroups within the cleavage dimension in the analysis; X_i is the proportion of the ith group's support given to the party; and $\bar{X}$ is the mean proportion of support for the party, calculated over all groupings, k. The quantity obtained is subtracted from 1.0 so that high scores signify high Group Appeal. Let us apply this formula to the Republican Party's appeal to gender groups in 1952.

In the 1952 ANES survey, 26 percent of males and 30 percent of females identified as Republicans. $\bar{X} = 28$

$$\sum_{i=1}^{k}|X_i - \bar{X}|^2 = |26 - 28| + |30 - 28| = 4$$

$$\sum_{i=1}^{k}|X_i - \bar{X}|^2 / k = 4 / 2 = 2$$

$$\frac{\sum_{i=1}^{k}|X_i - \bar{X}|^2}{k} / \bar{X} = 2/28 = .07$$

$1 - .07 = 0.93$

$0.93^2 = 0.86$

Republican Equal Group Appeal Score = 0.86

Start with the percentages, X_i, by which each group supports a party. Compute the average amount of deviation among the percentages by row (sum of absolute deviations, $|X_i - \bar{X}|$, divided by the number of groups, k) for each party.

Norm the average deviation by dividing by the mean, $\bar{X}$. (An average deviation of 1.0 percentage points is relatively small for a mean support level of 50 percent, but relatively large for a mean support level of only 10 percent.)

This example had only two groups, so the fractional term in the divisor = 1.0. That fractional term adjusts for having more than two groups. The Equal Group Appeal values produced by the formula within parentheses range from 0 to 1.0. Those values are then squared to normalize their distribution, which otherwise would be negatively skewed—i.e., a few scores tending toward 0 while many cluster toward 1.0.

Appendix B: Party Base Concentration Formula

The "base" of each major American party consists of voters who "think of themselves" as Democrats or Republicans. The Party Base Concentration formula measures the extent to which any social group dominates among party identifiers in the party's base. A Party Base Concentration score of 0.0 indicates that all significant groups in a social cleavage have the same proportion of party identifiers. A score of 1.0 indicates that one group contributes all party identifiers. Intermediate scores are calculated by this formula, which is similar to measures in economics of market concentration by firms:

$$Base\,Concentration = \sqrt{\frac{\sum_{i=1}^{k} Y_i^2 - 1/k}{1 - 1/k}}$$

Y_i is the proportion of a party's membership that comes from any significant group in a social cleavage; k is the number of significant groups in the cleavage. Let us apply this formula to the gender composition of Republican Party identifiers in 1952.

Republican party identifiers in the 1952 ANES survey consisted of 0.43 males and 0.57 females.

$$\sum_{i=1}^{k} Y_i^2 = 0.43^2 + 0.57^2 = 0.185 + 0.325 = 0.51$$

$$1/k = 1/2 = 0.5$$

$$\sum_{i=1}^{k} Y_i^2 - 1/k = 0.51 - 0.50 = 0.01$$

$$1 - 1/k = 1 - 1/2 = 0.5$$

$$Base\,Concentration = \sqrt{\frac{\sum_{i=1}^{k} Y_i^2 - 1/k}{1 - 1/k}} = \sqrt{\frac{0.01}{0.5}} = \sqrt{0.02} = .14$$

The Republican Party's Party Base Concentration score for gender in 1952 indicates some imbalance in party identification between men and women. Women accounted for slightly more Republican identifiers than men. At the time, sociologists contended that women, more than men, tended to be "culture carriers" and thus conservative and thus comfortable in the Republican Party.

Data for 2016 in Chapter 3 suggests that many women had become motivated to secure their own rights as culture innovators. They became less comfortable within the Republican Party, which changed to 0.53 men and 0.47 women. As the distribution equalized somewhat, the Republicans' Party Base Concentration score dropped to 0.05.

Appendix C: Poll Questions Asking Respondents' Ideology, 1935–1969

Found by iPoll search at Roper Center for Public Opinion Research

If there were only two political parties in this country—Conservative and Liberal—which would you join?
Gallup Poll; May 11, 1936–May 16, 1936

In politics, do you regard yourself as a liberal or conservative?
Gallup Poll (AIPO); Jan 20, 1938–Jan 25, 1938

Do you regard yourself as a conservative, or a liberal, or somewhere in between?
Roper/Fortune Survey; Aug 1, 1944–Aug 14, 1944

In politics, do you regard yourself as a liberal or conservative?
NORC Post-Election Survey 1944; Nov 26, 1944–Dec 3, 1944

Do you consider yourself to be a conservative or a liberal in your political views?
Gallup Poll; Mar 19, 1948–Mar 24, 1948

When it comes to national issues, do you regard yourself, in general, as a liberal, as a conservative, or as something else?
Foreign Affairs Survey; Jan 27, 1949–Feb 6, 1949

Do you consider yourself to be a conservative or a liberal in your political views?
Gallup Poll (AIPO); Mar 26, 1950–Mar 31, 1950

Taking everything into account, do you consider yourself, in general, as a liberal or as a conservative?
Gallup Poll; Feb 25, 1954–Mar 2, 1954

Taking everything into account, would you say that, in general, you think of yourself as a liberal—or as a conservative?
Gallup Poll (AIPO); Dec 31, 1954–Jan 5, 1955

Taking everything into account would you say that you, yourself, are more of a liberal or more of a conservative in politics?
Gallup Poll (AIPO); May 12, 1955–May 17, 1955

Taking everything into account would you say that you, yourself, are more of a liberal or more of a conservative in politics?
Gallup Poll (AIPO); Jan 17, 1957–Jan 22, 1957

Which of these probably comes closest to your position in politics? ... Conservative Republican, liberal Republican, Independent who leans Republican, Independent without party preference, Independent who leans Democratic, conservative Democrat, liberal Democrat?
National Labor Issues Survey; Dec, 1961–Dec, 1961

In politics, would you say you are a liberal or a conservative?
Survey Research Service Amalgam; Jun, 1965–Jun, 1965

What do you consider yourself in your political point of view—a conservative, a liberal or middle of the road?
Harris Survey; Jun, 1967–Jun, 1967

What do you consider yourself—conservative, middle of the road, liberal or radical?
Harris Survey; Sep, 1967–Sep, 1967

How would you describe your political beliefs—as conservative, moderately conservative, moderately liberal or liberal?
Gallup Poll (AIPO); Jul 10, 1969–Jul 15, 1969

References: Books, Articles, and Papers

Achen, Christopher H., "Parental Socialization and Rational Party Identification," *Political Behavior*, 24, No. 2, Special Issue: Parties and Partisanship, Part One (June, 2002), 151–170.

Adams, Robert McC., "Urban Revolution," in David L. Sills (ed.), *International Encyclopedia of the Social Sciences, Volume 16* (New York: Macmillan, 1968), 201–207.

Aden, Roger C. and Scott Titsworth, "Remain Rooted in a Sea of Red: Agrarianism, Place Attachment, and Nebraska Cornhusker Fans," in Adam C. Earnheardt, Paul M. Haridakis, and Barbara S. Hugenberg (eds.), *Sports Fans, Identity, and Socialization: Exploring the Fandemonium* (Lanham, MD: Lexington Books, 2013), 9–23.

Ahler, Douglas J. and Gaurav Sood, "The Parties in Our Heads: Misperceptions About Party Composition and Their Consequences," *The Journal of Politics*, 80 (April 27, 2018) at 965. Published online at http://dx.doi.org/10.1086/697253.

Aldrich, John, *Why Parties?* (Chicago: University of Chicago Press, 1995 and 2011).

Almond, Gabriel A. and James S. Coleman, *The Politics of the Developing Areas* (Princeton, NJ: Princeton University Press, 1960).

American National Election Studies (ANES) Cumulative Data File, 1948–2008 Codebook (Ann Arbor, MI: Inter-university Consortium for Political and Social Research, undated) at http://electionstudies.org/studypages/download/datacenter_all.htm.

American Political Science Association, "Toward a More Responsible Two-Party System," *American Political Science Review*, 44, II (September, 1950), 1–99.

Anunciacao, Luis, "An Overview of the History and Methodological Aspects of Psychometrics," *Journal for ReAttach Therapy and Developmental Diversities* (August, 2018), 44–58.

Azarian, Bobby, "An Analysis of Trump Supporters Has Identified 5 Key Traits," *Psychology Today* (December 31, 2017).

Ball, Terence and Richard Dagger, "Ideologies, Political," in George Thomas Kurian, *The Encyclopedia of Political Science, Volume 3* (Washington, DC: CQ Press), 759–762.

Barbour, Henry et al., *Growth and Opportunity Project* (Washington, DC: Republican National Committee, 2013).

Bartle, John and Paolo Bellucci, "Introduction: Partisanship, Social Identity and Individual Attitudes," in Bartle and Belluci (eds.), *Political Parties and Partisanship: Social Identity and Individual Attitudes* (London: Routledge, 2009), 1–25.

Bauman, Timothy, "Defining Ethnicity," *SAA Archaeological Record* (September, 2004), 12–14.

Bender, Thomas, "Urbanization," in Eric Foner and John A. Garraty (eds.), *The Reader's Companion to American History* (Boston: Houghton Mifflin, 1991), 1101–1104.

Bernstein, Mary, "Identity Politics," *Annual Review of Sociology*, 31 (2005), 47–74.

Bowler, Shaun, "Party Identification," in Justin Fisher, Edward Fieldhouse, Mark N. Franklin, Rachel Gibson, Marta Cantijoch, and Christopher Wlezien (eds.), *The Routledge Handbook of Elections, Voting Behavior and Public Opinion* (London: Routledge, 2017), 146–157.

Brooks, Clem and Jeff Manza, "Social Cleavages and Political Alignments: U.S. Presidential Elections, 1960 to 1992," *American Sociological Review*, 62 (December, 1997), 937–946.

Bryden, John and Eric Silverman, "Underlying Socio-political Processes Behind the 2016 US Election," *PLoS ONE*, 14(4), e0214854 at https://doi. org/10.1371/journal.pone.0214854.

Burke, Edmund, *Thoughts on the Cause of the Present Discontents* (1770).

Campbell, Angus, Philip E. Converse, Warren E. Miller, and Donald E. Stokes, *The American Voter* (New York: Wiley, 1960).

Chapin, F.S., "A Quantitative Scale for Rating the Home and Social Environment of Middle Class Families in an Urban Community: A First Approximation to the Measurement of Socio-economic Status," *Journal of Educational Psychology*, 19 (February, 1928), 99–111.

Cole, Alexandra, "Comparative Political Parties Systems and Organizations," in John T. Ishiyama and Marijke Breuning (eds.), *21st Century Political Science: A Reference Handbook* (Thousand Oaks, CA: SAGE, 2011), 150–158.

Converse, Philip E., "The Nature of Belief Systems in Mass Publics," in David E. Apter (ed.), *Ideology and Discontent* (New York: Free Press, 1964), 206–261.

Dean, John W., *Conservatives Without Conscience* (New York: Viking, 2006).

Dennis, Jack, "Political Independence in America, Part II: Towards a Theory," *British Journal of Political Science*, 18 (1988), 197–219.

Dietrich, Bryce J., "Using Motion Detection to Measure Social Polarization in the U.S. House of Representatives," *Political Analysis* (2020) at www.brycejdietrich. com/files/papers/Dietrich_cspan.pdf.

Dietz-Uhler, Beth and Jason R. Lanter, "The Consequences of Sports Fan Identification," in Lawrence W. Hugenberg, Paul M. Haridakis, and Adam C. Earnheardt (eds.), *Sports Mania: Essays on Fandom and the Media in the 21st Century* (Jefferson, NC: McFarland, 2008), 103–113.

Dionisio, Pedro and Carmo Leal, "Fandom Affiliation and Tribal Behaviour: A Sports Marketing Application," *Qualitative Market Research: An International Journal*, 11, No. 1 (2008), 17–39.

Downs, Anthony, *An Economic Theory of Democracy* (New York: HarperCollins, 1957).

Druckman, James N. and Matthew S. Levendusky, "What Do We Measure When We Measure Affective Polarization?" *Public Opinion Quarterly*, 83 (Spring, 2019), 114–122.

Druckman, James N., S.R. Gubitz, Ashley M. Lloyd, and Matthew S. Levendusky, "How Incivility on Partisan Media (De)Polarizes the Electorate," The *Journal of Politics*, 81 (December 3, 2018), 291–295 at 291–292.

Drury, John and Steve Reicher, "The Intergroup Dynamics of Collective Empowerment: Substantiating the Social Identity Model of Crowd Behaviour," *Group Processes & Intergroup Relations*, 2 (1999), 381–402.

Earnheardt, Adam C., Paul M. Haridakis, and Barbara S. Hugenberg (eds.), *Sports Fans, Identity, and Socialization: Exploring the Fandemonium* (Lanham, MD: Lexington Books, 2013).

Egan, Patrick J., "Identity as Dependent Variable: How Americans Shift Their Identities to Align with Their Politics," *American Journal of Political Science*, 64 (July, 2020), 699–716.

Fisher, Justin Edward Fieldhouse, Mark N. Franklin, Rachel Gibson, Marta Cantijoch, and Christopher Wlezien (eds.), *The Routledge Handbook of Elections, Voting Behavior and Public Opinion* (London: Routledge, 2017).

Galvin, Daniel J., "Party Domination and Base Mobilization: Donald Trump and Republican Party Building in a Polarized Era," *Forum* (2020).

Galvin, Daniel J., *Presidential Party Building: Dwight D. Eisenhower to George W. Bush* (Princeton, NJ: Princeton University Press, 2010).

Ghere, Richard K., "Review: *Uncivil Agreement: How Politics Became Our Identity*," *Public Integrity*, 21 (2019), 214–219.

Gill, Matthew, "Communicating Organizational History to Sports Fans," in Adam C. Earnheardt, Paul M. Haridakis, and Barbara S. Hugenberg (eds.), *Sports Fans, Identity, and Socialization: Exploring the Fandemonium* (Lanham, MD: Lexington Books, 2013), 151–164.

Goldman, Ralph M., *From Warfare to Party Politics: The Critical Transition to Civilian Control* (Syracuse, NY: Syracuse University Press, 1990).

Goldwater, Barry M., *The Conscience of a Conservative* (Princeton, NJ: Princeton University Press, 1960).

Green, Donald, Bradley Palmquist, and Eric Schickler, *Partisan Hearts and Minds: Political Parties and the Social Identities of Voters* (New Haven, CT: Yale University Press, 2002).

Greene, Steven, "The Social-Psychological Measurement of Partisanship," *Political Behavior*, 24, No. 3 (September, 2002), 171–197.

Gregersen, Erik, "History of Technology Timeline," *Encyclopaedia Britannica* at www.britannica.com/story/history-of-technology-timeline.

Grieve, Frederick G. et al., "Identification with Multiple Sporting Teams: How Many Teams Do Sport Fans Follow?" *Journal of Contemporary Athletics*, 3 (1999), 283–294.

Haridakis, Paul M. and Adam C. Earnheardt, "Understanding Fans' Consumption and Dissemination of Sports: An Introduction," in Adam C. Earnheardt, Paul M. Haridakis, and Barbara S. Hugenberg (eds.), *Sports Fans, Identity, and Socialization: Exploring the Fandemonium* (Lanham, MD: Lexington Books, 2013), 1–6.

Harmel, Robert and Kenneth Janda, *Parties and Their Environments: Limits to Reform?* (New York: Longman, 1982).

Hatemi, Peter K. and Christopher Ojeda, "The Role of Child Perception and Motivation in Political Socialization," *British Journal of Political Science* (February, 2020), published online by Cambridge University Press.

Hawkins, Stephen, Daniel Yudkin, Míriam Juan-Torres, and Tim Dixon, *Hidden Tribes: A Study of America's Polarized Landscape* (New York: More in Common, 2019) at https://static1.squarespace.com/static/5a70a7c3010027736a22740f/t/5bbcea6b7817f7bf7342b718/1539107467397/hidden_tribes_report-2.pdf.

Hooghe, Marc and Ann-Kristin Kölln, "Types of Party Affiliation and the Multi-speed Party: What Kind of Party Support Is Functionally Equivalent to Party Membership?" *Party Politics*, 26 (2020), 355–365.

Horn, Alexander, Anthony Kevins, Carsten Jensen, and Kees van Kersbergen, "Political Parties and Social Groups: New Perspectives and Data on Group and Policy Appeals," *Party Politics* (Paper submitted April 29, 2019; accepted for publication January 15, 2020).

Huddy, Leonie, Lilliana Mason, and Lene Aaroe, "Expressive Partisanship: Campaign Involvement, Political Emotion, and Partisan Identity," *American Political Science Review*, 109, No. 1 (February, 2015) online doi:10.1017/S0003055414000604.

Ignazi, Piero, *Party and Democracy: The Uneven Road to Party Legitimacy* (Oxford: Oxford University Press, 2017).

Iyengar, Shanto, Yphtach Lelkes, Matthew Levendusky, Neil Malhotra, and Sean J. Westwood, "The Origins and Consequences of Affective Polarization in the United States," *Annual Review of Political Science*, 22 (2019), 129–146.

Iyengar, Shanto, Gaurav Sood, and Yphtach Lelkes, "Affect, Not Ideology: A Social Identity Perspective on Polarization," *Public Opinion Quarterly*, 76 (Fall, 2012), 405–431.

Janda, Kenneth, "Cross-National Measures of Party Organizations and Organizational Theory," *European Journal of Political Research*, 11 (1983), 319–332.

Janda, Kenneth, *The Emperor and the Peasant: Two Men at the Start of the Great War and the End of the Habsburg Empire* (Jefferson, NC: McFarland, 2018).

Janda, Kenneth, "Interest Aggregation and Articulation," in George T. Kurian (ed.), *The Encyclopedia of Political Science, Volume 3* (Washington, DC: CQ Press, 2011), 798–799.

Janda, Kenneth, *Political Parties: A Cross-National Survey* (New York: The Free Press, 1980).

Janda, Kenneth, *The Social Bases of Political Parties: Democrats and Republicans, 1952–2012 and 2032* (eBook edition 1.0, February, 2013).

Janda, Kenneth and Robin Gillies, "Social Aggregation, Articulation, and Representation of Political Parties: A Cross National Analysis," paper delivered at the 1975 Annual Meeting of the American Political Science Association, San Francisco.

Janda, Kenneth, Jeffrey M. Berry, Jerry Goldman, Deborah Schildkraut, and Paul Manna, *The Challenge of Democracy: American Government in Global Politics* (Boston: Cengage, 2020).

Jones, David R. and Monika L. McDermott, "The Responsible Party Government Model in House and Senate Elections," *American Journal of Political Science*, 48 (January, 2004), 1–12.

Karpf, David, "Review: *The Revolution That Wasn't: How Digital Activism Favors Conservatives*," *The International Journal of Press/Politics*, 25 (2020) 538–544. DOI: 10.1177/1940161220902070.

Klar, Samara, Yanna Krupnikov, and John Barry Ryan, "Affective Polarization or Partisan Disdain? Untangling a Dislike for the Opposing Party from a Dislike of Partisanship," *Public Opinion Quarterly*, 82 (Summer, 2018), 379–390.

Knight, Kathleen, "Transformations of the Concept of Ideology in the Twentieth Century," *American Political Science Review*, 100 (November, 2006), 619–626.

Koc-Michalska, Karolina, Bruce Bimber, Daniel Gomez, Matthew Jenkins, and Shelley Boulianne, "Public Beliefs About Falsehoods in News," *The International Journal of Press/Politics*, 25 (2020), 447–468.

Krouwel, Andre, "Otto Kirchheimer and the Catch-All Party," *West European Politics*, 26 (April, 2003), 23–40.

Krouwel, Andre, "Party Models," in Richard S. Katz and William Crotty (eds.), *Handbook of Party Politics* (London: SAGE, 2006), 249–269.

Lapping, Brian, *End of Empire* (New York: St. Martin's, 1985).

Lee, Frances E., *Beyond Ideology: Politics, Principles, and Partisanship in the U.S. Senate* (Chicago: University of Chicago Press, 2009).

Lewis, I.M., "Tribal Society," in David L. Sills (ed.), *"International Encyclopedia of the Social Sciences, Volume 16* (New York: Macmillan and Free Press, 1968), 146–152.

Lewis, Verlan, *Ideas of Power: The Politics of American Party Ideological Development* (Cambridge: Cambridge University Press, 2019).

Lewis, Verlan, "The Problem of Donald Trump and the Static Spectrum Fallacy," *Party Politics* (July, 2019).

Limbaugh, David, *Guilty by Reason of Insanity: Why the Democrats Must Not Win* (Washington, DC: Regnery, 2019).

Lobban, Richard A., Jr. and Carolyn Fluehr-Lobban, "'Tribe': A Socio-Political Analysis," *Issues* (Rhode Island College Digital Commons, 1976), 143–165.

Lozada, Carlos, "Show Me Your Identification," *Outlook, Washington Post Book Review* (October 18, 2018) at www.washingtonpost.com/news/book-party/wp/2018/10/18/feature/.

Manza, Jeff and Clem Brooks, *Social Cleavages and Political Change: Voter Alignments and US Party Coalitions* (New York: Oxford University Press, 1999).

Mason, Lilliana, "'I Disrespectfully Agree'": The Differential Effects of Partisan Sorting on Social and Issue Polarization," *American Journal of Political Science*, 59 (January, 2015), 128–145.

Mason, Lilliana, "Losing Common Ground: Social Sorting and Polarization," *The Forum*, 16, No. 1 (2018), 47–66.

Mason, Lilliana, *Uncivil Agreement: How Politics Became Our Identity* (Chicago: University of Chicago Press, 2018).

Mason, Lilliana and Julie Wronski, "One Tribe to Bind Them All: How Our Social Group Attachments Strengthen Partisanship," *Advances in Political Psychology*, 39 (Suppl. 1, 2018), 257–277.

Meshi, Dar, Diana I. Tamir, and Hauke R. Heekeren, "The Emerging Neuroscience of Social Media," *Trends in Cognitive Sciences*, 19 (December, 2015), 771–782 at http://dx.doi.org/10.1016/j.tics.2015.09.004.

Miller, Warren E., "Party Identification, Realignment, and Party Voting: Back to the Basics," *American Political Science Review*, 85 (June, 1991), 557–568.

Morris, Richard B. (ed.), *Encyclopedia of American History, Bicentennial Edition* (New York: Harper & Row, 1976).

Müller-Wille, Staffan, "Linnaeus and the Four Corners of the World," in K.A. Coles, R. Bauer, Z. Nunes, and C.L. Peterson (eds.), *The Cultural Politics of Blood, 1500–1900* (London: Palgrave Macmillan, 2014) at https://link.springer.com/chapter/10.1057%2F9781137338211_10#citeas.

Neundorf, Anja and Kaat Smets, "Political Socialization and the Making of Citizens," in *Oxford Handbooks Online* (www.oxfordhandbooks.com), (Oxford: Oxford University Press, 2018) at p. 1.

Norusiš, Maria I., *SPSS Introductory Statistics Student Guide* (Chicago: SPSS, 1990).

O'Connor, Edwin, *The Last Hurrah* (Boston: Little, Brown, 1956).

Ojeda, Christopher and Peter K. Hatemi, "Accounting for the Child in the Transmission of Party Identification," *American Sociological Review*, 80 (2015), 1150–1174.

Orr, Lilla V. and Gregory A. Huber, "The Policy Basis of Measured Partisan Animosity in the United States," *American Journal of Political Science*, 64 (July, 2020), 569–586.

Pomper, Gerald M., "The Impact of *The American Voter* on Political Science," *Political Science Quarterly*, 93 (Winter, 1978–1979), 617–628.

Putnam, Robert, *Bowling Alone: The Collapse and Revival of American Community* (New York: Simon & Schuster, 2001).

Rae, Nicol C. and Juan S. Gil, "Party Polarization and Ideology: Diverging Trends in Britain and the US," in Terrence Casey (ed.), *The Legacy of the Crash: How the Financial Crisis Changed America and Britain* (New York: Palgrave Macmillan, 2011), 159–178.

Ratcliffe, Michael, Charlynn Burd, Kelly Holder, and Alison Fields, "Defining Rural at the U.S. Census Bureau," *American Community Survey and Geography Brief* (December, 2016). Available at www2.census.gov/geo/pdfs/reference/ua/Defining_Rural.pdf.

Rosenbluth, Frances McCall and Ian Shapiro, *Responsible Parties: Saving Democracy from Itself* (New Haven, CT: Yale University Press, 2018).

Safire, William, *Safire's Political Dictionary* (Oxford: Oxford University Press, 2008).

Schattschneider, E.E., *Party Government* (New York: Rinehart, 1942).

Schradie, Jen, *The Revolution That Wasn't: How Digital Activism Favors Conservatives* (Cambridge, MA: Harvard University Press, 2019).

Stapelbroek, Koen, "Pillarization," in George Thomas Kurian (ed.), *The Encyclopedia of Political Science, Volume 4* (Washington, DC: CQ Press, 2011), p. 1209.

Stone, Walter J., Ronald B. Rapoport, and Alan I. Abramowitz, "The Reagan Revolution and Party Polarization in the 1980s," in L. Sandy Maisel (ed.), *The Parties Respond: Changes in the American Party System* (Boulder, CO: Westview Press, 1990), 67–93.

Sugar, Bert (ed.), *I Hate the Dallas Cowboys: And Who Elected Them America's Team Anyway?* (New York: St. Martin's Griffin, 1997).

Tajfel, Henri (ed.), *Differentiation Between Social Groups: Studies in the Social Psychology of Intergroup Relations* (London: Academic Press, 1978).

Tajfel, Henri and John Turner, "An Integrative Theory of Intergroup Conflict," in W.G. Austin and S. Worchel (eds.), *The Social Psychology of Intergroup Relations* (Monterey, CA: Brooks/Cole, 1979), 33–47.

Tajfel, Henri, M.G. Billig, R.P. Bundy, and Claude Flament, "Social Categorization and Intergroup Behaviour," *European Journal of Social Psychology*, 1 (1971), 149–178.

Tamburrini, Nadine, Marco Cinnirella, Vincent A.A. Jansen, and John Bryden, "Twitter Users Change Word Usage According to Conversation-Partner Social Identity," *Social Networks*, 40 (2015), 84–89.

Theodorakis, Nicholas D., Ahmed Al-Emadi, Daniel Wann, Yannis Lianopoulos, and Alexandra Foudouki, "An Examination of Levels of Fandom, Team Identification, Socialization Processes, and Fan Behaviors in Qatar," *Journal of Sport Behavior*, 40 (January, 2017), 1–21.

Theodorakis, Nicholas D., Nikolaos Tsigilis, Daniel L. Wann, G. Lianopoulos, and Ahmed Al-Emadi, "Sport Spectator Identification Scale: An Item Response Analysis Approach," *International Journal of Sport Management*, 17 (2016), 178–196.

Theodorakis, Nicholas D., D.L. Wann, P. Nassis, and T.B. Luellen, "The Relationship Between Sport Team Identification and the Need to Belong," *International Journal of Sport Management and Marketing*, 12 (2012), 25–38.

Theodorakis, Nicholas D., Daniel L. Wann, and Stephen Weaverat, "An Antecedent Model of Team Identification in the Context of Professional Soccer," *Sport Marketing Quarterly*, 21 (2012), 80–90.

Tóka, Gábor, "The Impact of Cross-Cutting Cleavages on Citizens' Political Involvement," paper prepared for panel # 11/10, "Cleavages and Party Systems in Post-1978 Democracies" at the 2003 Annual Meeting of the American Political Science Association at Philadelphia, August 27–31, 2003.

Tyson, Joseph, "Fan Avidity as it Relates to Proximity of Minor and Major League Affiliates," *Sport Management Undergraduate* (2013), Paper 92.

U.S. Census, *Statistical Abstract* (Washington, DC: Government Printing Office, 1950).

Wann, Daniel L. and Nyla R. Branscombe, "Sports Fans: Measuring Degree of Identification with Their Team," *International Journal of Sport Psychology*, 24 (1993), 1–17.

Weakliem, David L., "The United States: Still the Politics of Diversity," in Geoffrey Evans and Nan Dirk De Graaf (eds.), *Political Choice Matters: Explaining the Strength of Class and Religious Cleavages in Cross-National Perspective* (Oxford: Oxford University Press, 2013), 114–136.

Weisberg, Herbert F. and Steven H. Greene, "The Political Psychology of Party Identification," in Michael MacKuen and George Rabinowitz (eds.), *Electoral Democracy* (Ann Arbor: University of Michigan Press, 2003), 83–124.

Wenzelburger, Georg and Reimut Zohlhöfer, "Bringing Agency Back into the Study of Partisan Politics: A Note on Recent Developments in the Literature on Party Politics," *Party Politics* (March, 2020) online.

White, Karl R., "The Relation Between Socioeconomic Status and Academic Achievement," *Psychological Bulletin*, 91 (1982), 461–481.

Wickham-Jones, Mark, *Whatever Happened to Party Government?* (Ann Arbor: University of Michigan Press, 2018).

Will, George F., *The Conservative Sensibility* (New York: Hachette, 2019).

Willis, Clint (ed.), *The I Hate Republicans Reader: Why the GOP Is Totally Wrong About Everything* (New York: Thundermount Press, 2003).

Wilson, A.N., "Afterword" in Charles Dickens, *A Tale of Two Cities* (New York: Signet Classics, 2007).

Winchester, Maxwell, Jenni Romaniuk, and Svetlana Bogomolova, "Positive and Negative Brand Beliefs and Brand Defection/Uptake," *European Journal of Marketing*, 42 (2008), 553–570.

Zelizer, Julian E., *Burning Down the House: Newt Gingrich, the Fall of a Speaker, and the Rise of the New Republican Party* (New York: Penguin, 2020).

References: Popular Periodicals and Websites

Allen, Steven J., "'We Have Lost the South for a Generation': What Lyndon Johnson Said, or Would Have Said if Only He Had Said It," *Capital Research Center* (October 7, 2014) at https://capitalresearch.org/article/we-have-lost-the-south-for-a-generation-what-lyndon-johnson-said-or-would-have-said-if-only-he-had-said-it/.

ANES Cumulative Data File, 1948–2008 Codebook (Ann Arbor, MI: Inter-university Consortium for Political and Social Research).

Baker, Peter, "Jackson and Trump: How Two Populist Presidents Compare," *New York Times* (March 15, 2017).

Bannon, Brad, "Whatever Happened to the Tea Party," *The Hill* (August 13, 2018).

Banville, John, "*The Shipwrecked Mind: On Political Reaction* by Mark Lilla Review—How Reactionaries Have Ruined Our World," *The Guardian* (December 14, 2016) at www.theguardian.com/books/2016/dec/14/the-shipwrecked-mind-on-political-reaction-by-mark-lilla-review.

Beauchamp, Zack, "'Hidden Tribes,' the New Report Centrists Are Using to Explain Away Polarization, Explained," *Vox* (October 22, 2018) at www.vox.com/policy-and-politics/2018/10/22/17991928/hidden-tribes-more-in-common-david-brooks.

Beychok, Bradley, "In 2020, Democracy Will Be Decided at the Margins," *The Hill* (November 18, 2019).

Bloomington *Daily Pantagraph* (February 9, 1953).

Bowman, Karlyn, "Who Were Trump's Voters? Now We Know," *Forbes* (June 23, 2017).

Boyd, James, "Nixon's Southern Strategy 'It's All In the Charts,'" *New York Times Magazine* (May 17, 1970), p. 105ff.

Brooks, David, "The Future of Nonconformity," *New York Times* (July 24, 2020), p. A23.

Budiman, Abby, "Asian Americans Are the Fastest-Growing Racial or Ethnic Group in the U.S. Electorate," Pew FACTTANK (May 7, 2020) at www.pewresearch.org/fact-tank/2020/05/07/asian-americans-are-the-fastest-growing-racial-or-ethnic-group-in-the-u-s-electorate/.

Bump, Philip, "Red vs. Blue: A History of How We Use Political Colors," *Washington Post* (November 8, 2016) at www.washingtonpost.com/news/the-fix/wp/2016/11/08/red-vs-blue-a-brief-history-of-how-we-use-political-colors/.

Burge, Ryan P., "Evangelicals Show No Decline, Despite Trump and Nones," *Christianity Today* (March 21, 2019), at www.christianitytoday.com/news/2019/march/evangelical-nones-mainline-us-general-social-survey-gss.html.

Burns, Nancy, "The Michigan, then National, then American National Election Studies," (2006) at www.isr.umich.edu/cps/ANES_history.pdf.

Byrne, Julie, "Roman Catholics and Immigration in Nineteenth-Century America," National Humanities Center at www.nationalhumanitiescenter.org/tserve/nineteen/nkeyinfo/nromcath.htm.

Carnes, Nicholas and Noam Lupu, "It's Time to Bust the Myth: Most Trump Voters Were Not Working Class," *Washington Post* (June 5, 2017).

Cohen, Micah, "Political Newspaper Endorsements: History and Outcome," *FiveThirtyEight* (October 26, 2011) at https://fivethirtyeight.com/features/political-newspaper-endorsements-history-and-outcome/.

Cohen, Nate, "Large Polling Leads Tend to Erode. Is 2020 Different?" *New York Times* (July 21, 2020), p. A14.

Cohn, D'Vera, "Census Bureau Considers Changing Its Race/Hispanic Questions," Pew Research Center (August 7, 2012).

Cole, Nicki Lisa, "Meet the People Behind Donald Trump's Popularity," *ThoughtCo.* (June 29, 2019).

Dean, John, "Trump's Base: Broadly Speaking, Who Are They?" *Legal Analysis and Commentary from Justia: Politics* (February 15, 2018).

Dole, Bob, "My Friend, George McGovern: He Was a Man Who Never Gave Up," Minneapolis *StarTribune* (October 22, 2012) at www.startribune.com/bob-dole-my-friend-george-mcgovern/175246371/.

"Fox News Voter Analysis," in cooperation with Associate Press and the National Opinion Research Center, at www.foxnews.com/elections/2020/general-results/voter-analysis.

Gallup Poll, "Party Affiliation," Gallup at https://news.gallup.com/poll/15370/party-affiliation.aspx on July 21, 2020.

Gao, George, "The Challenges of Polling Asian Americans," Pew FACTTANK (May 11, 2016) at www.pewresearch.org/fact-tank/2016/05/11/the-challenges-of-polling-asian-americans/.

George Washington Institute for Religious Freedom, "Religion in Colonial America: Trends, Regulations and Beliefs" at http://nobigotry.facinghistory.org/content/religion-colonial-america-trends-regulations-and-beliefs.

Hiegel, Taylor, "Remembering Kennedy's Micro-targeting in the 1960 Election," *NBC News* (November 22, 2013) at www.nbcnews.com/news/world/remembering-kennedys-micro-targeting-1960-election-flna2D11641336.

Ip, Greg, "It's Not the Economy Anymore, Stupid," *Wall Street Journal* (November 19, 2019).

Isaac, Mike, "Reddit Bans User Group Devoted to Trump," *New York Times* (June 30, 2020), p. B1.

John F. Kennedy Presidential Library and Museum, "Civil Rights Movement," at www.jfklibrary.org/JFK/JFK-in-History/Civil-Rights-Movement.aspx.

Jones, Jeffrey M., "Americans Lack Consensus on Desirability of Divided Gov't," *Gallup Poll Report*, June 10, 2010.

Kabaservice, Geoffrey, "When American Politics Turned Toxic," *New York Times* (July, 2020) at www.nytimes.com/2020/07/07/books/review/burning-down-the-house-julian-zelizer.html.

Levingston, Steven, "John F. Kennedy, Martin Luther King Jr., and the Phone Call That Changed History," *Time* (June 20, 2017) at https://time.com/4817240/martin-luther-king-john-kennedy-phone-call/.

References: Periodicals and Websites   169

Lewis, Matt, "America's Political Parties Are Just Tribes Now," *Daily Beast* (April 13, 2017) at www.thedailybeast.com/americas-political-parties-are-just-tribes-now.

Library of Congress, "Religion and the Founding of the American Republic: I. America as a Religious Refuge: the Seventeenth Century" at www.loc.gov/exhibits/religion/rel01.html.

Library of Congress, "Religion and the Founding of the American Republic: IV. Religion and the Congress of the Confederation, 1774–89" at www.loc.gov/exhibits/religion/rel04.html.

Library of Congress, "Religion and the Founding of the American Republic: VI. Religion and the Federal Government" at www.loc.gov/exhibits/religion/rel06.html.

Lincoln Project, "Dedicated Americans Protecting Democracy" at https://lincolnproject.us.

McElwee, Sean, "Data for Politics #14: Who Is Trump's Base?" *Data for Politics* (August 23, 2018).

McGinty, Jo Craven, "Documenting Race Proves Tricky for Census," *Wall Street Journal* (July 25, 2020), p. A2.

McMillan, Robert and Deepa Seetharaman, "Platforms Halt Forums for Trump Supporters," *Wall Street Journal* (June 30, 2020), p. B3.

Maddison, Angus, Statistics of the Ten Largest Economies by GDP (PPP) at https://en.wikipedia.org/wiki/Angus_Maddison_statistics_of_the_ten_largest_economies_by_GDP_(PPP).

Masciotra, David, "Anyone Who Says, 'It's the Economy, Stupid' Is Being Stupid," *Salon* (November 9, 2019).

Maxwell, Angie, "What We Get Wrong About the Southern Strategy," *Washington Post* (July 26, 2019) at www.washingtonpost.com/outlook/2019/07/26/what-we-get-wrong-about-southern-strategy/.

Morshedi, Mariam, "Prominent Conservative Voices Against Trump," *Subscript Law* (June 8, 2020) at www.subscriptlaw.com/blog/conservative-voices-against-trump.

Nasser, Haya El, "Most Major U.S. Cities Show Population Declines," *USA Today*, June 27, 2011.

"National Exit Polls: How Different Groups Voted," *New York Times* (November 3, 2020), at www.nytimes.com/interactive/2020/11/03/us/elections/exit-polls-president.html.

Newport, Frank, "The Partisan Gap in Views of the Coronavirus," *Polling Matters* (May 15, 2020).

Newsweek Staff, "Sen. Orrin Hatch Remembers Ted Kennedy," *Newsweek* (August 26, 2009), at www.newsweek.com/sen-orrin-hatch-remembers-ted-kennedy-78653.

"Nixon, Richard Milhous," The Martin Luther King, Jr. Research and Education Institute, Stanford University at https://kinginstitute.stanford.edu/encyclopedia/nixon-richard-milhous.

Nolan, Martin F., "Larger Than Life," *Boston Globe* (October 24, 1999).

Noonan, Peggy, "Burn the Republican Party Down?" *Wall Street Journal* (August 1, 2020), p. A13.

Packer, George, "A New Report Offers Insights into Tribalism in the Age of Trump," *New Yorker* (October 13, 2018) at www.newyorker.com/news/daily-comment/a-new-report-offers-insights-into-tribalism-in-the-age-of-trump.

170 *References: Periodicals and Websites*

Parker, Kim, Juliana Horowitz, Anna Brown, Richard Fry, D'Vera Cohn, and Ruth Igielnik, "What Unites and Divides Urban, Suburban, and Rural Communities," Pew Research Center (May, 2018).

Pew Research Center, "The American-Western European Values Gap," Pew Global Attitudes Project, November 17, 2011, at www.pewglobal.org/2011/11/17/the-american-western-european-values-gap/.

Pew Research Center, "A Brief History of Religion and the U.S. Census," *The Pew Forum on Religion and Public Life*, January 26, 2010, at www.pewforum.org/Government/A-Brief-History-of-Religion-and-the-U-S--Census.aspx.

Pew Research Center, "In a Politically Polarized Era, Sharp Divides in Both Partisan Coalition," (December 17, 2019) at www.pewresearch.org/politics/2019/12/17/in-a-politically-polarized-era-sharp-divides-in-both-partisan-coalitions/.

Pew Research Center, "Religious Landscape Study," (May 30, 2014) questionnaire at www.pewforum.org/religious-landscape-study/.

Pew Research Center, "Republicans, Democrats Move Even Further Apart in Coronavirus Concerns," (June 25, 2020) at www.pewresearch.org/politics/2020/06/25/republicans-democrats-move-even-further-apart-in-coronavirus-concerns/.

Pew Research Center, "Trust in Government, 1958–2019" (April 11, 2019).

Reuter, Tim, "Before Donald Trump, There Was William Jennings Bryan," *Forbes* (June 20, 2016) at www.forbes.com/sites/timreuter/2016/06/20/before-donald-trump-there-was-william-jennings-bryan/#a20c6a527926 forbes.com.

Roll Call, "Party Unity on Congressional Votes Takes a Dive: CQ Vote Studies" at www.rollcall.com/2019/02/28/party-unity-on-congressional-votes-takes-a-dive-cq-vote-studies/.

Roose, Kevin, "Reddit's C.E.O. on Why He Banned 'The_Donald' Subreddit," *New York Times* (July 1, 2020), p. B5.

Seib, Gerald F., "For Many Voters, It Isn't About the Economy," *Wall Street Journal* (January 21, 2020), p. A4.

Seib, Gerald F., "Trump—and Biden—Hunt for Hidden Voters," *Wall Street Journal* (July 21, 2010), p. A4.

Streitfeld, David, "Uncertain Payoff in an Apps Boom," *New York Times*, July 18, 2012, pp. 1 and 19.

Toukabri, Amel and Lauren Medina, "Latest City and Town Population Estimates of the Decade Show Three-Fourths of the Nation's Incorporated Places Have Fewer Than 5,000 People," U.S. Census at www.census.gov/library/stories/2020/05/america-a-nation-of-small-towns.html.

U.S. Census Bureau, "2019 U.S. Population Estimates Continue to Show the Nation's Growth Is Slowing," December 30, 2019.

U.S. Census Bureau, "Census Bureau Releases Results from the 2010 Census Race and Hispanic Origin Alternative Questionnaire Research," *News Release* (August 8, 2012) at http://2010.census.gov/news/releases/operations/cb12-146.html.

U.S. Census Bureau, International Data Base, at www.census.gov/population/www/projections/usinterimproj/.

U.S. Census Bureau, Quick Facts at www.census.gov/quickfacts/fact/table/US/PST045219.

U.S. Census Bureau, "Table 1. Urban and Rural Population: 1900 to 1990," released October, 1995 at www.census.gov/population/censusdata/urpop0090.txt.

U.S. Census Bureau, Chapter H, "Religions Affiliation, in *Historical Statistics of the United States: Colonial Time to 1957* (Washington, DC: Bureau of the Census, 1960).

References: Periodicals and Websites

U.S. History, "The Rise of the Common Man" at www.ushistory.org/us/24a.asp.

U.S. Senate, Washington's full address at www.senate.gov/artandhistory/history/resources/pdf/Washingtons_Farewell_Address.pdf.

Van Berkel, Jesse, "Rift Grows as Walz Weighs Mask Rule," Minneapolis *StarTribune* (July 13, 2020), p. 1.

Voter Study Group, "@019 VOTER Survey Full Data Set," (January 2020) at www.voterstudygroup.org/publication/2019-voter-survey-full-data-set.

Wikipedia, "List of Countries by GDP (Nominal)" at https://en.wikipedia.org/wiki/List_of_countries_by_GDP_(nominal).

Wikipedia, "Third Party Members of the House of Representatives" at https://en.wikipedia.org/wiki/Third-party_members_of_the_United_States_House_of_Representatives#1949–present:_Modern_era.

Wilkinson, Will, "The Density Divide: Urbanization, Polarization, and Populist Backlash," Niskanen Center Research Paper (June, 2019), at www.niskanencenter.org/the-density-divide-urbanization-polarization-and-populist-backlash/.

Zitner, Aaron and Dante Chinni, "Demographic Shift to Test Trump's Strategy," *Wall Street Journal* (January 4–5, 2020), p. A4.

Index

Note: Page numbers in *italics* indicate figures and in **bold** indicate tables on the corresponding pages.

Aaroe, L. 22
Adams, J. 6
Adams, J. Q. 6
Ahler, D. J. 28
Aldrich, J. 5
Almond, G. 47
American Daily Advertiser, The 133
American National Election Studies (ANES) 20–21, 28, 43, 64–65; on changing census categories 68–69; on educational levels 76–77, *77*; on ethnicity 94–95, *95*; on ideology 107–108; on income 59–61, *59–60*; on regions 53; on religion 83–86, *84–85*
American polity: changes over time in 1, 2–5, *3–4*; stability in 1–2
American Voter, The 20–21
Anderson, D. 102
Articles of Confederation 82

Bartle, J. 16
Bellucci, P. 16
Bernstein, M. 21–22
Biden, J. 149–150
Bowler, S. 16
Bowling Alone 16
Branscombe, N. R. 18
Brief Non-party Era, 1820–1824 6
Brooks, c. 38, 39, 54, 76
Bryan, W. J. 48, 49
Bryden, J. 136
Bureau of Labor Statistics 59
Burke, E. 13
Bush, G. H. W. 64, 149

Bush, G. W. 9, 10, 26, 49

Campbell, A. 20
Carlyle, T. 13
Carter, J. 102, 149
Carville, J. 64
Census Bureau 67–68, *68*, 94
Century of Consensus, A 105
Churchill, W. 151
Cinnirella, M. 136
civil rights era 8, 98, 99–101, 151
Civil War, the 7, 52
Clinton, B. 26, 64
Clinton, H. 9, 10, *11*, 39, 81, 149, 150
Coleman, J. 47
Communitarians 115
Conscience of a Conservative, The 147
Conservatives 115, 147–148
Conservatives Without Conscience 147–148
Converse, P. E. 20, 108
COVID-19 pandemic 4, 35, 65, 105, 128, 135, 149

Dean, J. 37, 147–148
Democratic Party: during the Civil War 7; ideological terms in platforms of *105*, 105–106; national headquarters 34; national party committee 34–35; origins of 6–7; *see also* political parties, American
Dewey, T. 100
Dickens, C. 1, 12, 13, 142
Dietz-Uhler, B. 16, 18–19
Dole, B. 5
Downs, A. 22

Index 173

Economic Theory of Democracy, An 22
educational levels: base concentration by 79, *79*; changes in, since 1952 76–77, *77*; equal group appeal by 77–78, *78*; group appeal and base concentration by, since 1952 80, *80*; reminiscing and summarizing on 80–81
Egan, P. J. 39
Eisenhower, D. D. 1, 4–5, 7–8, 28, 49, 58, 70, 94, 98, 100
emotions in social identities 27–28
Emperor and the Peasant, The 102
End of Empire 151
equal group appeal 43–45; across regions 54, *55*; base concentration vs. 130–131; by educational level 77–78, *78*; by ethnicity 95, *96*; formula 154–155; by ideology 110; by income *61*, 61–62; by religions 86; reviewing scores on 121–125, *122–124*; since 1952 56–57, *57*, *63*, 63–64, 72–73, *73*, 80, *80*, 87–89, *88–89*, 96–101, *97–98*, 111–113, *112–113*; by urbanization 70–71, *71*
ethnicity *93*, 93–94; equal group appeal by 95, *96*; group appeal and base concentration by, since 1952 96–101, *97–98*; party base concentration by 95–96, *96*; reminiscing and summarizing on 102

Feldman, R. 102
First Party System, 1796–1816 6
Fluehr-Lobban, C. 134
Forbes 37
French Revolution 12–13
French Revolution: A History, The 13
From Warfare to Party Politics 142

Gallup Poll 107, 108, **109**
Galvin, D. 49
Gentlemen's Agreement 90
Gill, M. 19
Gingrich, N. 140
Goldman, R. M. 134, 142–143
Goldwater, B. 8, 52, 64, 98, 100–101, 147–148
Gore, A. 9, 10
Green, D. 15, 27, 52
Greene, S. H. 20–21, 24

Hastert, D. 140
Hatch, O. 5

Hatemi, P. K. 23
Hayes, R. B. 99
Herfindahl-Hirschman Index (HHI) 46
Hidden Tribes 135
Hill, The 116
Hitler, A. 151
Hoover, H. 91
Horn, A. 43
Huber, G. A. 27
Huddy, L. 22
Humphrey, H. 8, 99

identity politics 21–22
ideology: causality and 113–115; changes in ideological self-placement and, 1952–2020 106–110, *108*, **109**; defined 104; in Democratic and Republic Party platforms over time *105*, 105–106; equal group appeal by 110; group appeal and base concentration by, since 1952 111–113, *112–113*; party base concentration by 110, *111*; poll questions asking about, 1935–1969 158–159; tribal politics and 115–118, *117*
income 59–61, *59–60*; equal group appeal and base concentration since 1952 *63*, 63–64; equal group appeal by *61*, 61–62; party base concentration by *62*, 62–63; reminiscing and summarizing on 64–65
information technology 136–138
International Journal of Sport Management and Marketing 17
Isaac, M. 137

Jackson, A. 6, 48, 49, 76
Jansen, V. A. A. 136
Jefferson, T. 6
Jensen, C. 43
Johnson, L. B. 8, 48, 64, 94, 100

Kennedy, J. F. 8, 91, 100, 123
Kennedy, R. 100
Kennedy, T. 5
Kevins, A. 43
Keynes, J. M. 134
Kim, D. 102
King, M. L., Jr. 100, 123
Kirchheimer, O. 22
Klar, S. 143
Krupnikov, Y. 143

Lanter, J. R. 16, 18–19
Lapping, B. 151
Lee, F. 104
Lewis, V. 104, 115, 116–117
Liberals 115
Libertarian Party 115
Libertarians 115
Lilla, M. 148
Lincoln, A. 6–7, 48, 49, 52, 94, 116
Linnaeus, C. 93
Lobban, R. A., Jr. 134

Manza, J. 38, 39, 54, 76
Mason, L. 22–23, 134–135
McCain, J. 63
McConnell, M. 140
McDaniel, R. 34
McElwee, S. 38
McGovern, G. 5, 24
McHenry, D. 102
media, mass 28–29
Meredith, J. 100
Millennial Generation 3e
Miller, W. E. 20, 21
Monroe, J. 6
Mussolini, B. 151

Newport, F. 4
New York Times 104, 137
Nixon, R. 5, 8, 24, 98, 101
Noonan, P. 142

Obama, B. 35, 49, 63, 101, 147
O'Connor, E. 147
Ojeda, C. 23
O'Neill, T. 5
Orr, L. V. 27

Palmquist, B. 15, 27, 52
Partisan Hearts and Minds: Political Parties and the Social Identities of Voters 16, 52
partisan identities: emotions in 27–28; in politics and sports 15–17; reminiscing and summarizing on 28–29; since 1952 23–26, *24–27*; social identity theory and political 19–23, *21*; social identity theory and sports 17–19; technology and 135–138
party base concentration 45–47; across regions 55–56, *56*; by educational level 79, *79*; by ethnicity 95–96, *96*; formula 156–157; group appeal vs. 130–131; by ideology 110, *111*; by income *62*, 62–63; by religion 86–87, *87*; reviewing scores on 125–126, *126–127*; since 1952 56–57, *57*, *63*, 63–64, 72–73, *73*, 80, *80*, 87–89, *88–89*, 96–101, *97–98*, 111–113, *112–113*; by urbanization 71–72, *72*
Paul, Rand 115–116
Paul, Ron 115
Peck, G. 90
Perez, T. 34
Phillips, K. 101
political parties, American: COVID-19 pandemic and 4, 135, 149; equal group appeal and (*see* equal group appeal); George Washington's warning about 133–134; national party committees 34–35; origin of 5–7; party base concentration and (*see* party base concentration); polarization of 4–5; presidential voting and stability and changes in 8–12, *9–12*; responsible party government and 141–143; social and party changes during current party system in 7–8; social groupings and 38–39; social identity theory and 19–23, *21*; tribal politics and 115–118, *117*, 134–135, 138–140; two methods of analyzing support for 39–42, **40**, *41*
population changes: across regions *53*, 53–54; changes in urban-rural distribution of, 1950–2018 67–68, *68*
presidential elections 8–12, *9–12*; 2020 149–151; George Washington and 5, 6, 133–134; party identification changes and 121; party loyalty in 24–25, *25*
Presidential Party Building 49
Priebus, R. 34, 35–36, 124
Psychology Today 37
Putnam, R. 16

Rayburn, S. 5
Reagan, R. 5, 48, 116
Reddit 137–138
Reflections on the Revolution in France 13
regions: equal group appeal across 54, *55*; party base concentration across 55–56, *56*; political changes in 52–53; population changes across *53*, 53–54; reminiscing and summarizing on 57–58

religion: American freedom of 82–83; base concentration by 86–87, *87*; changes in religious composition and, 1952–2020 83–86, *84–85*; equal appeal and base concentration by, since 1952 87–89, *88–89*; group appeal by 86; importance of, in American life 83; reminiscing and summarizing on 89–91, *90*

Republican Party: during the civil rights movement 8; during the Civil War 7; ideological terms in platforms of *105*, 105–106; national headquarters 34; national party committee 34–35; origins of 6–7; Trump campaign: 2016, and 35–36, 147–148; 2020, and 36–38; *see also* political parties, American

responsible party government 141–143

review of survey data: equal group access scores 121–125, *122–124*; party base concentration scores 125–126, *126–127*; reinforcing social cleavages 127–130, **128**, *129*

Roosevelt, F. D. 7, 48, 49, 67, 70, 86, 90–91, 93, 116

Roper Center for Public Opinion Research 107

Routledge Handbook of Elections, Voting Behavior and Public Opinion 16

Ryan, J. B. 143

Schattschneider, E. E. 5–6
Schickler, E. 15, 27, 52
Schradie, J. 137–138
Second Party System, 1828–1856 6
segregation, racial and religious 57–58, 90, 99–100
Silent Generation 2
Silverman, E. 136
slavery 6–7
Smith, A. 91
social cleavages: electoral politics and 138–140; reinforced with survey data 127–130, **128**, *129*; technology and 135–138
social groupings 38–39
social identity theory: emotions in social identities and 27–28; political partisans and 19–23, *21*; sports partisans and 17–19
social media 136–138
socio-economic status (SES) 59

Sood, G. 28
sports: politics and 15–17; social identity theory and 17–19
Sports Fans, Identity, and Socialization 16
Sport Spectator Identification Scale (SSIS) 18
Stevenson, A. 1, 28, 98
Stokes, D. E. 20

Tajfel, H. 16, 17, 21, 23
Tale of Two Cities, A 1, 12, 142
Tamburrini, N. 136
Tea Party movement 116
technology 135–138
Third Party System, 1860-present 6–7; social and party changes during 7–8
Thurmond, S. 100
Tóka, G. 39
tribal politics 115–118, *117*, 134–135, 138–140
Truman, H. 70, 86, 100
Trump, D. 1, 3, 9, 10–12, *11*, 39, 49, 101, 116, 141; 2016 campaign of 35–36, 124–125, 148; 2020 campaign of 36–38, 147, 148–151; base supporters of 39, 42, 49, 81; evangelicals and 91; media and 137–138; national party committee and 34–35; regional support for 53
Turner, J. 16, 17, 21, 23

Uncivil Agreement: How Politics Became Our Identity 16
United States, the: Articles of Confederation of 82; changes since the Great Depression in 2–5, *3–4*; Constitution of 2; growth of 1–2; as representative democracy 2; responsible party government in 141–143; uniqueness of two-party system stability in 8–12, *9–12*
urbanization: base concentration by 71–72, *72*; changes in, 1952–2018 68–70, *69*; changes in urban-rural population distribution, 1950–2018, and 67–68, *68*; defined 67; equal appeal and base concentration by urbanization, since 1952 72–73, *73*; group appeal by levels of 70–71, *71*; reminiscing and summarizing on 73–74
urban-rural population distribution changes, 1950–2018 67–68, *68*

van Kersbergen, K. 43

Wallace, G. 8
Wall Street Journal 36, 37–38, 39, 65
Wann, D. L. 18
Washington, G. 5, 6, 133–134

Weisberg, H. F. 20–21
Why Parties? 5
Wright, J. 140
Wronski, J. 134–135

Zeilzer, J. 140